Forget
"HAVING IT ALL"

Forget
"HAVING IT ALL"

How America Messed Up
Motherhood—and How to Fix It

by Amy Westervelt

SEAL PRESS

Seal Press
Hachette Book Group
1290 Avenue of the Americas, New York, NY 10104
www.sealpress.com
@sealpress
Printed in the United States of America
First Edition: November 2018

Published by Seal Press, an imprint of Perseus Books, LLC, a subsidiary of Hachette Book Group, Inc. The Seal Press name and logo is a trademark of the Hachette Book Group.

The publisher is not responsible for websites (or their content) that are not owned by the publisher.

Print book interior design by Six Red Marbles Inc.

Library of Congress Cataloging-in-Publication Data

Names: Westervelt, Amy, author.
Title: Forget "having it all": how America messed up motherhood-and how to fix it / by Amy Westervelt.

Description: First edition. | New York, NY: Seal Press, [2018] | Includes bibliographical references.

Identifiers: LCCN 2018031136| ISBN 9781580057868 (hardcover) | ISBN 9781580057882 (e-book)

Subjects: LCSH: Motherhood—United States. | Working mothers—United States. | Stay-at-home mothers—United States. | Work and family—United States. | Feminism—United States.

Classification: LCC HQ759 .W535 2018 | DDC 306.874/3—dc23

LC record available at https://lccn.loc.gov/2018031136

ISBNs: 978-1-58005-786-8 (hardcover), 978-1-58005-788-2 (e-book)

LSC-C

10 9 8 7 6 5 4 3 2 1

To my boys: Matt, Archie, and Roscoe.

Table of Contents

CHAPTER

1

Being a Mother Shouldn't Suck

I am writing this book hip-deep in the chaos that is modern American motherhood. My children are young (two and six), my bills are high, and my career is in an industry that is a uniquely bad fit for parents: journalism. In the course of my research, my bank account has been overdrawn half a dozen times, I've lost health insurance and then managed to get it again, and I've had my car repossessed. I've had to find new childcare arrangements twice, and threatened to divorce my husband at least as many times. But while the impetus to write this book came from my own life, and I will refer to my own experiences off and on throughout, this story is not really about me. Nor would I claim to have represented all types of mothering experiences, which are as many and varied as women themselves (or men, for that matter). I began to research motherhood—our perceptions of it, the ways we talk about it, the expectations placed on and around it—not only because I believe it remains, as some feminist scholars have posited, a key frontier in the fight for gender equality, but also because I see changing ideas about motherhood as the lynchpin to systemic transformation toward greater equality for all.

Our ideas of women and men have evolved over the decades, pushed by cultural dialogue and shifting policies. We

1

have softened some of the lines around gender, broadened roles, relaxed rules, gotten more intersectional in our understanding of identities and oppression but where mothers are concerned, we have clung more persistently to rigid ideas and expectations, which limit not just mothers but all women, irrespective of their reproductive choices. Ideas of motherhood influence everything from workplace dynamics to policies and laws that impact all women and men as well, underpinning everything from gender expectations to parental leave policies to which public bathrooms have changing tables.

And while women have steadily earned more rights and status within the patriarchal system, that was never really the goal of feminism. It's not enough to replace men with the occasional woman in a patriarchal system; the system needs to be replaced, not remodeled, and mothers are one key to that endeavor.

The popular old feminists' tale was that the world was matriarchal before it was patriarchal—in some ways, it was pleasant to think of a time ignorant of paternity, when people believed that women just bore children the way trees bore fruit. But anthropologists have found little evidence for this notion of paternity-ignorant humans. It is true that many ancient cultures were matriarchal, and some still are. But this origin story also proved dangerous, an idea quickly picked up by misogynists who used it to illustrate that patriarchal societies represented progress forward, away from a primitive matriarchal past.

In fact, where human evolution is concerned, the opposite is true: Read any anthropologist's description of the defining traits of chimpanzees, the closest monkey relative to humans, and it's likely to include words like "aggressive," "competitive," "focused on domination," and "reflexively xenophobic." In other words, patriarchal. If that's making you think, "Hey! I'm a man and I'm not like that," or "I know many fine men who are not like that," it's important to understand that my use of "patriarchy" here references the values that have come to be associated with this system, not any sort of gender definition. In fact, men are not destined to be patriarchal any more than women are destined to be matriarchal. Patriarchal women are the patriarchy's biggest and most ardent champions. Instead of simply signaling "ruled by men" or "ruled by women," I'm using these terms to describe systems governed by particular values—because over time, these are the values that have been demonstrated most often by each system. Patriarchal systems tend to be governed by competition and domination, which means they also tend to be characterized by aggressive and xenophobic behavior. Matriarchal systems are governed by care and collaboration, and their hallmarks are communication and inclusivity. Very few people are entirely patriarchal or matriarchal, irrespective of the sort of system they live in, but in a patriarchal system that rewards patriarchal values, those values will tend to get stronger over time, just as in a matriarchal system matriarchal values are strengthened over time. As primates evolved, we have progressed in ways that could make our societies more matriarchal (or matrifocal), which again, does not mean "a patriarchy, but with women in charge," but rather a society with a heavy emphasis on collaboration, equality, and communication, all things that bigger brains enable and that, in turn, enable the growth of bigger brains.

In observing matrifocal societies in both Indonesia and in some neighborhoods of East London, feminist theorist Nancy Chodorow explained these societies as simply cultures that value women and men equally.

Women's kin role, and in particular the mother role, is central and positively valued. Women gain status and prestige as they get older. At the same time, women may be important contributors to the family's economic support, as in Java and east London. And in all three societies they have control over real economic resources. All these factors give

*women a sense of self-esteem independent of their relation-
ship to their children. Finally, strong relationships exist
between women in these societies, expressed in mutual cooperation and frequent contact. A mother, then, when her
children are young, is likely to spend much of her time in
the company of other women, not simply isolated with her
children.*

Chodorow contrasts this general positivity about women
and womanhood (including positive mother-daughter relationships) with the low self-esteem she observed in the daughters of American middle-class families. "For the daughter of
a Western middle-class family, feminine gender identification
means identification with a devalued, passive mother, and
personal maternal identification is with a mother whose own
self-esteem is low," she wrote.

Several decades ago in the book *Of Woman Born*, Adrienne
Rich differentiated between motherhood, which she defined
as the patriarchal institution of motherhood—male-defined
and often oppressive to women—and mothering, the female-
defined experience of being a mother, which Rich described
as potentially empowering to women. Dozens of scholars followed in Rich's footsteps, examining both the experience of
mothering and the institution of motherhood from a feminist
perspective, and in 2006, feminist theorist Andrea O'Reilly
pioneered the field of motherhood studies and matricentric
feminism. O'Reilly positions "mother" as an identity separate
from "woman" and thus in need of an intersectional lens. "Indeed, mothers are oppressed under patriarchy as women and
as mothers," O'Reilly writes in *Matricentric Feminism*. "Con-
sequently, mothers need a matricentric mode of feminism
organized from and for their particular identity and work
as mothers. A mother-centered feminism is needed because
mothers—arguably more so than women in general—remain
disempowered despite 40 years of feminism."

Of course, there are far more than forty years of feminism, and there are many other groups of women who have been unjustly ignored by the movement, but O'Reilly is pointing largely to feminist legislative efforts to create equality between the sexes. And she's right; they've generally left mothers behind.

Ideas about motherhood are inextricably linked to cultural values, which is why we need to treat motherhood rhetoric as the powerful force that it is. How is it that in so many ways we still treat all women as "pre-pregnant" even if they have no intention of bearing children? Why do we praise conservative women (think Phyllis Schlafly or Anita Bryant, or more recently Sarah Palin or Kellyanne Conway) for "having it all" but criticize progressive women who try to? Or praise some women (white, middle or upper class) for having kids and vilify others (everybody else) for doing so? Why is it that attributing a maternal lens to a political cause is seen as effective by some but undermining by others? And how the heck do we expect men to want to co-parent when we place no social value on caregiving? These are just some of the questions I began with as I looked for an answer to the question I kept asking: Why does motherhood in America kinda suck?

Motherhood and Women's Rights

Much has been written, and will be written, about the myriad ways in which we embed gender rules and roles in both women and men at an early age. We learn early on—from our parents, extended family, teachers, religious leaders, society—which tasks and behaviors are expected and acceptable for boys and girls, and those ideas persist well into adulthood. In fact, various studies have pointed out the connection between what kids see in their households growing up and how they expect the division of labor in their homes and families to be divvied up as adults. We often encourage girls to be nurturing right from the start, buying them baby dolls or suggesting babysitting as a first job. If the reaction to my then four-year-old son asking for a baby doll for his fifth birthday is any indication—people either thought it was a weird request or a clear indicator of his homosexuality—the notion that babies are for girls is still very much entrenched in American culture. And that impacts who seems qualified to care for children farther down the road. As Brigid Schulte, former *Washington Post* reporter and current director of New America's Better Life Lab, notes in her excellent book, *Overwhelmed*, "Both men and women are naturals at child care. It's just that the culture has given women more time to get good at it."

For me, the impact of sexism is at least as much about financial stability and basic survival as about more ephemeral things like feeling valued as a woman or a mother. Don't get me wrong—both are important, and they tend to go hand in hand—but 70 percent of mothers in this country work, with mothers serving as the primary or sole earners in 40 percent of American households, and in recent years forces have conspired to make it exceedingly difficult to be a working mother in America unless you're very rich. Sexism contributes to lower wages, particularly for mothers, and then there's the high cost of childcare, diminished access to positions of power, and the expectation that women always put family before career.

In January 2016, I was walking down my street and had a revelation: At some point, mainstream feminism became more about teaching women how to game capitalism than it was about actually replacing or improving a system that fails both genders. Many people have continued to suffer under this approach, and mothers have been particularly screwed.

While chewing on this admittedly unoriginal idea, I shuffled my two-weeks-post-partum body down the street to the mailbox. There was a check waiting for me, which was a huge relief because rent was due, and I had no idea how we'd pay it if that check was late. On my way back home, I patted myself on the back. Having a second baby had not slowed me down at all! I was supporting all of us, and I had only had to take an afternoon off to give birth. I was emailing from the recovery room, and I hit a big deadline two hours after delivery. No one I worked with even knew I'd had a baby. Go me! Power woman!

Except, wait a minute. Why on earth was anything about that scenario good? Why did I feel that was an accomplishment— or that I couldn't tell people I was having a baby? And why did that seem somehow stronger or more feminist than taking a normal amount of time to recover from giving birth and to bond with my child?

In the year after his birth, this was my average day:

4:00 a.m.	Wake up (I use the phrase "wake up" loosely as it implies actually being asleep at some point. With an infant and a toddler, this is not a given.)
4:15 a.m.–6:15 a.m.	Work
6:15 a.m.–7:30 a.m.	Make and eat breakfast
7:30 a.m.–8:15 a.m.	Pack lunches and snacks while husband gets kids dressed
8:30 a.m.	Drop off kids at day care
8:45 a.m.–4:15 p.m.	Work
4:30 p.m.	Pick up from day care
5:00 p.m.–5:30 p.m.	Make dinner
5:30–6:00 p.m.	Eat dinner
6:00 p.m.–7:00 p.m.	Hang out with baby, put him to bed
7:00 p.m.–8:00 p.m.	Hang out with preschooler, husband puts him to bed
8:00 p.m.–midnight	Work

It was grueling, and that's with being able to afford part-time day care. Before you say, "Where the hell was her spouse?" consider that in 30 percent of American families, one person is doing all of this. In my case, my husband was there, putting the toddler to bed, and often picking the kids up or making dinner, and looking after the baby half the time so we didn't have to pay for full-time day care. But he was also trying to get a company off the ground and trying to rustle up other paid work so that I wouldn't have such a crazy schedule (and for the record, I like to cook and I'm picky about what I eat and what the kids eat, so I'm not great at letting him help on the food front). I have, of course, made several personal choices that contribute to the current state of affairs in my own life: I chose to have kids, I chose to live in a small town, and back when I was nineteen and couldn't predict the media apocalypse, I chose to hitch my career to an industry that's been paying steadily lower wages since 1970.

Still, the idea that any one person's choices are the only thing to blame for misfortune in a system that in reality offers limited choices is problematic, as Ann Crittenden spends an entire chapter detailing in her best-selling book *The Price of Motherhood*. The notion that women deserve to be paid and promoted less because they choose to have kids, and thus spend time on something other than a career, Crittenden points out, "assumes that raising a child is just another lifestyle option, like choosing to run long distance or play serious tennis":

> The consequences of those decisions are private, of no con-
> cern to the rest of us. If people who opt to nurture and
> educate the next generation are systematically handicapped
> in the labor market, if they find it hard to make a decent
> living or get ahead without neglecting their children, why
> should we care? It's their choice.... The big problem with
> the rhetoric of choice is that it leaves out power. Those who
> benefit from the status quo always attribute inequities to
> the choices of the underdog. The modern version of the old
> "true woman" argument—the true woman appreciates that
> her proper place is in the home—is the "choice" argument.

Crittenden goes on to point out the stark lack of choice available in work arrangements in the United States, particularly in comparison to various European countries (Sweden, of course, and also the Netherlands), where a variety of well-paid part-time jobs are available. In fact, in the years since her book was first published, the European Union has mandated parity in wages and benefits for part-time workers, providing working parents with valid choices.

The "myth of choice" is particularly problematic for women of color. As Michelle Alexander points out in *The New Jim Crow: Mass Incarceration in the Age of Colorblindness*, the idea of personal responsibility and choice enables both institutions and individuals to justify every form of systemic oppression, telling themselves that the oppressed "deserve" their fate.

In the course of researching this book, I spoke to literally hundreds of women from all walks of life. I keep coming back to something one of them, Shirley, a former Mormon and mother of four grown children, said: "When my children were young, I just understood that that was not my time, that that was a period of time in my life that was really for my children."

In some ways, it's a lovely sentiment, the picture of maternal devotion. It's somewhat appealing too. It feels simple and stress-free to be pulled only in one direction. But for me it was also deeply rattling, and not just because it assumes that all mothers can afford this level of self-sacrifice (in my case, as in the case of many mothers, it was not an option to give up work, financially). Mostly it bothered me because it insinuates the need for a prolonged "time-out" for mothers that I see as unrealistic and not entirely healthy. It underscores an expectation of selflessness in mothers that's a trap for women. It also implies that any mother who works for reasons other than financial security is selfish. But it's not as though you can just cease being a human because you have a child.

Furthermore, what happens when that child no longer needs your time? How does one reboot back into a sentient being? I'm not saying that children don't need an adult, ideally a parent or at least a close relative, around in their early years. And of course, it's important for mothers to bond with their children and vice versa. But ultimately, I don't believe that choosing to have kids should have to mean the total self-abnegation and self-betrayal that it continues to require of women.

That belief is bolstered by the fact that motherhood doesn't eliminate the individual identities of women in this way in many other developed countries, most of which, ironically, do not fetishize motherhood nearly as much as Americans do. In Sweden, for example, both parents are encouraged to take parental leave when a child is born and expected to equally divide child-rearing tasks as that infant becomes a toddler. In the Netherlands, flexible work schedules and well-paid part-time work are available to both mothers and fathers as a way to reduce the amount of time children have to be in day care. The United States has none of these options, but we do have a burgeoning industry that provides mothers with business cards featuring such titles as "Mom in charge" or "Mother of Angela and Tony," or "CEO of the Smith household." We also continue to require women without children to justify their decision over and over again, and doctors still ask women for permission from their spouses should they wish to opt for permanent birth control, despite the fact that that practice has not been legal for years. Our maternal mortality rate is increasing—unheard of in any other developed nation—during the same period of time in which we have turned a baby shower into an over-the-top, multi-event affair that now includes such things as a "gender reveal party" and a "naming party," not to mention increasingly elaborate first birthday parties.

As I struggled to juggle kids, career, and marriage and maintain some semblance of my own identity, I wondered how it was that a culture that superficially holds motherhood in such high esteem could in fact have so little regard for women who have children.

The Pendulum

Hoping to move beyond being pissed off, I started where I always do when I have a question about why something is the way it is: the past. I wanted to understand how society got here, how our understanding and expectations of mothers evolved, what our definition of motherhood says about our culture, and how our perceptions of motherhood affect our understanding of women in general. What I discovered was that we've been grappling with these questions for a very long time and that there are plenty of other and better ways to do it (many of them right here in our own country).

First, it's impossible to understand anything about American culture without, again, acknowledging that this country was colonized by people who believed very strongly in the power of the self. The uniquely American mix of entitlement and individualism is an undercurrent to everything we are as a country today, a fact that has led to both greatness and depravity. In the case of motherhood, Anglo America has always seen children as solely the purview of their parents—not their extended family (who, in many cases, were back home in England, or elsewhere in western Europe) and not their community, which was new and tenuous.

That was the case for white colonial Americans. For Native Americans and enslaved African Americans, the origins of "American motherhood" look quite different, and I believe understanding these differences and creating an inclusive dialogue about mothering is key to approaching the problems that plague motherhood today. Today, we very much talk about motherhood in the framework of the history and experiences of middle-class, straight, white women in this country, which leaves the majority of American mothers out. As Chimamanda Ngozi Adichie has said: "The single story creates stereotypes. And the problem with stereotypes is not that they are untrue, but they are incomplete. They make one story become the only story."

It's worth noting that pundits and public intellectuals, philosophers, psychologists, and religious thinkers have been worrying about "the Woman Question" in America—what the proper role and authority of women should be—for as long as the country has existed. Abigail Adams was lecturing her husband John about it back in the 1700s, Ida Tarbell was writing about it in 1915, and we're still talking about it today. We also have a long history in this country of asking mothers, in particular, to perform a specific role, and then placing them within a legal, economic, and political system that makes that role impossible to adequately perform. It started with the idea of what historian Linda Kerber terms "republican motherhood"—the notion that mothers are responsible for the moral fiber of a nation, that they alone have the power to create and nurture great new citizens. It's an idea that has roots in western Europe, but gained new urgency in the New World, where early colonizers were suddenly concerned with both creating a larger population and ensuring that those new citizens were raised to be productive and moral members of society.

In her seminal book *Mother Love: Myth and Reality*, French philosopher Elisabeth Badinter traces the rise of republican motherhood in Europe and, particularly, France during the late eighteenth century. Badinter frames ideas about motherhood in the context of ever-shifting roles and power between mother, father, and child, noting that for women, during periods of history when the role of "mother" is given power, as in the case of republican motherhood, it often means that the individual woman is stripped of certain rights and freedoms.

This certainly held true in America where, at the same time that everyone from Benjamin Franklin to the popular press was telling mothers that it was their job, nay their duty, to raise virtuous citizens, our forefathers were creating a legal system that gave women no rights to protect their children, physically or financially. White mothers of America were tasked with being solely responsible for their children's futures while being told they had no legal right to keep them from being abused. They also had no legal right to their own money or property. African American mothers, meanwhile, had no claim at all to their children and had to bear the unique torture of birthing children into a world of abject horror.

White American mothers were not only expected to form model citizens while having little actual authority over them, but also were expected to do so with zero external support. The idea of the nuclear family was not unique to America at this time, but its prevalence certainly was. One of the more unusual aspects of white American motherhood is the cultural tendency to place more importance on the individual and, in the case of motherhood, on each individual family than on the collective good. In his musings on America in the seventeenth and eighteenth centuries, French philosopher Alexis de Tocqueville noted this repeatedly, calling Americans by turns lonely, isolated, and self-sufficient. What that translated to for mothers was a shift away from the "it takes a village" philosophy that had governed motherhood in nearly every other culture and toward every mother as an island, solely responsible for the children she was raising.

This, of course, did not hold true among slave families, which were being upended so constantly and capriciously that what sociologist Patricia Hill Collins calls "othermothering" and anthropologist Sarah Hrdy calls "alloparents"—the practice of various adults in a community, not just biological parents, sharing responsibility for its children—were critical to survival in this "new world." Slavery, wherein mothers were expected to return to work almost immediately after birth, and any morning might turn out to be the day your children are sold away from you—strengthened the notion of what anthropologists call "fictive kin," and the formation of communities where everyone felt a lot more sense of responsibility for children, irrespective of whose biological offspring they were. Older women, too weak to work the fields, often looked after the children of multiple families. Now, Collins and many other feminist writers have pointed to the models of othermothering and community mothering (the role many Black women take on to nurture not just individuals within a community, but the community as a whole) as practices that could and should be emulated writ large, as they seem to best support the working mothers and single mothers who represent the vast majority of American mothers today.

Most Native American tribes, particularly the Iroquois, Navajo, and Kootenai/Salish, also placed an emphasis on community mothering, a tradition that was upended by colonialists and the drive to separate American Indian children from their mothers and their communities, and strip them of their language and culture. Native American communities across the country are still reeling from this ugly, painful period and working to reinstate a culturally appropriate approach to motherhood.

The scientific understanding of women's reproductive systems also had an important impact on forming our notions of motherhood. In the nineteenth and twentieth centuries, men started to invade the traditionally female domain of childbirth. Prior to this period of history, late pregnancy and childbirth were entirely female realms. Men were excluded, sometimes for several weeks, and it was a time of female solidarity over which the presiding expert was a female midwife. In the nineteenth century, midwives were shunted aside and childbirth was taken over by male doctors who said midwives had been doing it all wrong, despite hundreds of years of success. Along with uniquely tortuous ideas about how childbirth should be done, these male doctors introduced American society to the idea of eugenics, an insidiously racist notion about which types of women should or shouldn't breed and which sorts of children have value.

It was also around this time that American women started to get their sea legs and begin fighting back. Women like Lucretia Mott, Harriet Tubman, Susan B. Anthony, Elizabeth Cady Stanton, Maria Stewart, Sarah and Angelina Grimké, Lucy Stone, Sarah Douglass, Sojourner Truth, and the Forten women (mother Charlotte; daughters Sarah, Margaretta, and Harriet; granddaughter Charlotte L.)—many of them inspired by exposure to the more gender-equal Native American communities of the northeast—were formidable forces in the nineteenth- and twentieth-century fights for women's suffrage and the abolition of slavery, two causes that often (though not always) found the same champions. In the early twentieth century, Margaret Sanger, who would eventually have her own ugly story with eugenics, began preaching the gospel of birth control and kicked off a century-long fight over women's reproductive rights that we're still battling today.

This Progressive Era (from the 1890s to the 1920s) seemed like it might become the new normal. With white and middle-class women entering the workplace more frequently, and more women remaining single and self-sufficient well into adulthood (and in many cases for their whole lives), the idea of women working became more normal across racial and economic strata. In the twentieth century, as the country engaged in not one but two world wars, women were needed more than ever in the workplace, and the US government even funded a national day care system to better enable mothers to participate in meeting the economic and military needs of the day.

Eleanor Roosevelt was providing a new model for First Lady, championing civil rights and the New Deal as opposed to hosting teas and galas. By most accounts it was her husband's philandering that helped turn Eleanor into the force she was. After discovering an affair between her secretary, Lucy Mercer, and her husband in 1918, Eleanor offered Franklin a divorce, but his mother threatened to cut off his inheritance should the couple split and his advisors believed it would end his political aspirations. In agreeing to stay with him, Eleanor had two demands: first, he would break it off with Mercer (he failed at this but was exceedingly discreet) and second, that he would never again share Eleanor's bed (he had an easier time with this one, go figure). Although devastated by her husband's betrayal, it freed Eleanor from various social rules: she began standing up to her tyrannical mother-in-law, and she was empowered to do and say as she pleased. In so doing, she set an example for other white women, further inspiring Progressive reforms.

But the pendulum was destined to swing back. As World War I came to an end and the economy recovered from the Great Depression via World War II, white America rushed to the safety of the past, which included the idea of sweet, domestic women who fulfilled the roles of wife and mother and were happy to commit to those roles alone. The day care system was dismantled. When the idea of subsidized childcare was raised again in the 1970s, thanks to a bill Congress passed with bipartisan support, the religious right, with Pat Buchanan at its helm, warned that such a thing would signal the end of the traditional family, and Nixon vetoed the bill.

Back and forth the pendulum has swung, but for every Betty Friedan and Phyllis Schlafly, for every bell hooks and Christina Hoff Sommers, every Patricia Hill Collins and Alveda King, every Offred and Serena Joy, our ideas around motherhood have changed, and those perceptions have shaped the lives of women, for better or worse, for centuries.

It's a fascinating history and one that fills me alternately with optimism and a wave of grim acceptance. It's galling to look back at the early 1900s and think in some ways it may have been a more progressive time than now. But it's also inspiring to read about women who were out there in these streets talking about birth control at a time when women weren't even allowed to vote. It's depressing to think that the United States once had a vast network of government-supported day care centers that it dismantled after World War II, or that Congress passed a universal childcare bill in the 1970s only to have Nixon veto it at the urging of a man who had no children himself. But it's also encouraging to realize that we managed it once—because it means we could do it again.

Watching the pendulum swing has helped me to see our current predicament in the context of all that came before and all that might come next. In some moments that's grounding and helpful; in others I am furious thinking about the ways in which motherhood has been used to shame, constrain, and judge women, how even the reverence and respect sometimes shown to mothers can be a double-edged sword that cuts women off at the knees.

Perhaps most importantly, in studying each step along the way I've found solutions, ranging from the practical (government-subsidized day care) to the philosophical (we need to value caregiving and community more). And I've met fiercely inspiring women. Women who were part of past fights for equal rights. Women who are paving a path forward today. Mothers, grandmothers, and women who have opted out of having children. Men who take issue with the role patriarchal society has carved out for them, all working toward creating a more equitable society for everyone. I've traveled throughout the country, interviewing hundreds of people from all backgrounds who have put together their families in a variety of ways. And then, because my sense is that American progressives have tended to pine for policy solutions that would be difficult to implement without massive cultural and economic change, I went not to Sweden, that mythical land of utopian gender equality that every book about work-life balance points to, but to Japan—a country with a political and economic system similar to that of the United States, with similar ideas about "the ideal worker." If you want to substantially change anything in America (or any country, really), you need both cultural change and policy change. If America were to roll out Swedish policies tomorrow, they would likely fail in ways we might not even be able to predict today. That is why at the end of each chapter in this book, you'll find a suggested cultural change and its complementary policy change.

In fact, Japan has been doing exactly that—slapping Scandinavian-style policies on a committedly patriarchal capitalist society—for decades, in the hopes of upping its plummeting birth rate by creating a society in which people want to have more children. This, of course, is partly necessary because of the country's staunchly anti-immigration policies; if the current (and recurrent) trend of anti-immigration sentiment continues in the United States, combined with steadily decreasing birth rates, we may find ourselves in a similar position, in need of incentivizing both reproduction and working mothers. In fact, conservative politicians in particular have been chastising American women for years for not having more children, while at the same time implementing policies that make it increasingly difficult for working families to survive in this country.

What I learned in Japan is that there is exactly the sort of gap between conditions and behavior that you might expect to see in the United States were the government to roll out new family-friendly policies tomorrow. As Masako Ishii-Kuntz, a researcher who has been studying Japanese fatherhood for more than thirty years, put it to me, "Everyone wants to embrace these new ideas, but no one feels comfortable doing it, yet."

Still, there is progress being made there, and there are lessons to be learned about which cultural norms most need to change if a country wants family-supportive policies to work.

The conclusion is simple: We need to push for a society that values caregiving as much as individual success, a world in which neither men nor women are shamed for doing the "women's work" of caring for other humans. We can't wait around for a knight in shining armor to show up and deliver "work-life balance," and women need to stop buying our way into the patriarchy, reaping the rewards of a system that is fundamentally unfair. Our focus should not be gaming the patriarchy to seek revenge on men. No. We're Americans after all; breaking our ties to old systems and starting over is who we are. Or at least that's the story we tell ourselves. So let's make it real: Instead of tweaking the old system here and there, let's build a new society, one that reflects true "family values."

CHAPTER

2

Pioneer Women

"I have family members who were taken from our tradi-tional lands in Montana and shipped off to the East Coast, hundreds of miles away to deter them from escaping, to turn them into non-Indian, to 'kill the savage,'" native public-health researcher Janelle Palacios (Salish/Kootenai) told me recently, as we watched her daughters play in the distance. Palacios grew up on the Flathead Reservation in Montana and now researches public health in Native American communities. "We have whole generations of kids who were in a sense lost, because if you take a kid out of their home when they're four, and you hold them hos-tage until they're 18, 19, and you take away their cultural environment, and take them away from their family and friends, it's difficult to have a shared language or shared values. And you grow up with the indoctrination that you should strive to be different, that you should hate what you look like, that you should hate your roots. That theme has continued to this day."

Palacios's grandparents were taken during what's known as the "boarding school years" from the late 1800s to the early 1900s, when Indian children would be sent to boarding schools that aimed to "kill the savage and save the man." Thousands of these children were literally killed, and many more were abused. Just as the boarding schools were shutting down, the Indian Adoption Project began removing children from their families and placing them with either white families or religious groups. White social workers active on Indian reservations at the time often saw the family structures and mothering practices there—with children being watched by extended family members or community members, especially if their parent worked a lot or was dealing with a substance abuse problem—as deviant, justifying the removal of children.

"You can really see the impact today," Palacios says. "The more functional, healthy tribes? They're usually the ones that were in a geographic location where it was easier to hide your kids."

You can't really talk about American anything without first looking at who colonial Americans were. In history textbooks, the depiction of these people—Puritans, mostly in the Calvinist tradition—is often quite romantic: They came to this "new" land in search of religious freedom or, later, adventure. Seen from a different lens, they were also zealots intent on creating a theocracy or, as they put it, a "godly commonwealth." There were economic drivers as well. The migration of some 20,000 Puritans from England to New England consisted primarily of people well off enough to be able to afford passage to the New World, but who saw little chance for upward mobility in the restrictive aristocratic class structures of the Old World, whereas the colonies afforded the opportunity for "free" land and fast wealth. These early American colonialists saw themselves as the next iteration of the Israelites, freed from the oppression of England by God and given a new land in which to worship freely. They were so convinced that God wanted to give this "new" land to them and only them that they thought nothing of killing the people who were already living on that land and taking what they wanted for themselves. With a mandate from God and a narrative that all people who were not converted to Puritanism and thus marked by God for salvation were sinners condemned to eternal damnation, it was easy to justify as a religious crusade what was actually murder and theft for personal gain.

"And then you think about the people who decided to push farther West and go out on their own, you're really talking about sociopaths willing to destroy anything standing between them and their own individual success," Palacios says.

It's important to remember that these early white Americans were children of the Reformation, and decidedly so. Puritans who followed the teachings of John Calvin believed in the all-powerfulness of God, the Bible as a book from God (written by Him) that should be followed literally, and the innate evil of all humans who had been born with original sin that needed to be cleansed via prayer and devout living. Although historians now refer to the New England Puritans as Calvinists, they did not think of themselves as following Calvin; the prevailing view of the time was that individuals could and should interpret for themselves what the Bible meant and that everything written there was to be taken and interpreted literally.

This emphasis on each person's individual and personal relationship with the Bible, in part a reaction to the ecclesiastical hierarchies and aristocratic bishops and cardinals of the Catholic Church, laid the groundwork for the rise of the individual in America and a deep-seated mistrust of experts. As early governments and courts were established, the Puritans based law on the Bible as well, again with a Reformist approach. While England had more than one hundred crimes on the books that could result in hanging, in the colonies, there were only ten capital crimes, in keeping with the Ten Commandments.

Women, and especially mothers, were seen as subservient, which Puritans found justification for in the Bible. It was in this context that the Anglo American family was born, an island unto itself beholden to no one and reliant on nothing but its own labor. The nuclear family had been a dominant structure in England for several centuries, and the Puritans particularly embraced it in order to ensure that men had total control over their wives and children, whose salvation was their responsibility. That idea—that each family should take care of itself, that children are the sole responsibility of their biological parents—persists today, the rotten foundation on which modern American parenting stress is built.

Despite their insular nature, in the early days of colonial America families did tend to be fairly large, which helped with turning uncultivated land into productive farms for both subsistence and the growth of wealth. Under both English and colonial law, men ruled their wives, children, and any servants. Thanks to the Old World law of "couverture," married women had no legal identity of their own nor any economic status; they had no claim to property or money, even if they had brought it into the marriage or earned it while married, and no legal rights to their children. Married women could not sign contracts or make wills, and they were not allowed to inherit their husband's money should he die, either. The most a widow could inherit was one-third of her husband's estate, which would be controlled, naturally, by her son if she had one. Colonial American families tended to be very large because there was nothing but an upside to having more children in the New World, and a woman's value was a function of her fertility. The average colonial American white woman spent about twenty-five years pregnant and nursing babies.

A silver lining to the absolute power of men in Puritan households was that fathers were quite involved in childrearing. They were seen as responsible for the moral character of their children, as Puritans believed that women were inherently weak and that mothers lacked the strength to administer the sort of strict discipline required to rid a child of the stain of original sin. The notion of "breaking a child's will" shows up repeatedly in historical texts from America in the 1700s, and Puritans were pretty hard-core about it, frequently beating their children with canes and, as historian Jodi Vandenberg-Daves points out in her book *Modern Motherhood: An American History*, swaddling them with wooden rods and encouraging walking at an early age.

The idea that children are born sinners who needed to have the evil beaten out of them was prevalent in much of western Europe at the time as well. It wasn't until the late 1700s to early 1800s, well into the Age of Enlightenment, that the idea of children as innocents, an idea passionately espoused by French philosopher Jean-Jacques Rousseau, began to take hold.

As their American sisters were setting up homesteads, in France and England mothers used this time, when they were seen as nonessential parents and when sinful children could just as easily be sent away to wet nurses, to develop fairly active public lives. Intellectual women in France hosted salons and held court. The focus for women was more on their roles as wives than as mothers, and the notion of maternal instinct had not yet taken hold.

In colonial America, viewing children as miniature adults wasn't just in keeping with religious principles but also happened to line up neatly with economic concerns: Building the colonies required child labor. This was true both in the case of family homesteads and on larger properties in the southeast, which relied on the labor of both enslaved African American children and minor indentured servants shipped over from England to harvest cash crops like tobacco. It was convenient, then, not to view children as "innocents" but rather as sinners who could be cleansed through the virtue of hard work.

As is so often the case, it was a combination of economic and military concern, and fear of female autonomy, that prompted society to shift its ideas about children and to turn its gaze toward mothers. Infant mortality rates were sky-high at a time when most nations were intensely concerned with nation building. Something needed to be done about both the quantity and the quality of humans being produced. After all, how can you build an imperial army if half of your babies are dying and the other half are sickly?

First, politicians and philosophers pointed to the custom of employing wet nurses as a problem: Women should be nursing their own children, they said, rather than sending them off to low-income women who couldn't afford to take care of themselves and thus must be producing subpar nutrition for the nation's babies. To give you a sense of how massive a shift this was in how children were raised, in Paris in 1780, out of the roughly 21,000 children born, 20,000 were sent away to wet nurses.

French feminist scholar Elisabeth Badinter notes that Frenchwomen were the first to send their children away to wet nurses, although Englishwomen soon followed suit. Initially, it was an extension of the idea of children being born sinful or, as Augustine described it, the embodiment of evil. Sixteenth-century preacher Juan Luis Vives, for example, cautioned mothers against nursing their children "too voluptuously."

"Bodies are as much delights as weaknesses; and so mothers damn their children when they nurse them voluptuously," he said. With this in mind, in the seventeenth century, upper-class Frenchwomen began routinely sending their babies away to wet nurses. The bourgeoisie soon followed, and by the eighteenth century, the practice had expanded across all segments of society.

Badinter positions this practice as part of a larger move by women to distance themselves from motherhood in order to gain rights as individuals. "To understand the rejection of motherhood by women, we must remember that at this period the mother's work received no attention and was not valued by society," she writes in *Mother Love: Myth and Reality*. "At best, it [motherhood] was considered normal; at worst, vulgar. Women gained no credit for being mothers, and that was their main function. They understood that to have the right to some esteem, they had to choose a path other than motherhood."

For working-class and some middle-class women, it was also an economic necessity—women's labor was needed to tend to farms or family businesses, and thus infant childcare had to be outsourced. But Badinter's most shocking discovery breached national boundaries, applying to (and massively offending) mothers everywhere: While there were always mothers who loved their children, "mother love" was not always considered a universal, natural sentiment.

In other words, the modern, Western understanding of maternal instinct—an innate nurturing ability that all women have the capacity for, which need only be activated by another mammal in need (not necessarily a child, although that's economically and militarily preferable)—is a social construct, created largely to reduce infant mortality rates and curb women's independence. Which makes it easier to understand why entire cities full of women thought nothing of sending their newborns off to wet nurses before this construct took hold. Before you send an indignant email or search the Internet for pictures of me to throw things at, let me add: There *is* such a thing as maternal instinct, or more accurately instincts, but what anthropological, social, behavioral, and neurobiological studies conducted over the past two decades tell us is that to the extent that maternal instinct exists, it is as ancient as it is precarious, and as complicated as it is mutable.

John Bowlby, the sociologist whose work on child attachment lay the groundwork for what Dr. William Sears would later turn into the attachment-parenting craze, hypothesized that what he called the "attachment system"—a largely fear-driven system that triggers the need for attachment (and thus survival) in children and, ideally, caregiving in mothers—evolved in humans around 5 million years ago, during the Pliocene and Pleistocene epochs. While neurobiological research conducted since the 1990s has corroborated much of what

Bowlby hypothesized, it has also expanded our understanding of caregiving, the interaction between caregiving and attachment, and the emotional and neurobiological drivers of each. Studies in comparative evolution have found that in fact caregiving and attachment have been evolving for at least 180 million years, with caregiving in its rudimentary (mostly feeding-based) form evolving in the reptilian precursors to mammals as a prerequisite for the evolution of attachment.

Meanwhile, genomic studies conducted in the two decades since Badinter formulated her hypothesis have pinpointed "imprinted genes," genes that are expressed from a single parental allele, related to particular maternal behaviors or the lack thereof. Two genes in particular, *Peg1* and *Peg3*, when mutated, result in reduced maternal care by mutant mothers.

"Mutant mothers": That's a trigger isn't it? So we know that human mothers and children have evolved to activate certain behaviors in each other at a biological and genetic level. Maternal instinct, right? Not quite. What we also now know, from the anthropological studies of Sarah Hrdy, the behavioral biology work of Melvin Konner, and the developmental psychology research of Stephen Suomi and his colleagues at the National Institute of Child Health and Human Development, is twofold. First, primate mothers have always had to balance their own survival and that of their offspring, which Hrdy points to in her work, showing that maternal ambivalence and the competing drives of ambition and caregiving are not, as some cultural critics would have us believe, a new phenomenon created by increased rights and education for women; and second, genes and "instinct" do not necessarily a good mother make. Konner has painstakingly revealed how hopelessly intertwined genetics, biology, and environment are and always have been, while Suomi's work has been instrumental in showing both how much one's own upbringing, particularly in the first years of life, can impact one's ability and desire to parent, and that those impacts can be mitigated with a lot of hard work. As Konner puts it in his classic book on the biological constraints on human behavior, *The Tangled Wing,* "on average, early experience matters, and any relationship depends to some extent on prior ones."

In her comprehensive tome on how motherhood evolved in primates and humans (*Mother Nature*), Sarah Hrdy traces the competing demands, between their own survival and that of their offspring, that have always plagued mothers. "Throughout human history, and long before, mothers have been making tradeoffs between quality and quantity, managing reproductive effort in line with their own life stage, condition, and current circumstances," she writes. "As a result, infancy has not always been the warm, safe-in-the-arms-of-love tableau many of us imagine."

"Whatever maternal *instincts* are they are not automatic in the sense that most people use that term," Hrdy concludes. While the prevailing notion has been (and remains today) that mothers once had an innate, selfless reflex toward their children that has been polluted by centuries of female ambition, Hrdy's extensive research shows that no, in fact, primate mothers have always balanced nurturing with ambition, mother love with sexual love, ambivalence with devotion.

This remains a hard pill for women to swallow. Every woman friend I talked to, and even several of the researchers I interviewed while writing this book, shifted uncomfortably when this topic came up. But it's difficult to dismiss the evidence. Historical documents from western Europe, just before the first Americans migrated, make it clear that white, European society neither believed that mothers had a sort of natural instinct or bond with their children, nor expected that they should. And so, not all did. Of the sixteenth to eighteenth centuries, Badinter writes, "mother love was not at that time a social and moral value," which enabled some women—those who could afford financially to keep and raise their children but who simply didn't want to—to outsource the job to someone else. "It seems they considered this [motherhood] an unworthy occupation and chose to get rid of the burden," Badinter writes. And again, because mother love was not considered a virtue or a requirement of "true womanhood" at the time, Badinter notes, "They did so, too, without eliciting the slightest protest."

For centuries, historians have assumed that these mothers sent their children away as a sort of emotional self-defense tactic, given the high infant mortality rates of the day. But Badinter found no proof of this after extensive research. "It was not so much because children died like flies that mothers showed little interest in them," she writes, "but rather because the mothers showed so little interest that the children died in such great numbers. In our search for evidence of the existence of love, we must be prepared, should we not find it, to conclude that love simply did not exist."

Badinter's bombshell, of course, wouldn't drop until after a couple of centuries' worth of philosophy, religion, and politics had built the notion of mother love into the powerful force it is today, beginning with the Age of Enlightenment. Rousseau and other Enlightenment philosophers began to preach the gospel of childhood innocence in the eighteenth century, greatly influencing ideas about motherhood. In this new framework, mothers were more than just physical vessels. They were the sacred caretakers of God's innocents, charged with nurturing and protecting new souls. (Never mind that the children they nourished would then be consumed by military or economic pursuits.)

In both France and England, men with power began encouraging women back into their homes, highlighting the importance of mothers' involvement in safeguarding and raising their children, and accusing any mother who didn't nurse and keep her children of being unnatural. In France, Rousseau consistently promoted the idea of women's roles as mothers and wives, dependent on men. "Men and society could not prevent the desire for emancipation from taking hold, but they very skillfully managed to create obstacles to the acquisition of power and return the woman to the role they felt she should never have left: that of mother," Badinter writes. "As a bonus, they would get their wives back."

In England, public health officials focused on mothers as both the source of and solution to infant mortality. Extensive programs aimed at maternal nutrition and skills were put in place, and the idea of eugenics—preventing some deaths while allowing others, in the interest of preserving the white race (the definition of which was constantly changing), began to take hold.

At the same time, the importance of white women's labor to the economic success of their households, although often quite substantial, especially in the colonies, was increasingly diminished, paving the way for increased focus on the role of mother. Meanwhile, what historians Margaret Marsh and Wanda Ronner have called the "motherhood mandate"—the idea that all women must be mothers—remained strong. Even through the early colonial period in America, when there was no special spiritual or emotional role assigned to mothers, when fathers were responsible for spiritually protecting and guiding their children, the idea that a woman's only worth lay in her ability to produce children was not questioned.

de Tocqueville and "The Three Races"

Just as you can't talk about American ideas without placing them in the context of the first European transplants to America, you can't use "American" as an adjective without evaluating your subject in the context of the various realities of American-ness. The evolution of the white, European (and then American) family bears little resemblance to that of Native American or African American families, or subsequent

immigrant families. In his observations of American democracy in the mid-1800s, French philosopher Alexis de Tocqueville noted the different realities for what he called "the three
races" living in America at the time: African Americans, Native Americans, and white Europeans. "Considering what happens in the world, it seems that Europeans are to men of other
races what human beings are to animals," he wrote. "They
use them to serve themselves, and when they do not submit,
destroy them."

Echoes of that European domination still reverberate
through American society and are particularly obvious in
the African American community. Slaves in the United States
came predominantly from West Africa, where societies were
more matrifocal, mothering was a much more communal affair, and children were considered the responsibility of the
community. In her research on matriarchal societies, German philosopher Heide Goettner-Abendroth notes that he-
reditary queens held important positions for thousands of
years in West Africa, a practice that continued until fairly
recently. "This is not a question of scattered instances of individual queens ruling in patriarchal monarchies," she notes,
"but situations where uninterrupted regency or co-regency by
women is the norm."

Matrifocal, community-oriented social structures were critical in the context of slavery, when mothers were forced back
into the field days after giving birth and children were largely
raised by older enslaved women. And in another departure
from the way things were done in Europe, colonial America did
not always confer rights via paternity. The fact that the children
of an enslaved woman were automatically slaves, irrespective of
who their father was, left nothing but incentives for masters to
rape these women, which they did frequently for both pleasure
and profit. Once born, whether the offspring of two slaves or
of a slave and a master, the children of enslaved women were
the master's property and could be sold away at any moment.

Enslaved mothers, then, had to trust that the women of their extended community would look after their children.

There has been such evil in enslaving people and in the trauma inflicted upon African American families by slavery and, later, by institutions that have perpetuated many of the same conditions. Black mothers through American history confronted first slavery, then economic slavery, and now persistent institutional racism—demanding resilience and ingenuity that is not often acknowledged by mainstream culture. As soon as Black women were freed from slavery, the importance of self-reliance took hold. "The cultural expectation that you should be economically self-reliant has persisted for Black mothers for more than a century," points out Dawn Dow, a research associate of feminist scholar Patricia Hill Collins at the University of Maryland. "That's a longstanding idea in the Black community that's only recently emerged in women's rights conversations that center white women."

Dow points out that in the same way that white American motherhood has been constructed as the result of a constellation of historical, cultural, and economic drivers, Black motherhood ideologies are the result of various historical, economic, and social processes. "The dominant models of motherhood are often talked about from the framework of assumptions about what motherhood is supposed to be, what an ideal or good mother is," Dow says. But there is no universally accepted idea of the "good mother" in America, particularly across racial and ethnic groups. "Different groups of mothers have had different economic, cultural, and social experiences and come from different traditions and backgrounds, and so they conceive of the 'good mother' in different ways," Dow says. "Because these alternatives to the dominant model have often overlapped with people who are lower income or more racially stigmatized, people often look at those experiences from a deficit perspective—what's wrong with them? Versus let's look at this holistically and evaluate the strengths and weaknesses of this approach versus other approaches."

Native American women, for example, had an approach to mothering that resulted from more community-minded social structures and, in many tribes, a history of matrilineal leadership. The European attempt to "break the savages" or "kill the savage and save the man" would repeat from early colonial days through various cycles of brutality in the subsequent centuries, and still plays out in systemic ways today. Still, many Native women, like Black women, have managed to maintain a form of communal mothering that has proven far more resilient, and adaptable to modern times, than the nuclear family model embraced by Europeans.

"Children are all of our responsibility," Janelle Palacios says. "I'll never forget being on the reservation as a child and there was some sort of sporting event at the school and I was running around outside causing trouble and an old auntie lectured me and sent me inside. That sort of thing is common in Indian communities."

"Through collectivism, spirituality, and the application of sovereignty, Native mothers have shaped empowered mothering experiences in spite of the capitalist, Christian, and colonial frameworks that have worked together to support patriarchal western motherhood in Native communities," explains indigenous feminist theorist Kim Anderson in her essay "Giving Life to the People: An Indigenous Ideology of Motherhood" (published in *Maternal Theory: Essential Readings*). According to Anderson, in Native communities, men and women, fathers and mothers inhabit roles seen as "interdependent, equally valuable and flexible." Because indigenous economies were upheld through kinship systems, Anderson explains, "mothers lived and worked in extended families, precluding the possibility of an isolated and subordinate mother as family servant."

There are examples of this sort of kinship childcare arrangement in white European families as well. A Bulgarian mother I interviewed for this book said her mother moved in to help raise her children while she worked. "Her mother did it for her; I'll do it for my kids. It's just what we do," she said.

In her research on middle-class African American mothers, Dawn Dow has found that even those who can afford to pay for childcare often opt for either family or community childcare instead (which is presumably free or cheaper), if it's available. "There's a tradition of that in Black families, where there's very much a sense of 'my mother helped me, I'll help you' that gets passed down the line," she says.

It turns out that the notion of community parents—also referred to as "alloparents"—is a fundamental part of how humans were able to evolve beyond our animal ancestors. Hrdy argues in her book *Mothers and Others* that social support was crucial to human success, that compared with other primates, humans are uniquely cooperative, and that it was precisely cooperation in childcare that gave rise to this fundamentally human trait.

"In my view, cooperative breeding (as sociobiologists term the reproductive strategy in which alloparents help both care for and provision young) came before big brains," Hrdy wrote in a piece in *Natural History* magazine in which she argues against the prevailing theory that humans evolved empathetic skills only after their brains grew. What Hrdy calls "cooperative reproduction"—the emergence of alloparents—began in our early evolutionary ancestors and ultimately led to smarter brains and better social skills. It set the stage for children to grow up slowly and remain dependent on others for many years (thanks, chimps) and paved the way for humans with bigger brains. In other words, it was only when caring became a core value and a key aspect of group organization that humans were able to evolve into the thinking apes we are today.

The more evolved form of parenting, then, is to take a communal approach. And fortunately, there are many examples of how to do that—it's just a matter of looking for and valuing them.

Cultural Fix: Move Toward an Intersectional Understanding of Motherhood

For all the talk of intersectionality these days, I'm amazed at how siloed the motherhood realm remains. In surveying literally hundreds of motherhood-focused magazines and websites, mommy blogs, and podcasts, I find that the norm by far is that anything related to Black motherhood or Latinx motherhood, Asian American motherhood, lesbian motherhood—any motherhood that isn't heterosexual and white—is relegated to niche outlets that clearly target those demographics, while mainstream publications center the experience of white mothers (generally heavy on figuring out work-life balance and steeped in the notion that these two realms—work and motherhood—must always and inherently be in opposition to each other and in competition for resources). This perpetuates a society in which we do not learn from each other, and in which what is held up as "good" mothering is a very particular form of white, middle-class mothering that doesn't apply to all women (including many white women).

Academic research is beginning to get better about this, thanks in no small part to Collins's groundbreaking work, but there is still plenty of work to be done there to provide an intersectional lens on motherhood studies. In mainstream media, we've got an even longer way to go. Women's magazines have historically steered clear of anything that touches on motherhood, let alone an intersectional lens on the subject. However, this barrier is beginning to soften thanks in part to a boom in media about motherhood, from books like Sheila Heti's *Motherhood* to shows like Netflix's *The Letdown* and comedians like Ali Wong and Laurie Kilmartin, motherhood has infiltrated so many other realms of media that magazines have had to relent. Five years ago an editor who had worked at *Marie Claire* and then *Elle* told me, when I asked her advice on pitching a story related to motherhood, "Oh, you can't bring that to any of the women's magazines. They all have a rule against covering motherhood." But in 2017, both magazines published a handful of essays and, in *Elle*'s case, even a cover story on issues related to motherhood. Still, it would be great if more women's magazines would include the topic, and if these publications would make an effort to include intersectional discussions of motherhood, and hold up examples of "good" mothers of color in ways that benefit all women (rather than perpetuating yet another harmful expectation—the "strong Black mother" who never needs, and shouldn't need, any help).

And we need to be intersectional in ways that go beyond race, as well, taking class into account in all that work-life balance advice and looking at ways to make parenting more equal across gender lines as well. For example, almost every woman I know made her first dollars babysitting. That's true of precisely none of the men I know (although I realize that, of course, some young men do babysit!) Were we to encourage men to take on more caregiving jobs earlier, to include them in those conversations from a young age, the transition to fatherhood might not be so jarring. In continuing to perpetuate the idea that little girls get baby dolls and then start babysitting as preteens while little boys get cars and take on manual labor as their first jobs, we set both up to struggle with parenthood. Giving both genders broader ideas and experiences early on would go a long way toward balancing out parental roles later in life. Had my husband logged some years babysitting infants, as I did, for example, or been surrounded by the general cultural notion that he should know what to do with a baby, he might have either known better or felt like he should when he was given the responsibility of a newborn. Instead, he threw up his hands about two months in, and I worked extra hours to hire part-time help. Similarly, had the notion that I could throw up my hands and admit defeat ever occurred to me when I first became a mother and felt completely out of my depth, having a bit of extra help might have, well, helped.

We also need to be willing to look for and try new solutions. It's easy enough to say, "Hey, community mothering is awesome!" or "We really ought to get more boys babysitting!" But actually putting those beliefs into action requires taking practical steps. If living near family or asking for family help is not an option, consider creating your own group of alloparents, forming a tight-knit group of other parents in your community, people with whom you would comfortably swap parenting duties. I began trying this out in a year that was particularly challenging on both the work and home fronts. I asked one friend to pick up my son from school and take him for a playdate for a couple of hours—it helped both of us because it kept his son busy enough for him to finish up some work, too. I partnered up with a mom friend whose husband is away for work frequently (as mine was at the time) to swap family dinners at our respective houses. I agreed to trade date nights with another mom friend so that both couples could get out occasionally without having to pay for babysitting.

Policy Fix: Government-Subsidized, Equal, Use-It-or-Lose-It Family Leave

The community and family infrastructure that Dawn Dow points to is difficult to replicate for families who don't come from this tradition or don't live near their families. Dow says middle-class Black moms she's spoken with who don't have the option of family childcare find the lack of extended family support to be a strain on their careers and on their lives in general. "Because if you can, say, have your mom pick your kid up from day care, all of a sudden your day is extended and you can get a little more work done, and people feel differently about their child spending some time with grandma than they do about a part-time nanny picking him or her up from day care," she says.

Renita Parker-Mobley, a working mom who lives in Washington, D.C., a couple of hours from where she grew up in Maryland, says her dad or sister will occasionally take her son for a night or weekend, but not having the sort of reliable family help that her mom had when raising her is difficult. "It just feels like it's all on us, and if we need help it requires a lot of money and planning and it's just stressful," she told me.

It's a strain we see in myriad books and articles about the challenges of modern mothering. The solution—creating communal parenting networks in the absence of extended family—can only work if new parents are given the time and support needed to create and nurture these networks. And to do that, we need government-subsidized parental leave. It cannot just be maternity leave, and it cannot be unequal, with mothers being given more time than fathers, as tech investor Tim Ross discussed with me recently. "I used to be of the mindset—and I thought I was being really progressive and a good ally with this—that we should give women all the maternity leave they want and did not think men needed yet another benefit," he said. "But then I realized that, no, that just makes it easier to perpetuate the idea that women are the ones who should be at home raising children, and it inevitably leads to companies paying women less, promoting them less, and giving them less responsibility because the bottom line in that scenario is that they cost more, on average. It has to be equal or the outcome will be unequal elsewhere."

Still, Ross points out that in some ways the cultural, economic, and physical considerations around motherhood often

conflict. "Culturally, both genders ideally bear equal responsibility and have equal expectations," he says. "And then economically, you have to make the cost of leave equal for men
and women if you want to prevent the otherwise inevitable
hiring and pay discrimination. But medically, women obviously have unique recovery needs after birth."

Perhaps the solution then, is to consider a sort of swap-
ping system, wherein mothers get the first three weeks off,
paid, while fathers get one or two weeks. Then one parent
takes the next twelve weeks off paid and the other takes the
following twelve weeks off paid, with companies paying for
recovery weeks and the government paying for each of the
twelve-week periods, which companies are mandated to allow. Companies and their staffs could work out any number
of variations within these parameters—perhaps the parents
switch off every four weeks for twelve weeks each or go back
to work part-time after eight weeks and keep a part-time
schedule for another eight weeks. With such an approach,
we could ensure that women get recovery time; that the economic costs for men and women are relatively equal, which
minimizes the potential for discrimination; and that we set up
the cultural expectation that both parents are approximately
equally involved in raising children. Making the government
pay keeps companies from discriminating (as much) against
reproductive-age employees. In addition, we give both men
and women stretches of solo parenting time, so they have to
really figure parenting out, and by staggering the leaves, parents can go about twenty-nine weeks before they need to hire
childcare, which helps reduce the cost of going back to work.

Annie Dean, cofounder and CEO of Werk, a consulting
firm that helps Fortune 500 companies do a better job of re-
cruiting and retaining working mothers, has a personal lens
on this issue. When Dean had her children, she was working
at a law firm with a generous maternity leave policy. "I had
two six-month maternity leaves," she says. "But during those

leaves my husband had two to four days off." Not only does that make him inherently less costly to his company, reinforcing discriminatory hiring and payment of mothers, but also it sets fathers up from the beginning to be the secondary parent. "I'm the only one home for the first six months, so only I know the schedule and the care providers, and all the daily stuff. If we don't give men the same opportunity to participate in parenthood the way women have always been expected to, that bias and systemic role assignment persists," Dean says.

The same thing happened to me with my first child. I put my career on hold completely, while my husband took one week off. He was allowed two weeks, but he saved one for when his mother was coming over from Scotland a few months later (yes, that argument still comes up). A week after our son was born, he was back at work, leaving the house at 6 a.m. and typically returning around 8 p.m., missing the daily routine of an infant entirely. So much so that when our second child was born and the shoe was on the other foot—my husband needed to be the primary parent while I worked—he was absolutely unprepared for how difficult it is to deal with an infant. "He cries a lot! He's a fussy baby," he would say to me. And I would respond, "Yeah, he's a pretty normal newborn." The net result for us was that I had to work even more hours to pay for additional childcare because my husband could not really hack it. That's a bit harsh, I realize, but I'm a tired working mom and have no energy left to sugarcoat this. He was given the responsibility of another human for the very first time at the age of thirty-seven, and he wasn't quite up to the challenge. Had he been encouraged to babysit or look after younger cousins, as I've suggested we encourage boys to do more of, this transition might not have been so difficult to manage.

Joan Williams, the founding director of the Center for WorkLife Law at the University of California at Hastings, has been a proponent for years of equal paternity and maternity leave, and progressive companies that want to retain top talent are beginning to take notice. When men are not just given, but actually take paternity leave (a key distinction), they often provide more support—physical, financial, and emotional—for the mothers of their children to return to work. Men and women taking equal leave also makes the workplace more egalitarian in general.

Hillary Frank created the popular parenting podcast, *The Longest Shortest Time*, one of the few parenting podcasts that does try to take an intersectional lens. In late 2017, she produced a series called *It's a Real Mother* about discrimination against working mothers, with the final episode focused on solutions. "We really wanted there to be like this one thing that we could tell people to do, but that was hard to find," she says. "And then when we did find something, we all groaned... Sweden again!"

What she found was that even with its amazing options for both maternity and paternity leave, Sweden was seeing gender inequality in terms of who took leave and for how long, which was correlating with pay and promotion gaps. "They were able to implement all the things on our wish list—these amazing leave policies and they even have a Minister of Gender Equality—but they were still seeing discrimination against working moms," Frank says. "Moms would still take leave more than dads, and for longer periods of time, and so companies still saw hiring or promoting mothers as a risk."

Americans still looking wistfully at Sweden-style policies would do well to consider an example a bit closer to home, economically and politically: Japan. For decades, Japan's government has been attempting to institute policies that would encourage women to have more kids. Thanks to restrictive immigration policies and the fact that fathers have traditionally done almost nothing to help with children, Japan has been battling a declining birth rate for decades, prompting concerns over workforce shortages and economic losses. To combat the problem, since 2010, the government has instituted generous parental leave policies for men and women, estab-lished a government-subsidized day care system, and, through its "*ikumen* project" (*ikumen* roughly translates to "involved dad"), promoted positive cultural representations of fathers and encouraged companies to offer working dads flextime.

"It hasn't really worked. We have a gap between context and conduct," sociology researcher Masako Ishii-Kuntz told me in her office at Tokyo's Ochanomizu University. "So, they are allowed to go home early—or really just at a normal time, since it's really common for Japanese men to work late, un-til 10 or 11 at night—and they are allowed to take paternity leave, but hardly anyone is doing it."

Ishii-Kuntz has been researching fatherhood in Japan for three decades, during which time she also spent several years in the United States and in Scandinavia. "I've interviewed hundreds of Japanese dads, and I'd say probably about a third of them really want to be more involved with their kids and are into the *ikumen* thing," she says. "But according to the lat-est data only 3 percent of men are actually taking advantage of these policies."

In part, that has to do with some glitches in implemen-tation (there are nowhere near enough day care centers, for example), but the primary culprit, according to Ishii-Kuntz, is the culture. "No one wants to be the first guy in their office to take paternity leave or leave early," she says. "And bosses are from a time when that was not done, so they have a hard time establishing a workplace in which that's okay."

Similarly, US academic settings with egalitarian parental leave policies have not really moved the needle on equality. Men often benefit from a fatherhood bonus due to the fact that women still take a dominant role in child-rearing, par-ticularly in early infancy if the mother is breastfeeding. If a married couple of university professors have a baby and both get the same amount of leave, for example, while the mother is dealing with feedings every two to three hours and thus

forced to truly take leave of her work, the father often benefits from time off from his daily teaching or advisory duties
to pursue research. In her research on mothers in academia,
Andrea O'Reilly found that the number-one indicator of success for women was the type of marriage they had and how
egalitarian it was, even more so than whether or not they had
children, or how egalitarian parental leave policies were.

The solution? In 2017, Sweden instituted equal leave policies for mothers and fathers, and a mandate that requires
that you use the leave or lose it. "So basically, you're stupid
if you don't take it," Frank says. Men and women are already
taking leaves of more similar lengths, and that has evened out
the risk and cost for companies.

Ishii-Kuntz sees this as the sort of policy needed if you hope
to change both culture and policy. To combat the conduct-
context gap in Japan, the government there is now rolling out
training for executives at companies throughout the country,
through the IkuBoss program, showing bosses how to encourage their staff to take advantage of parent-friendly policies and
how to manage the workplace in ways that minimize whatever
productivity loss they fear they will incur by doing so.

But simply mandating equal leave might be a more efficient
route. Frank says she has high hopes for such an approach
working in the United States. "It's the one thing I could imagine being implemented and changing things pretty quickly, at
scale," she says.

Of course, once they go back to work, many parents will
also need some amount of paid childcare, which is not only
exceedingly costly in the United States, but also saddled with
centuries of downright weird notions about the idea of anyone but primary parents being responsible for children. It's
another system that needs overhauling, and we'll get to it in
the coming chapters.

3

Birthing a Nation

"I increasingly view motherhood as a form of activism," says Danielle Lovell-Jones, a lawyer-turned-impact-investing-consultant. Lovell-Jones lives in London but grew up in Miami, watching her mother advocate for the kids who didn't have someone like her in their corner. "My mom was just sort of a radical, and so she knew what it was like to feel like the 'other' and she spotted that in other kids— usually large, Black boys that everyone else was afraid of. She would always talk to them and help them out, and so she modeled for me very early on that no matter how different someone is from you, you never know what their back story is, and everyone deserves to be treated with respect."

That laid the groundwork for Lovell-Jones's own approach to parenting, in which she emphasizes balancing respect for oneself with respect for others, and teaching her daughters to be thoughtful in their approach to the world and to other people. As a Black woman raising two future Black women, she has to give them the skills to protect themselves while not instilling fear or stereotypes too deeply in them. "It's hard, because you know, as a mother you want to protect your children. At the most basic level, that's what you're supposed to do. But then you have to think: What am I protecting them from? Is that fear valid? Is there a way to make them more accepting and better able to co-exist with a variety of different types of people? Because that ability is what I think we're really missing today."

Before she had kids, Lovell-Jones says she wanted to "change the world on a big scale; the more people the better." Now, although she hasn't given up on big-scale change, she also sees the value in the small scale. "So I've gone from the whole world to two specific humans," she laughs. "But I do feel like that's important. And I also feel like that work gives me strength to push for larger changes, too."

In researching various maternal-activist organizations, Lovell-Jones says she was somewhat disappointed in what she found. "There's a way that a lot of their messaging comes across—whether the issue is gun control or drunk driving, whatever it is—it just feels like it's coming from a place of frailty a lot of the time. And I'm not frail. I don't think of myself as this soft, sentimental mother. Motherhood doesn't make you weak; it makes you strong. We need to be harnessing that strength for large-scale political change."

In the late eighteenth and early nineteenth centuries, the Enlightenment brought about a revolution in both thought and practice. A belief in self-government and the rejection of old ideas in favor of new and youthful ones swept the world, changing both countries and families. In its love of all things youthful, the Enlightenment produced new ways of thinking about children, namely that they were innocents who ought to be protected and nurtured, rather than sinners who needed to have their spirits crushed. But while the Enlightenment might have improved the lot of children, it wasn't so great for mothers.

One outcome of this line of thinking during and after the American Revolution was the notion of "companionate marriage," which provided a slightly more egalitarian model of marriage in which men and women were mates rather than master and his human chattel. Still, the concessions offered to women during this time fell far short of actual equality. At a time when the innate rights of kings and men to rule was being questioned around the world, the white, propertied men who wrote the Constitution made sure to keep in place institutions like couverture and slavery that maintained their positions atop the social and political order.

There were women who saw in the Enlightenment a path to freedom. "Remember the Ladies, and be more generous and favourable to them than your ancestors," Abigail Adams famously told her husband John. "Do not put such unlimited power into the hands of the Husbands. Remember all Men would be tyrants if they could."

But instead of true independence, women were offered better versions of marriage and motherhood. It was during this time that the notion of republican motherhood came about, accompanied by its more spiritual cousin "moral motherhood," which is an extension of the Victorian notion of the "Angel in the House"—the woman who acts and speaks only for others, who lives only to rule the private sphere of the home and keep everyone in it happy and comfortable. As the understanding of children as innocents was emerging, along with it came the idea of women as the ultimate protectors and nurturers of that innocence. The notion of maternal instinct emerged in full force during this time period as well. The motherhood mandate had long posited that all women should, by nature, be mothers, and the idea of maternal instinct extended that idea, asserting that all women must naturally be good at mothering and love their children unconditionally.

This created pressure on women not only to be perfect mothers but also to feel perfectly motherly. It eliminated any room for what psychologists call "maternal ambivalence." Psychoanalyst Barbara Almond defines maternal ambivalence in her book *The Monster Within* this way: "Conflict is the bedrock of human psychology and is always manifested in some form of ambivalence, the word we use for feelings of both love and hate toward the same person, goal, or desire in our lives. It is a completely normal phenomenon. What we love can disappoint us. What we love, we can also lose. What we lose causes us pain. That mothers have mixed feelings about their children should come as no surprise to anybody."

I can't even begin to explain what a wave of relief reading that paragraph brought to me. I adore my children, and sometimes I want to run away from them. Even in our current "bad mom" culture, that feels taboo. We only celebrate the "bad mom" when she's doing something amusingly wrong like baking terrible cupcakes. Maternal ambivalence is as verboten as it ever was.

In *Mother Love/Mother Hate: The Power of Maternal Ambivalence,* therapist Rozsika Parker lays out a view of maternal ambivalence as stemming from the often opposing yet simultaneous desires of mother and child, which Parker argues need not be negative if they are simply accepted as a fact of life: "The conflict between love and hate actually spurs mothers on to struggle to understand and know their baby. In other words, the suffering of ambivalence can promote thought—and the capacity to think about the baby and child is arguably the single most important aspect of mother."

For both Parker and Almond, the only real problem with maternal ambivalence is that it has become a social taboo. As Almond puts it: "I believe that today's expectations for good mothering have become so hard to live with, the standards so draconian, that maternal ambivalence has increased and at the same time become more unacceptable to society as a whole."

With these new expectations on mothers and motherhood came new ways of judging women who did not meet them. Not that the notion of maternal instinct is terrible, or that it hasn't served many positive purposes: adding to the enjoyment of motherhood for women, assigning social and moral value to the connection between mother and child, aiding in the protection and nurturing of children, and so forth. But it is also a social construct that neatly served not only to keep women in a place that men found comfortable but also to contribute to the enterprise of nation building.

As newly minted moral guardians, colonial American mothers were key to building up the citizenry of a new nation. Republican motherhood as an idea placed the responsibility of grooming new citizens on mothers, which also had the effect of ensuring that women would focus on attaining status via motherhood rather than through independent public life. However, women did use the new value placed on motherhood to demand certain things, starting with education.

If mothers were going to be responsible for the citizenry of a new nation, after all, they should probably know something about reading, writing, arithmetic, and history. "Between the 1780s and 1820s, American women acquired education during an expanding but experimental stage when scores of female academies proliferated across the new nation, yet decades before colleges or other institutions of higher ed admitted women," historian Lucia McMahon writes in *Mere Equals: The Paradox of Educated Women in the Early American Republic*. In this sense, too, even the motherhood mandate had a silver lining: If all women were expected to one day become mothers, all must be educated.

Of course, this education had its limits. It was intended to make women more entertaining wives (for their companionate marriages) and more skilled mothers. James Neal, a teacher at the Young Ladies' Academy of Philadelphia in the 1700s, noted that proper attention to education enabled women to be "more perfect ornaments of society, fully calculated to render happy beyond expression those who participate with you."

As more women became educated, the need to reinforce the boundary between women and lofty intellectual pursuits grew. It wasn't long before various ideas associating infertility with advanced education in women came about, just in case these ladies got any ideas in their heads about shirking the duty of childbearing. In her book *Disorderly Conduct: Visions of Gender in Victorian America,* Carroll Smith-Rosenberg describes the emergence of this thinking: "A girl who curtailed brain work during puberty could devote her body's full energy to the optimum development of its reproductive capacities. A young woman, however, who consumed her vital force in intellectual activities was necessarily diverting these energies from the achievement of true womanhood. She would become weak and nervous, perhaps sterile, or more commonly, and in a sense more dangerously for society, capable of bearing only sickly and neurotic children."

Male doctors who began gaining power over reproduction toward the end of the nineteenth century (more on that in Chapter 5) were hugely influential in promoting this idea. Doctors routinely wrote and spoke about the fact that women, already weak by nature, would only be further weakened by education, which would in turn weaken their progeny.

At the same time, education began to increasingly be seen as beneficial for children. As a new country, America had no generational wealth to speak of, and there was less land available to be grabbed, stolen, or bought cheaply, so expanding the family's finances by acquiring more land was now more challenging. Given the financial instability of American families, many saw college education as a way in which their sons might eventually bolster the family fortune. Women were still decades away from gaining access to higher education, but it was generally thought that the mothers of future college students should not be left entirely uneducated.

Shifts in religion during the 1700s and 1800s also contributed to changing ideas about women and, in particular, motherhood. Women made up 70 percent of the Protestants in New England and contributed to what historians have described as a "feminization" of the religion, most notably with the attribution of the traditionally feminine characteristics of humility and self-sacrifice to Jesus Christ. Women's roles in their churches also helped them wrest the mantle of "morally superior sex" away from men. In writings from the early to mid-1800s, we see men talking about the need for women's tempering influence rather than the other way around.

But while white mothers' roles and responsibilities were expanding, the rights of women in general remained constrained. The emphasis on the importance of being a good wife and a good mother made for a general social and cultural push of white women into their homes. As concerns rose that men's morality would be sullied by the influence of both money and alcohol, the idea that this risk could be mitigated by pious women who kept out of the dirty business of politics and business provided both an important role for women and a way to keep them home at the same time. The "cult of domesticity" or "cult of true womanhood"—the idea that "true women" are pious, pure, domestic, and submissive—emerged in the early nineteenth century and worked to keep a large portion of the female population out of the public sphere.

"By shaping the next generation of leaders and citizens, mothers held the key to their children's—and the nation's—future," McMahon writes. "Yet such influence came at a price. Nineteenth-century educators increasingly abandoned the idea of 'mere equality' [between men and women] to promote a hierarchical ordering of the family, insisting that mothering remained 'subordinate, as it respects the father.'"

"Though her station is subordinate," Joseph Emerson rationalized at the time, "yet in a great measure, she carries in her heart, and holds in her hand, the destinies of the world."

African American women, meanwhile, were still enslaved for the greater part of this century and, once freed, generally lived in poverty, which required them to work outside the home. This had the added impact of automatically disqualifying them from being "true women," further devaluing Black women in society's hierarchy.

Moral Motherhood and Race

The emphasis on moral motherhood and maternalism after the American Revolution was a double-edged sword for
women of color. While it served to further degrade many
women of color, particularly Black women, by defining their
motherhood practices as inherently flawed, inferior, and unnatural (you couldn't be a "moral mother" if you worked outside the home, which nearly all Black women did at the time),
it also provided an on-ramp to abolitionism for many white
middle- and upper-class women. If motherhood was sacred,
the thinking went, then it was unconscionable that some
mothers should be enslaved and lack any rights to keep or
protect their children.

Abolitionists frequently referenced the impact slavery had
on the mother-child bond, particularly when speaking to religious white audiences. "The domestic hearth, with its holy
lessons and precious endearments, is abolished in the case of
a slave mother and her children," Frederick Douglass wrote.

As white women were reducing the sizes of their families,
enslaved Black women were bearing the brunt of the end of
the international slave trade. With no way to bring in more
slaves, American slave owners had to make do with what they
had, which increased their view of enslaved Black women as
breeding stock. At the same time, slaves were traded within
the country at a record rate, which more often than not meant
the breakup of families. In the first half of the nineteenth century, 875,000 slaves were moved from the Upper South to the
Lower South. Those mothers who were allowed to raise their
children often did so with no involvement from fathers, who
were either their masters or fellow slaves who had been sold
off to another plantation. Black mothers had to balance the
need to physically protect their children with the need to help
them find dignity and self-respect in a situation that afforded
neither.

The contradiction between moral motherhood and slavery was impossible to ignore, and that contrast rallied many white middle- and upper-class women to the abolitionist cause. However, it's also an early example of the sort of problematic #whitefeminism we still see today. For many women, what stirred their desire to support abolitionism was not an aversion to slavery per se, so much as a desire to confront any situation in which the ideal of moral motherhood was impossible to attain. They were fighting, then, for Black mothers to be more like white mothers, never mind whether Black mothers wanted moral motherhood, or that such a lens reinforced the idea that Black motherhood was inferior.

It's the same line of thinking that eventually had middle- and upper-class white women invading the homes of poor white women, immigrant women, Black women, and Native women to show them how to "properly" mother, which resulted in a whole host of new problems (more on that in Chapter 4). At the same time, in invoking moral motherhood to advocate for abolition, white women often played up the idea of the self-sacrificing mother who wants nothing more than to care for her family, perpetuating a prescription for motherhood that both restricted white women and implicitly criticized Black mothers.

Meanwhile, the abolitionist movement was often dismissive of the women joining its ranks. In fact, it was the treatment of women at an abolitionist convention that led to the formation of the first women's rights convention, in Seneca Falls, New York, in 1848. Issues on the agenda included abolition, property rights for married women, access to higher education and, for the first time ever, the right to vote.

Suffragists like Elizabeth Cady Stanton pointed to the more equal rights of women in Native American tribes as inspiration for American women to demand equality. "In the councils of the Iroquois every adult male or female had a voice upon all questions brought before it," Stanton reported

in *The National Bulletin* in 1891. "[They] were essentially democratic in their government....The women were the great
power among the clan."

Stanton described how clan mothers had the responsibility for nominating a chief and could remove that chief if he
did not make good decisions. "They did not hesitate, when
occasion required, 'to knock off the horns,' as it was techni-
cally called, from the head of a chief and send him back to the
ranks of the warriors."

Matilda Joslyn Gage, in her 1893 book *Woman, Church,
and State*, described the Haudenosaunee neighbors she had
observed growing up: "Division of power between the sexes in
this Indian republic was nearly equal," she wrote. "The common interests of the confederacy were arranged in councils,
each sex holding one of its own, although the women took the
initiative in suggestion, orators of their own sex presenting
their views to the council of men."

Both women were amazed at the matrifocal nature of
Native communities. While in colonial America at the time,
paternal rights were absolute and mothers had no legal claim
to their children, in Native communities, children always belonged first and foremost to their mothers. "It appears the
children belonged to the mother, not to the father, and that he
was not allowed to take them even after the mother's death,"
Stanton wrote.

A proponent of divorce, particularly for women who were
in abusive or loveless marriages—and attacked almost as much
for this viewpoint as for her stance on women's suffrage—
Stanton admired the Iroquois approach to this issue as well.
"No matter how many children, or whatever goods he might
have in the house, the husband might at any time be ordered
to pick up his blanket and budge; and after such an order it
would not be healthful for him to attempt to disobey."

Despite her respect for Native communities, Stanton
was racist toward Black men and women. She believed in

abolition, but when rifts arose between abolitionists and suffragists over who should get the vote first—black men or white women—she made various ugly comments about how much more worthy of the vote white women were. And for all their breathless excitement over egalitarian Native communities, even the most radical of suffragettes was not yet advocating for any major change in gender roles or access to meaningful political power. Rather, they used maternalism to their benefit—speaking out about slavery because it hindered women's ability to mother, and about property rights and the vote because such legal tools would better enable women to protect their children. Women's rights activists were content to focus on voting rights, and even then, many suggested a limited vote, pegged to the temperance movement.

Temperance—a movement to limit and, in some cases, prohibit consumption of alcohol—wound up being a cause that could represent intersectional interests, including both abolition and women's rights. Temperance was used as a wedge issue for women's rights: It was easier to make the case that it was unfair that women could be left destitute by an alcoholic husband and thus needed some amount of economic independence, for example, or that women ought to be able to have a say in whether alcohol was sold in their neighborhoods, than it was to make the case that women were equally human and thus deserved equal rights under the law. The connection between temperance and abolition was more nuanced, but Frederick Douglass, a leader in both movements, connected the degrading condition of slavery with the penchant for drunkenness, the self-control denied by slavery and the loss of self-control wrought by alcohol. Many Black abolitionists of the day also saw an alliance with the temperance movement as a way to establish moral credibility among white activists indoctrinated to think of African Americans as morally inferior.

Ultimately, the women's rights and abolitionist movements split amid arguments about whether to pursue the vote for

Black men or for women first, with Susan B. Anthony, Matilda Joslyn Gage, and Elizabeth Cady Stanton heading up the National Woman Suffrage Association, which advocated for women first, and Lucy Stone, Frederick Douglass, and Gerrit Smith forming the American Woman Suffrage Association, which supported suffrage for Black men first and then all women. Once slavery ended, the abolitionist movement had turned, shortly after the Civil War, to the idea of universal suffrage for all—initially, Black men and all women. But over time, it became clear that these efforts would need to be staggered, and factions within the movement disagreed over who should go first. For the record, Black men got the vote in 1870, while Black women (all women) would have to wait for the passage of the Nineteenth Amendment in 1920. Its association with the temperance movement ultimately worked against the women's rights movement—the Woman's Christian Temperance Union backed women's suffrage beginning in 1879 as a means to advance a conservative Christian agenda that has largely worked to undermine women's rights.

From their first forays into public life, American mothers have often worked against each other. Mothers, like women, are not a monolith. There have always been, and are today, women who are quite comfortable within and willing to fight to preserve a patriarchal system. There are mothers who believe that stay-at-home mothers are better than working mothers, that white mothers are better at mothering than women of color. Motherhood rhetoric has been used just as frequently to further ensnare mothers in the cult of domesticity as it has been used to further social justice.

Linguistics scholar Lindal Buchanan points to Sarah Palin as a recent example of this in her textbook *Rhetorics of Motherhood*. Palin often had her disabled son on stage with her as a visual representation of her views on abortion, Buchanan points out. "While it was possible to disagree with and debate Palin's stance on abortion, it was virtually impossible to contest her visual rhetoric without appearing loutish and insensitive," Buchanan notes. "The candidate's invocation of motherhood tapped into the overarching system of gender and made her appeal difficult to refuse or refute directly."

Motherhood rhetoric has also been used to pit mothers against women without children and married women against single women, as Buchanan points out. Buchanan notes that American culture tends to contrast Woman—what she calls a "devil term"—with Mother, a "god term," attributing selfishness, hysteria, sex, work, sensuality, irrationality, and so forth to the Woman, and love, empathy, protection, home, altruism, and nourishment to the Mother.

Nonetheless, whether she did so intentionally or not, Palin may also have indicated tacit approval for mothers of young children to work in ambitious, demanding jobs. "I think '08 fundamentally changed the terrain," Jennifer Lawless, director of American University's Women and Politics Institute said in a 2012 interview about women getting into politics. "The Republican Party is the party that would be the most inclined to embrace traditional roles and responsibilities. When they had, as their vice-presidential nominee, a female candidate with very young children, they were saying by default that this was okay. So I think it becomes difficult for there to be backlash against that statement now, given who was on their ticket in 2008."

That seems logical, but voters are still anything but logical, especially when it comes to women. The same person who loved Sarah Palin's hockey mom shtick in 2008 could very easily hold motherhood against a candidate whose views don't align with his or her own. Moreover, if history shows anything, it's that patriarchal people are quite effective at applying "means to an end" logic when it comes to working mothers: It's okay for Palin to take on an ambitious political job as a young mother because that will give her the power necessary to pass laws that enforce traditional gender norms.

Cultural Fix: Reclaiming Republican Motherhood

Republican motherhood was something of a trick pulled on nineteenth-century mothers—it had a whiff about it of "if we tell them motherhood is important, maybe they'll be content with a supporting role and not ask for more." It also only included white women. What if we turned republican motherhood on its head and encouraged mothers to take charge of the world they and their children live in? To change the systems we live in, either from within or without, to view, as lawyer/mother/activist/podcast host Danielle Lovell-Jones described it to me, "motherhood as activism," not in a way that limits women with children but in a way that expands their role into one that takes the entire local, national, and even global community into account.

So far, only Republican (as in GOP) mothers have been allowed to use being a mother as a qualification for anything—think Sarah Palin's constant "hockey mom" and "mama bear" shout-outs—and it's often wielded as a sword against those seeking more rights for women and against women who don't have children. This is maternalism at its worst. And motherhood rhetoric tends to remain a dangerous tool in today's world. Any appeal to the maternal is inherently colored by today's gender norms, which means it has tremendous potential to backfire. As an example, Buchanan highlights the varying viewpoints of the Million Mom March for gun control, which took place on Mother's Day in 2000. The march was seen by some as so imbued with gendered stereotypes—the enraged mother, the mama bear or lioness protecting her cubs—that it undermined the argument, painting it as an emotional reaction rather than reasoned analysis. Others argued that initiatives like the Million Mom March merely introduce the notions of caring, empathy, and nurturance to political discourse and that there's nothing inherently wrong with those things, that they have only been devalued by a patriarchal society that views all things coded as "feminine" as inherently weak and unstable. Buchanan espouses more of a both-and understanding of maternalism. "Tapping into shared cultural understandings of motherhood produces rich rhetorical resources capable of advancing women and their civic agendas while simultaneously reinforcing limiting stereotypes and inequitable gender relations," she writes. "Motherhood's cultural entrenchment is the source of both its rhetorical power and its potential detriment to women."

The key, then, is to be very conscious of the potential detriments of maternalism—that frailty that Lovell-Jones sensed in the marketing of some mother advocacy organizations, for example—and build a system and a way of thinking and talking about motherhood that is matrifocal. "In the necessary push for equality, there's been a push against traditional roles, which has resulted in delegitimizing mothers' voices," says Kristin Rowe-Finkbeiner, CEO and cofounder of MomsRising, which boasts more than a million members. That's happened on both the right and the left, and mother-activist groups today are working to regain a place of strength for mothers in local, state, and national political discussions. Part of that, according to Rowe-Finkbeiner, is meeting moms where they're at. After all, you can't advocate for working moms without realizing that they probably don't have a ton of hours to volunteer. "Moms are an incredibly powerful force and when we join together we can move mountains," she says.

Right now, we face an incredible maternal barrier—mothers are hired less, paid less, and judged more harshly in the labor force. Mothers are the fastest-increasing segment of minimum-wage workers. We are more likely to live in poverty than either non-mothers or men. Our hurdles are great and that puts enormous time constraints on us in

our ability to be engaged in politics. So we're opening mul-
tiple avenues to give their voices impact—whether they
have five minutes, five hours, or five days. People need to
be able to take time to do what they can do in the moment.
It all adds up.

MomsRising has seen several wins as a result of that ap-proach, including some key local and state family-leave laws. Similarly, Moms Demand Action for Gun Sense in America has strategically gone after state and local legislators in the absence of federal leadership on gun control and posted a long list of legislative wins in 2017. Their message is targeted, angry, and effective.

Patricia Hill-Collins has written extensively in defense of activist, community mothering, which she sees as a nat-ural extension of Black mothering approaches. Some main-stream white feminist groups have criticized what they call "maternal politics" in the past for locking women into the idea that their only value is motherhood and that mother-hood is the only role that gives legitimacy to their voices. "This type of thinking sets up a hierarchy of feminisms, as-signs the type engaged in by U.S. Black women and women in Africa a secondary status, and fails to recognize moth-erhood as a symbol of power," Collins writes in *Black Feminist Thought.* "Instead, the activist mothering associated with Black women's community work becomes portrayed as a 'politically immature' vehicle claimed by women who fail to develop a so-called radical analysis of the family as the site of oppression similar to that advanced within Western feminism."

It's time to rethink and reclaim the notion of republican motherhood as a potential force for good, and a useful tool in the creation of a new system that places equality, the public good, and fairness at its core.

Policy Fix: Get More Working Mothers
into Government

While researching this book, I wanted to find out how many mothers of young children are working in the government today. That stat is nowhere to be found, so I spent several weeks combing the Internet to compile a database of congressional parents. There seem to be only two women in the Senate with children under twelve, Kirsten Gillibrand and Tammy Duckworth, both Democrats, and fourteen men (eight Republicans and six Democrats). It's hard not to see that as yet another proof point that fathers are often more encouraged and supported in their ambitions than mothers. In the House, there are eight mothers of children under twelve (evenly split between Democrats and Republicans). That means that Congress-wide, 1.8 percent of our representatives are working mothers. In order to push through policies that benefit working mothers, that needs to change. Of course, not all working-mother politicians will advance an agenda that improves the lot of other working mothers. Anti-feminist culture critic Phyllis Schlafly was the ultimate example of this: She worked tirelessly to vilify working mothers and move against policies that would support them, all while being a working mother herself—but having more working mothers weigh in on the policies that impact them is likely better than having no say at all.

Brigid Schulte draws attention to this gap between what's going on with the general public and the reality of life for most politicians: "While only a small percentage of American families can afford to have one parent at home full-time, the vast majority of congressional representatives have a spouse at home dealing with child care needs and household duties," she writes.

That's if they still have kids at home at all, which very few do. The small minority of congressional representatives with young children are overwhelmingly men with a stay-at-home spouse, which makes it difficult for them to understand what life is like for the vast majority of American families.

Regina Bateson, a candidate for Congress from California's District Four (the district that includes Yosemite and Lake Tahoe) says this is part of what prompted her to run, albeit begrudgingly at first. "I benefitted greatly from the maternity care afforded by the Affordable Care Act, and I know what policies would help me most as a working mom," she told me recently. "But I hardly mentioned my kids in my campaign because it's just a lose-lose—either you're penalized for taking on something like a political campaign when you have young kids, or then you have one of my primary opponents, a woman who doesn't have kids and she was penalized for that…And how many women with young children are in Congress right now? A small handful. So the people deciding the policies that impact us are either long past the point of raising children or didn't have them."

Kristin Rowe-Finkbeiner echoes this sentiment. "There's been a lot of talk about the 'balancing act' and a lot of blame— if you can't fit everything in your cute little calendar it's your fault as a woman," she says. "Bringing the actual stories of real women to our elected officials shows them that this many people are having the same issues at the same time, so it's not an individual failing, it's a structural issue, and fixing it could help everyone. Most of Congress right now, they don't know what it really means to have child care cost more than college, and how that impacts, for example, grocery purchases. And how that affects the rest of the economy given that moms are the top consumers."

4

The Industrial Revolution and the Division of Labor

"I was working at the hospital from 3 p.m. to midnight every day. I was married and had two children, and I did everything around the house and for the children, too. Coming from Mexico, the idea was that the man was in charge of the woman, and the woman had to take care of the house and the kids and everything." Leticia Aguilar is in her sixties now, her children are grown and have their own children, and she continues to run a preschool and work with dozens of Latinas in her town to teach them how to forge more equitable marriages. *"There was an older woman at the hospital, Adrie, and she gave me a ride one day and sat down with me at lunchtime and said, 'Leticia, let me tell you something. From what I see and what you're telling me, he's controlling you 100 percent and you're doing everything he wants you to do. I think you need to try to change things.' She listened to me, and she let me cry about everything I was doing. That lady helped me, that one lady. Because I was seeing what she noticed, too, but I wasn't ready to say, 'Yes, this needs to change.' It was like I was waiting for someone else to tell me,"* Aguilar says. *At the time, she never left the house without asking her*

husband's permission. A few weeks after their conversation at the hospital, Adrie invited her out for dinner. "And that was the first time I told my husband, you know, 'Honey, I'm gonna go with my friend that works in the hospital.' He looked at me and said, 'Where are you going? Who gave you permission?' And I said, 'I'm not asking you. I'm just telling you that I'm going to have dinner with my friend.' And he looked at me and just turned to himself and laughed, and I just went and I said, Enjoy, Leticia. And when you come back you can resolve the problem, but you gonna enjoy. *That was the first time I left. And I said,* Okay, now I know that I can be myself and I can be...he's my partner but he's not my papa." *Eventually, Aguilar put herself through school and started a business. "He threatened to divorce me for years," she says. "But I just kept saying, 'I love you, but I need to do this for me. If you have to divorce me, I understand.'" The divorce never materialized, and years later, when they spoke about that period in their marriage, she says her husband admitted to her that, because she's fifteen years younger than him, he was scared she would meet someone else at school and leave him. He also had a hard time dealing with the fact that she was working for money, and that they needed her to after he injured his back and the mill he worked at shut down. "He said, 'I was worried because, you know for me, the idea is that the wife doesn't need to work or make money.' For years I was the one raising the family and I was the one making the money. He was mad about that. Because this macho idea, they don't let the wife support the husband. That was really hard on him." Aguilar says it took decades, but her husband gradually changed his thinking. "Now he says to me that he feels so proud when he goes to the store or anywhere in town and everyone always asks him, 'How's Leticia? How's her business going?' He says, 'I feel so lucky that you are my wife.'"*

In recent years, Aguilar has devoted much of her time to helping other immigrant women in her small California mountain town to find more equality in their marriages. Hosting what she calls "child nutrition workshops," she gets these young mothers out of their homes and talks them through strategies for gaining more control in their marriages, more equality and respect from their husbands, more control over their own labor and finances. "I just want these girls to understand that they are humans who are just as valuable as their husbands, and they do all this work for everybody, and it's okay to ask for some respect for themselves."

The Industrial Revolution brought more people—both women and men—out of their homes for paid work. Prior to the late 1700s, the majority of Americans lived on farms or in small towns. Most families and communities were largely self-sufficient, growing and preparing their own food, and making their own clothing and various other essentials of everyday life. It took quite a while for this to change, even as factories became more and more common. By 1880, nearly one-half of Americans were still farmers. This changed dramatically in the early 1900s, as the supply and lowered costs of manufactured goods created a consumer revolution for both urban and rural households. The advent of commercial electricity in the late nineteenth century made the creation and operation of large factories feasible in cities, sparking a massive migration to America's cities.

This mechanization of labor affected both men and women and changed how many families functioned. The introduction of large-scale sewing machines, for example, radically disrupted the textile industry, which had supported a large network of at-home seamstresses, most of them low-income women who needed this work to support their children. These women couldn't compete with textile factories; most had to take jobs in them, which took them out of the home and often left them scrambling for childcare.

The country was changing in other ways, too. The Progressive Era, on the heels of the Industrial Revolution, overlapped with the country's second big wave of immigration. By 1920, half of the American workforce was composed of immigrants and their children, who accounted for more than one-third of the total population. When more restrictive immigration policies were enacted in 1920, American companies turned to their other source of undervalued labor—Black people, who were recruited in droves from the rural South to come work in the urban centers of the North.

By the early twentieth century, labor shifts were having an impact on families and gender roles, too. In middle- and upper-class white families, it was increasingly common for men to go out to work while women stayed home and tended to children, and the "male breadwinner" and "female homemaker" roles emerged. Now, not only were women culturally seen as responsible for children and home, but also they were often the only ones physically at home.

The gendered division of labor is seen very differently through the dominant white, middle-class lens than it is by various other ethnic and economic groups in the country. For many racial and ethnic minorities, women working outside the home had already been the norm for decades, and so-called reproductive labor—the birthing and rearing of children—and the "motherwork" of dealing with both children and home were often seen as being in service of the group, both in terms of the family and the larger community, rather than in the service of the man in charge of any particular family. "Women's reproductive labor—that is, feeding, clothing, and psychologically supporting the male wage earner and nurturing and socializing the next generation—is seen as work on behalf of the family as a whole rather than as work benefiting men in particular," observes Asian American sociologist Evelyn Nakano Glenn, writing about Asian American families. While hetero white moms certainly stay at home with their children for the sake of the kids at least as often as they do so to support their male spouses, there seems to be more conflict around this decision in white communities, with numerous books and articles devoted to the trade-offs between children and career that don't exist at anywhere near the same numbers in communities of color, where it's just assumed that most people irrespective of gender will do some mix of money-work and care-work, and where the latter is valued nearly equally to the former. Collins points out that for most women of color, their primary conflict is not within but outside the home, "as women and their families engage in a collective effort to create and maintain family life in the face of forces that undermine family integrity."

Still, the gendered division of labor that occurred during the Industrial Revolution changed the lives of everyone in the country, and continues to have an impact on all working women today: Employers tended to be white, middle- or upper-class men who took the view that all women were married and being supported by a husband, and thus could be paid less because their income was merely supplemental, or that women who were working when they had children at home were inferior women, an assumption bolstered by racism and xenophobia if they happened to also be women of color or immigrants (and most were). Even late-nineteenth-century Marxists, who were already working for expanded rights for the proletariat and fighting against capitalism, saw women's involvement in the workplace as problematic. While the Progressive Era in the late nineteenth and early twentieth centuries brought white women more options for work than women of color, almost all women in the workforce were concentrated into a handful of low-paying jobs (various secretarial and domestic jobs, textile work, and teaching). Although the capitalist powers that be ostensibly wanted to hire women—a cheap labor force—society at large still relied on women's labor in their homes. "They ultimately underestimated the strength of the pre-existing patriarchal social forces with which fledgling capital had to contend and the need for capital to adjust to these forces," feminist economist Heidi Hartmann explained in her groundbreaking 1979 paper on the notion of the "family wage" that emerged during the Industrial Revolution. "The Industrial Revolution was drawing all people into the labor force, including women and children; in fact, the first factories used child and female labor almost exclusively. That women and children could earn wages separately from men both undermined authority relations and kept wages low for everyone."

Marxist philosopher Karl Kautsky complained of this in an essay penned in 1892, writing, "The activity of woman today in industrial pursuits means an increase of her former burden by a new one. But one cannot serve two masters. The household of the working-man suffers whenever his wife must help to earn the daily bread."

Under the auspices of protecting women from, as Kautsky put it, serving "two masters," reformers used motherhood to justify labor laws that ultimately undermined women workers. In the late 1800s, reformers began lobbying for limitations on women's hours in the workplace. Labor unions had been lobbying for shorter workdays in general, a request that was shot down repeatedly when it pertained to men. For women, however, motherhood was used as a special circumstance requiring unique attention. In 1908 a high-profile Supreme Court case upheld an Oregon state law that limited women's workdays to ten hours. In the majority decision, Justice David Brewer wrote that "as healthy mothers are essential to vigorous offspring…the physical well-being of woman becomes an object of public interest and care in order to preserve the strength and vigor of the race." Thus, "differentiated by these matters from the other sex, she is properly placed in a class by herself, and legislation designed for her protection may be sustained, even when like legislation is not necessary for men and could not be sustained."

What these well-intended "protective labor laws" did was make women less competitive in the marketplace and less appealing to employers. It also helped employers justify paying women less. As Jodi Vandenberg-Daves so aptly puts it, "By making women a special class of employee, regardless of whether they were actually mothers, protective labor legislation contributed to women's secondary and segregated roles in the workforce."

They allowed men to continue to dominate higher-paying jobs while also reinforcing the status quo of the gendered division of labor at home, as Hartmann points out in her explanation of the "family wage":

> While the problem of cheap competition could have been solved by organizing the wage-earning women and youths, the problem of disrupted family life could not be. Men reserved union protection for men and argued for protective labor laws for women and children.... Men sought to keep high wage jobs for themselves and to raise male wages generally. They argued for wages sufficient for their wage labor alone to support their families... Instead of fighting for equal wages for men and women, male workers sought the "family wage," wanting to retain their wives' services at home.

These laws enabled employers to justify paying women less for years. And while unionized men would go on to negotiate shorter days for themselves as well, they also had access to a variety of better-paying jobs that women were barred from. The family wage setup ensured that women would be paid little, which encouraged them to, as Hartmann puts it, "choose wifery as a career." It also ensured that women would be in charge of child-rearing. It's no surprise, then, that this era saw the establishment of home economics classes in schools, targeted toward girls only, naturally.

It should be noted that despite shifts in the labor force, the "American family" as discussed in the media and politics throughout the eighteenth, nineteenth, and early twentieth centuries remained quite narrowly defined, not only as a white, middle-class family, but also as a heteronormative nuclear family, with a mother and father and four children on average. In recent decades, economists and philosophers have pointed out that this arrangement didn't just arrive out of nowhere—it was the familial arrangement that best served capitalism. Marxist philosopher Friedrich Engels, in *Origins of the Family, Private Property, and the State*, attributed the rise of this model to the emergence of the notion of private property, noting that in bourgeois families, women had to serve their masters, be monogamous, and produce heirs to inherit property. The danger here, as Hartmann later pointed out, is the assumption that in the absence of capitalism, sexism would disappear. We know from history that it does not.

As feminist philosopher Marjorie Jolles points out, in part that's because there is an inherent economic value and power in female reproduction that people living in any sort of societal structure want to control. "Women have a vital contribution to make to the human race in the form of motherhood," she says. "That capacity has been harnessed by other powers since the beginning of human history. There have been many ways motherhood has been monetized, capitalized, and controlled, so I don't know that we could ever talk about motherhood being distinct from the political world or the economy. It is women's primary value—not even actually giving birth, but the capacity to. The value placed on women has been related to fertility since forever."

According to Hartmann, the laws and practices put in place during the Industrial Revolution, which included not only limits on the length of women's workdays but also bans on particular types of work (usually the well-paid kind), continue to harm women even today. "The family wage is still the cornerstone of the present sexual division of labor—in which women are primarily responsible for housework and men primarily for wage work," she wrote in 1979, and continues to repeat in her regular reports on the gender pay gap and division of labor for men and women today. "Women's lower wages in the labor market (combined with the need for children to be reared by someone) assure the continued existence of the family as a necessary income-pooling unit. The family, supported by the family wage, thus allows the control of women's labor by men both within and without the family."

Irrespective of the economic and labor shifts happening throughout the eighteenth and nineteenth centuries, children still needed to be cared for. The economic realities of the Industrial Revolution, well into the twentieth century, further underscored the need for community mothering networks in all but middle-class white communities, and home-based day care centers began to emerge at this time as well, almost exclusively in low-income neighborhoods. Progressive reformers also began to tackle poverty systematically, pushing for the creation of the first US welfare systems.

In 1909 President Theodore Roosevelt held the White House Conference on the Care of Dependent Children, at which reformers agreed that some sort of funding was needed to enable low-income mothers to keep their children with them, rather than giving them up to various institutions. At the time, orphanages included more children with living parents who just couldn't afford to keep them than actual orphans. Shortly after the national conference, several states began passing legislation that appropriated funds for "mothers' pensions." The idea was to provide a modest income to poor mothers without a breadwinning husband in order to enable them to stay at home with their children. Feminists at the time encouraged experimentation with shared child-rearing and collective housework in addition to mothers' pensions as a way to free women from their economic dependence on men. This thread of feminism persists, increasing in relevance at times (as the number of divorced women increased in the 1980s, for example, and the realization dawned that a stay-at-home mom who divorces in midlife is destined for poverty).

In the Progressive Era, reformers believed that it was simply unfair that a mother's ability to keep her children depended on whether she was married. This was yet another place where the temperance and women's rights movements intersected, because many reformers felt that women were being adversely impacted by drunkard husbands who would desert their wives, leaving them in such abject poverty that they often couldn't keep their children. While Progressive reformers chafed at such injustice, they did not take it so far as to push for increased wages or more work options for mothers; few but the most radical of feminists believed at the time that mothers should be working.

Many of the reformist mothers of the Progressive Era, who often thought they were doing God's work, undermined their own stated goals, especially when working with low-income women and women of color. By viewing everything through the lens of a white, middle-class motherhood ideal, they attempted to impose structures on other mothers that not only didn't work in their context but actually made their situations worse. The Woman's Christian Temperance Union often cast poverty as a sort of moral failing on behalf of mothers, as though for some reason they were choosing tenement living—leaving young children home alone while they worked or, worse, allowing them to roam the streets—instead of the order of a middle-class household. This view turned family assistance and social work into a sort of cultural imperialism, a need to "reform" rather than help any mother who didn't adhere to white, middle-class norms, a view that ultimately influenced the US welfare system, which continues to place the blame for poverty on the poor today.

What middle-class Progressive reformers couldn't grasp was that many low-income mothers had no choice but to work. From 1890 to 1940, women's labor force participation grew from 18 percent to 25 percent, and by 1920 African American women were about twice as likely to be working outside the home as white women. Women of color were almost exclusively confined to low-paying domestic work, and to make ends meet, many of their children worked too. Hartmann notes in her treatise on the family wage that the productive labor value of children helped fathers to maintain custody of them during this era. Although rare, when custody battles did happen, it was a foregone conclusion that children would remain with their father, and the necessity of fathers in children's lives was a core cultural belief. It's a belief that makes a lot of sense when you consider that the economic stability of women and children was dependent on men—being deserted by the man of the house was a tragedy not because of some sort of romantic notion about marriage but because it meant that a woman and any children she had were almost guaranteed to be destitute. As child labor laws made children less valuable monetarily, thinking began to shift toward children being the purview of mothers, and mothers were almost exclusively awarded custody in disputes.

America's First Day Care Centers

For decades, American women have been finding creative ways to keep their kids alive while they worked, either inside or outside the home. Sonya Michel, a sociologist at the University of Maryland, details these methods in an essay on the history of childcare in the United States: "Native Americans strapped newborns to cradle boards or carried them in woven slings. Colonial women placed small children in standing stools or go-gins to prevent them from falling into the fireplace. Pioneers on the Midwestern plains laid infants in wooden boxes fastened to the beams of their plows. Southern dirt farmers tethered their runabouts to pegs driven into the soil at the edge of their fields."

But working mothers in cities were under increasing pressure to provide more oversight of their children—allowing them to stay home alone or roam the streets was seen as unseemly by the middle- and upper-class powers that be. Progressive Era maternalist reformers started the country's first "day nurseries" in cities in the late 1800s as a way to help women who earned so little and worked so much that they would otherwise have to leave their children in almshouses, in orphanages, or with family. It was a godsend for poor working-class women, but one that came with a large heaping of morality: day care leaders shamed mothers for using the nurseries and actively discouraged their use, undermining the system they were in the process of building. Josephine Dodge, president of the National Federation of Day Nurseries for three decades, repeatedly and publicly said day nurseries were a crisis solution only and that in the ideal situation, mothers would be at home with their children. That line of thinking persists today, with day care centers being seen as a sort of necessary evil or stopgap for families in crisis, and at least one big media story per decade highlighting the negative impacts of day care on children.

In order to reconcile the notion of working mothers as "bad" with the good work of caring for children, nursery founders spoke of their work as an effort to reform bad mothers and reduce the impact their work schedules might have on their poor, innocent children. To that end, they took it upon themselves to "educate" these mothers in "proper" child-rearing practices, often holding up day care as ransom for various changes they wanted to see mothers make at home.

The idea of settlement houses—homes in low-income communities where middle-class reformers would live so as to integrate themselves into the communities with which they were working—made its way from the United Kingdom to the United States in the late 1800s and provided Progressive reformers with a more holistic view of poverty and a better understanding of the myriad structural drivers of it. In the diaries and published observations of these Progressive white women, their admiration for the work ethic of the families they assist is clear. Still, many of these early social workers sought to impose middle-class white values on families, offering advice where it wasn't needed and assuming that any mothering practices that differed from the white, middle-class approach were "bad."

This sense of "knowing better" bled into the creation of the formalized child welfare system, which began to take shape in the early 1900s, first in the form of state-run programs that doled out pensions to mothers, and the federally supported Children's Bureau, the stated purpose of which was to investigate and report "upon all matters pertaining to the welfare of children and child life among all classes of our people." The Children's Bureau also provided a vital lifeline to the country's mothers, particularly those living in rural areas, mailing a regular newsletter full of information about everything from maternal nutrition to the latest child development research, and answering letters asking for advice from mothers all over the country.

At the time, feminist Crystal Eastman argued that mothering was work of value to the larger society, "requiring a definite economic reward and not merely entitling the performer to be dependent on some man." Amen, Crystal. Alas, Eastman's vision was not to be. Still, with local laws that enabled mothers' pensions, first in Illinois and then in forty-one other states, reformers did provide some amount of support for impoverished mothers. These pension programs led to the formation of the federal Aid to Dependent Children (ADC) program as part of the Social Security Act of 1935. Eventually renamed Aid to Families with Dependent Children (AFDC), it lasted until 1996.

Unfortunately, the pensions were, as historian Jodi Vandenberg-Daves puts it, "stingy, discriminatory and [available to] only a fraction of single mothers." Data gathered by historian Gwendolyn Mink shows that in the 1920s, the average assistance grant in thirty-nine of forty-two states was below the cost of living by 20 percent or more. For many women, especially women of color, the grants were simply unavailable. Some states argued that African American women could support themselves and thus did not need public aid, for example. To counteract this, the middle-class Black women who formed the National Association of Colored Women in 1896 made improving working conditions for Black mothers a strategic priority. They supported various initiatives to increase wages and improve working conditions for domestic workers, for example, and threw their full-throated support behind the idea of childcare for working mothers, without any of the tension exhibited by their white reformer counterparts.

States also used various morality tests for their family assistance programs to disqualify women who were divorced or deserted, who were seen as promiscuous or irreligious, who didn't keep tidy homes, and, in many states, who were working out of the home and whose children could feasibly earn wages (despite the fact that one of the points of the pension programs in the first place was to reduce or even eliminate child labor). In other words, the mothers' pensions programs encouraged women to take on only work that could be done at home, with their children around, which also happened to be the lowest-paid sort of work available.

It's hard not to look at the early family welfare programs and not see the tentacles of modern-day workplace and welfare policies. Discriminatory? Check. Unsupportive of working mothers? Check. Weirdly involved in women's sex lives? Check again.

Welfare as Cultural Imperialism

The pensions and later the AFDC also formalized a sort of cultural imperialism that lives on in the country's welfare systems today, as reformers and social workers imposed their viewpoints on the families they worked with, who in turn toed the line in order to access health care, childcare benefits, and financial assistance. In the West, for example, white reformers encouraged Mexican American mothers to replace their traditional tortillas and beans with "American" foods, particularly in school lunches, to help their children assimilate.

But no community was harder hit by this odd combination of social welfare and imperialism than Native Americans. During the late 1800s and early 1900s, tens of thousands of Native American children were removed from their families—often forcibly—and sent to so-called Indian boarding schools, the intent of which was to effectively destroy any connection they might have to their heritage, language, or cultural framework. The loss of any connection to their biological families was considered an acceptable sacrifice in the effort to "civilize" them. Many children died, the result of malnourishment or harsh punishment. Those who lived were eventually returned to families they did not know, in communities that were completely foreign to them. For the most part, "assimilation" didn't open educational or economic opportunities to these children; it merely made them feel worthless in the larger society and foreign in their own families.

"The effect of that period of time, when so many Indian families were just broken, really can't be overstated," says native public-health researcher Janelle Palacios.

This break in the family line disrupted mothering practices as well, creating a gap in knowledge that had been
passed down from woman to woman over time. Many native
women have had to relearn ancient customs, or had to persist
in following their traditions during periods when they had to
butt up against a dominant Anglo culture that views them as
primitive or laughable. Baby-wearing, for example, the pride
of attachment moms everywhere today, is a long-standing native tradition that was roundly dismissed by child development experts for decades.

The Drudgery Must Still Be Done

While much of the documentation of the Industrial Revolution
has centered on work outside the home, there's an important
story about domesticity to be told as well. For middle-class
women (mostly, although not always white), being at home,
looking after homes and children, was far from a leisurely existence. It felt like, and was, work, despite the fact that it was
not valued culturally or economically. Clothes were washed
by hand, and cooking was a fairly involved manual affair,
particularly for families living in rural settings.

Upper-class white women who could afford to outsource
some of this labor did so, exclusively to other women. In
many African American families, the mother was performing this domestic labor, for very little pay, for other families,
which often meant that children had to help pick up the slack
at home.

The facts that children have needs and that a certain
amount of labor is required to keep a home maintained are
immutable. Those realities are not inherently oppressive but
have become so as a function of society's insistence that this
work be done by a child's biological mother and, barring that,

by another woman (usually one who is also a mother). The further insistence that this labor be performed unpaid or paid at a very low rate magnifies the oppression associated with tending to a community's basic needs. It was this constellation of factors that prompted Anna Marie Jarvis to advocate for the creation of Mother's Day in 1910. Anna's mother, Ann Maria Reeves Jarvis, was a socialist and a feminist in the 1800s when being either of those things, let alone both, was pretty rare. During the Civil War, she organized women to tend to wounded soldiers, irrespective of which side they fought for. After the war, she organized the first mothers' groups—but these were not moms' groups as we might think of them today. Jarvis was focused on labor rights and women's rights and began advocating for some system of remuneration for what was (and still is) derogatorily referred to as "women's work." She called for a "Mothers' Work Day," and it was a radical idea—to spend a day protesting to promote the idea that what mothers do is work and that mother-workers should be organized in the same way as miners and factory workers. Jarvis dedicated her life to this cause, and after her death in 1905 her daughter continued her work.

Anna Jarvis spent the rest of her life giving speeches, writing letters to politicians, and producing pamphlets espousing her mother's idea of the Mothers' Work Day. She ultimately succeeded in getting the day recognized; it became a national holiday in 1914. But rather than functioning as the sort of rabble-rousing middle finger to the establishment that her mother had wanted, Mother's Day became the ultimate exercise in sentimentality, a day of superficial mother-love that her mother would have hated. Anna Jarvis spent years trying to restore the original meaning to Mother's Day, but it had taken on a life of its own and she died furious about it.

Community Mothering

Also critical to the well-being of society as the twentieth century began and more low-income mothers in particular began to work outside the home was what Patricia Hill Collins has called "community mothering." While it includes the notion of various members of the community helping working mothers with their children, community mothering has a broader political and philosophical component to it as well, having to do with the work that women—often mothers—do to keep communities together and maintain certain cultural traditions.

This was particularly important for African American and immigrant families—African American women were instrumental in forming and nurturing communities as slavery ended and families found themselves either sharecropping in the rural South or crowding into small apartments to take new jobs in America's burgeoning cities.

Community mothering and the very idea of female leadership was also vital to Native American families, whose traditional culture was always under threat. "Equality per se may have a different meaning for Indian women and Indian people," Assiniboine feminist scholar Dr. Kathryn (Kate) Shanley wrote in *Thoughts on Indian Feminism* in 1988. "That difference begins with personal and tribal sovereignty, the right to be legally recognized as people empowered to determine our own destinies." Part of that sovereignty, Shanley argues, lies in defining family and motherhood differently than in the dominant Anglo-European culture. "The nuclear family has little relevance to Indian women," she writes. "In fact, in many ways, mainstream feminists now are striving to redefine family and community in a way that Indian women have long known."

Feminist historian Barbara Alice Mann (Seneca) extends this thinking, noting that Anglo America has largely forgotten that a highly functional matriarchy existed right here on this land for hundreds of years: the Iroquois Nation. "I am continually astounded by the apparently fixed idea of even left-of-centre academics that women are, by definition, a powerless group," she wrote in a paper on the Iroquoian model of woman-power.

> *The* Gantowisas, *or woman of the sisterhood of the lineage, boldly led her nation in politics, economics, social life, and spirituality. She was more than a little instrumental in creating the constitutional government that established their civil, political, economic, social, and spiritual rights. The notion of such formalized woman-power may startle Europeans and their descendants, but it is an old and mature idea among Native Americans, especially those east of the Mississippi River. All eastern Nations recognized the political, economic, spiritual, and social roles of Clan Mothers.*

But while female leadership and community motherwork are valued in various communities of color, they can also put an additional layer of pressure on mothers. "On the one hand, racial ethnic women's motherwork for individuals and the community has been essential for their survival," Collins writes in her essay "Shifting the Center: Race, Class, and Feminist Theorizing on Motherhood," adding, "On the other hand, this work often extracts a high cost for large numbers of women, such as loss of individual autonomy or the submersion of individual growth for the benefit of the group."

Look Out, Here Comes Oedipus

You can't talk about motherhood during the twentieth century without talking about the broad cultural influence of

Sigmund Freud—an influence that would only strengthen and spread as the century wore on. Even today, we reference Freud frequently, despite the fact that many of his theories have since been disproven; we joke casually about mommy or daddy issues, Freudian slips, or arrested development.

As would be the case for many of the psychologists and scientists to follow him, for Freud, women and their complexities were often an annoying anomaly in his theories, the subject he couldn't explain, the data set that always complicated things. When he got all the way through a theory and realized it didn't apply to women, Freud seemed to have just shoehorned us in where he could. So, to extend the Oedipal idea to women, for example, he came up with female castration and "penis envy."

As feminist Lili Hsieh has pointed out, Freud did the same with female sexuality. For him there was no female sexuality: All sexuality was masculine, which women could tap into to varying degrees.

> *Although boys are caught in the constant threat of castration, girls on the other hand are in this sense already castrated, and thus are faced with an irreparable damage— "they feel seriously wronged ... and fall victim to 'envy for the penis'" ... Freud suggests that for women there are two possible ways out of penis envy—besides the more strenuous ways such as neurosis or "masculinity complex"—one of them is a "capacity to carry on an intellectual profession" ... the other is having a baby. Both are thus substitutes for the penis.*

For mothers, Freud influenced perceptions in two ways: First, he saw women's reproductive capacity as inherently limiting to their development, intellectually and sexually. That did not differ much from what people generally thought at the time, except in the extent to which he saw the female mind as being troubled by this. In terms of child-rearing, however, Freud was the first to underscore the importance of the child-hood origins of adult personality. This helped mothers, in some ways, to be more mindful about the sorts of people they were raising, but it also helped to launch a seemingly end-less thread of mother-blame in the American consciousness, and fed into the belief of behaviorists like John B. Watson that mothers could effectively "ruin" their children in the first three years.

Cultural Fix: End the Gendered Division of Labor in the Home

One key way to ensure that women aren't continuing to shoul-der an unfair burden of household and childcare tasks is to model a gender-neutral division of labor in the home. This sounds simpler than it is.

In an informal survey I conducted in 2017 of a diverse group of 200 parents, two things stood out: one, women are still definitely doing more home and childcare than men, par-ticularly when it comes to the under-the-radar tasks that keep home and family life running (recent data from Pew supports this as well); and two, people who plan to be parents are of-ten not thinking and talking through how they will run their households once they have kids. A whopping 68 percent of respondents answered the question "Before having children, did you discuss division of labor with your co-parent?" with "Not at all" or "Not really." While of course, the division of labor in a home is something that evolves over time, I believe the fact that so many people don't discuss it before children enter the picture is a big part of why it often ends up being unequal. Creating equality requires intention and effort.

In my own case, about a week before my first child was born, my husband casually said to me: "Oh yeah, I guess we didn't really talk about this, but I assume you're okay with staying home with the baby for a while?" He was joking, but there was a kernel of truth to that joke that, honestly, made me want to slap him. We hadn't talked about it, and I felt like I had no idea what life would look like after the baby was born, which resulted in some tough times that probably could have been avoided. I don't expect every couple to have the time or inclination to go full nerd on a spreadsheet capturing every detail of their home life, but understanding what's involved in managing a household and figuring out how that labor will be divided is fundamental to righting some of the imbalances inherent to motherhood in America today.

No matter what your living situation, whether you're the only adult in the house or not, it's also critical to avoid gender-stereotypical chores wherever possible. Kids are born a particular sex, but they learn gender roles and they learn them early. In their influential 1987 article "Doing Gender," Candace West and Don Zimmerman note: "What is produced and reproduced [by housework] is not merely the activity and artifact of domestic life, but the material embodiment of wifely and husbandly roles, and derivatively, of womanly and manly conduct."

In a 2011 study of boys growing up in single-mother households, researchers Clara Berridge (University of California at Berkeley) and Jennifer Romich (University of Washington) found that the mothers, who taught and expected their sons to participate fully in household chores, felt strongly that they were both preparing their children to be self-sufficient—a skill necessary for boys and girls—and that, in teaching their sons in particular to play a meaningful role in the household, they were preparing them to be good husbands and fathers. That finding dovetails with Vânia Penha-Lopes's 2006 analysis of Black men's recollections of the housework they performed as boys; they felt that "having done housework early on better prepared them for adult life." A 1999 study by Constance

Gager, Teresa Cooney, and Kathleen Thiede Call about professional husbands and wives sharing housework also established that having done a type of housework as a child was related to a greater likelihood of doing that task as an adult.

I see this play out in my own house every day—my husband's mother insisted that he do his own laundry starting around age ten, and he has always insisted on doing it himself in our partnership. When we have talked about divvying up household chores, he always, always calls dibs on laundry as something that he doesn't mind doing and feels he can keep on top of easily. Cooking, however, which was always the domain of women in his household, is much harder for him to wrap his head around—not because he doesn't want to or because he insists on being passively bad at it so that I will take it on (what Arlie Hochschild calls "disaffiliation"), but because he sees it as much harder and more complex than it is, simply because he never learned to do it.

To ensure my own kids don't fall into this trap, we've undertaken the occasional family cooking lesson, where I teach both the kids and my husband some basics. Because there was a period of about two years where I also had to travel for work quite a bit while my husband manned the home front, my boys have grown up in a house where it is every bit as normal for dad to make a meal as mom, every bit as normal for dad to pick them up after school, get them dressed in the morning, make their lunches, give them a bath, and so forth. We didn't plan it that way, and it was a hard time on us financially, but I'm extremely glad my children are growing up in a household where domestic tasks are not particularly gendered.

This sort of role swap is becoming increasingly common, not only as more women take on the breadwinner role in their families, but also as more couples—both heterosexual and homosexual—take a "seesaw" approach to marriage, where the adults trade off being more career- or home-focused for periods of time. Another way to ensure that kids aren't just seeing one type of person doing domestic labor, according to feminist philosopher Petra Bueskens, is to arrange what she calls "strategic absences," or periods of time when the mother is not available. This is easier to do if the mother has work that requires travel, but can be planned as well. Bueskens found that what she called "revolving mothers" were able to subvert—intentionally or not—the gendered dynamics of childcare, leisure, and work in the home.

Scholar Andrea O'Reilly has contributed some interesting research in this realm as well. At the 2018 Matricentric Feminism Conference in Florence, Italy, she presented her research on the subject of "wife work," noting that after having studied several women who had dropped out of academia despite being on a path toward success, she had found that husbands had at least as much, if not more, to do with those dropout rates as children. "Any of the women who had children had all chalked up the loss of their academic careers to children," O'Reilly said. "But when I asked for details, for examples of the sorts of tasks or responsibilities that had interfered with their research, it turned out that what they were really talking about was not mothering work, but wife work: taking charge of the design of their homes, performing various chores for their spouse, which ran the gamut from picking up dry cleaning, or adding a stop on the grocery run for a particular food item he liked to remembering his family members' birthdays to maintaining the social calendar of both the couple and the family to the emotional labor of supporting his needs and his career."

In other words, when we begin to unpack the impacts of the gendered division of labor in nuclear American families on women, if those women are in heteronormative marriages, we have to look not only at the expectations put on them as mothers but also as wives.

Policy Fix: New and Improved Home Economics

A 1980s study by time-use study expert John Robinson proclaimed that working mothers were spending far less time with their children than previous generations of mothers. The media exploded with headlines reinforcing the long-held belief that mothers in the workplace would result in the total destruction of the American family. Far less reported, of course, was the correction Robinson made shortly after publishing his findings. He had miscalculated.

The damage was done, and the race for working mothers to spend increasingly more time with their children—usually at the expense of sleep, exercise, and personal hygiene—was on. Today's working mothers spend about as much time with their children as stay-at-home moms did in the 1960s. Married women in the United States do 70 to 80 percent of the housework, and the amount of housework they do tends to triple once they have children, irrespective of whether or not they work. In other words, the "second shift" that sociologist Arlie Russell Hochschild laid out in her book of the same name back in 1989 is still something most working mothers have to contend with.

The issue of women continuing to take on more of the household and childcare duties on average has been exacerbated for the middle class by the rise, from the 1990s to today, of what feminist scholar Sharon Hays calls "intensive mothering" in her 1998 book *The Cultural Contradictions of Motherhood*. We'll delve into this more in Chapter 8, but in a nutshell, intensive mothering is the notion that mothers should spend every resource they have, including energy, time, and money, on ensuring the success and happiness of their children.

One way to engender a cultural shift on the home front may, paradoxically, be to go back to an early twentieth-century policy: mandated home economics classes. Once vilified, rightly, by feminists for targeting women only and promoting a sexist view of household gender roles, home economics classes have all but disappeared from American schools. But what if such classes could teach both boys and girls not only basic housekeeping skills like cooking and cleaning, but also get them thinking about what's required to run a home and who does that labor?

In Japan, sociology researcher Masako Ishii-Kuntz has high hopes for the power of holistic home economics classes—courses that teach real, practical family planning and encourage balanced gender roles—to shift culture. It's a required class there, co-ed, for elementary through high school students. And because Ishii-Kuntz trains many of the nation's home economics teachers, the role of fathers and the importance of their involvement is a module in the courses. She's now trying to convince the Ministry of Education to make home economics part of the school entrance exams that Japanese students take whenever they're moving from one stage of school to the next. "If it's not on the exams, it's too easy for the students to tune out," she says. "If we make sure they're paying attention, they're engaged in these classes? That's where I think we can really start to see a shift."

5

Scientific Motherhood and Modern Reproduction

———————

When I found out I was pregnant with my second child, I was not happy about it. He was unplanned and, to put a more brutal point on it, unwanted. I had decided a year before that I wanted only one child. Then, on the first night my husband and I had had alone together in the three years since our first son was born, I drank far too much and all that planning went out the window.

Ultimately, I wrapped my head around the idea of having a second child, but I spent much of that pregnancy enraged. At the fact that I was having more children than I'd planned to, at the fact that my career would continue to be derailed for another few years, at the fact that we were far too broke for me to take more than an afternoon off to give birth. And most nonsensically, at my husband for doing this to me.

It was hard for me to feel anything but angry in those months, which I feared would harm my son. When I voiced that concern to a therapist she said, of course, "What's the alternative, trying to suppress those feelings? Surely that would be equally as harmful."

And so I raged and shouted my way through nine months and was not at all the happy and glowing pregnant person people wanted me to be. And I spent several months after his birth complaining as well—about having been strapped to a bed in the delivery room, about having my water broken without my consent, about being given Pitocin after my son's birth without my consent, about the backwoods doctors who had botched an otherwise straightforward birth so badly, and of course, always, about having to go back to work the next day. Still, deep within this very long and very committed pity party, I knew something absolutely: In fact I had made a choice—many choices. And I was fortunate to be a woman who could choose, and upon whom no reproductive activities had actually been forced.

I am fighting the very strong urge to assure any reader that for all of my misgivings during his pregnancy, I adore my youngest son. Because the fact that all that rage and ambivalence can exist within months of unconditional love and delight shouldn't be hard to believe, but it is given the mystical, superhuman ideas and expectations we continue to impose on mothers.

From the mid-nineteenth to early twentieth centuries, American thinking on birth control and abortion began to change significantly, evolving into much the same framework that we have today, with a clear division between birth control and abortion and varying degrees of support for each.

It was not always so. It's hard to believe that at a time when religious thought was so dominant, in a country founded in part with the intention of being entirely devoted to God's wishes, birth control and abortion were far less fraught topics in the early eighteenth and nineteenth centuries than they would become by the twentieth century, or even than they are today. But logically, it makes sense: In order to accomplish the lofty goals of moral and republican motherhood, of course, women needed to have fewer children—you can't groom model citizens if you're raising a dozen children at once.

Abortion before "quickening"—the fetus's first movements, which usually happen around the four-month mark—was both legal and, by all accounts, fairly casual up to the early nineteenth century. Quickening was considered the start of life, in part because no one could really know for certain that a woman was pregnant before then. Abortion undertaken before this point was seen as an extension of the family-planning strategies women were increasingly deploying to limit the number of children they had and thereby ensure that they could remain good companions to their husbands and involved, moral mothers to their children. Women went to midwives for help with abortion or consulted homeopathic healers who knew of various herbs and teas that would do the trick safely. By the mid-nineteenth century there was a wide selection of abortifacient products on the market (not all of which actually worked), including pills, teas, and oils, all marketed as menstruation regulators. Of course, products that helped bring a woman's period back were generally those that ended a pregnancy, but this allowed everyone to continue to think about it as just reproductive regulation, an extension of birth control. Historian James Mohr estimates that abortion rates may have increased from about one in every twenty-five live births at the end of the eighteenth century to one in every five or six by the middle of the nineteenth century.

Medicalized Reproduction

At the same time that mechanized processes revolutionized the economy and, with it, work, America was being mechanized in other realms as well. While many married middle-class women saw themselves increasingly confined to the roles of homemaking and child-rearing as their husbands went out into the world to earn a living, single women and poor women had various new types of jobs open to them in offices and factories. People of both genders increasingly saw themselves commoditized as cogs in the machine of industrial progress.

This era also saw the medicalization of reproduction as male doctors began taking charge of female reproduction, pushing out the female midwives who had long presided over this cycle of life. Medicalized birth went hand in hand with what historians call "scientific motherhood," a concept promoted by the behaviorists of the time (most vocally John B. Watson), which encouraged mothers to leave emotion out of child-rearing, stick to strict schedules and routines with their children, and obsess over their progeny's development. The child development/parenting self-help genre exploded during this time as mothers looked for expert advice, usually from men (many of whom did not have children).

The medicalization of birth was something of a trade-off, with many women willing to put up with the invasiveness and humiliation of a man in the birthing chamber in exchange for the sweet relief of medical painkillers. At least that was the case for middle-class white women. Many enslaved African American women had male doctors foisted upon them as the unwilling guinea pigs of American gynecology, which made them understandably suspicious of doctors as free women. These women endured countless surgeries, fertility treatments, and extreme measures without consent. Alabama physician J. Marion Sims, still commonly referred to as "the father of gynecology" and to whom various statues are dedicated (including one in Brooklyn that was finally removed in 2018), frequently performed gynecological surgeries on enslaved African American women without anesthesia (he started using anesthesia when he began performing surgeries on white women). He also often invited several colleagues to observe his procedures, a common practice and again, one that gave no thought at all to consent from the patients. While the doctors who so imposed themselves on these women thought nothing of doing so on account of their race, they also still clearly thought of their patients as women whose bodies could teach them about all women's bodies. It's no wonder, then, that emancipated African American women were often skeptical of doctors, a skepticism that deepened decades later with the infamous Tuskegee study. The Tuskegee Study of Untreated Syphilis in the Negro Male, conducted by the US Public Health Service from 1932 to 1972, promised free medical care to impoverished male African American sharecroppers. The program did provide some amount of free medical care, but the secret intent of it was to study the effects of untreated syphilis on African American men. Men who had been previously diagnosed were purposely not treated, while those diagnosed after the study began were neither told they had the disease nor treated, even after it was discovered that penicillin effectively cured the disease. A study that was supposed to last six months lasted more than forty years and unnecessarily caused severe heart issues and even death among many of its participants, not to mention the impact on their spouses and children, several of whom also contracted syphilis.

With such a dark medical history, it's easy to understand why the African American community remained distrustful of the medical establishment well past the end of Jim Crow. And still today there are reasons for skepticism, amid unusually high maternal mortality rates for African American women. According to the Centers for Disease Control and Prevention (CDC), in the United States today, Black mothers die during childbirth at three to four times the rate of white mothers, a disparity due to a complex web of factors driven by systemic racism: lack of access to healthy food and health insurance, safe drinking water, safe neighborhoods, and reliable transportation; the likelihood of giving birth in a hospital still dealing with the effects (and lack of funding) of historical segregation;

and the effects of unconscious (or conscious) bias in doctors who don't believe their patients when they complain of a particular problem. The ongoing stress of dealing with racism on a daily basis is also at play. In her research on Black maternal mortality, Haile Cole at Amherst University has replicated what various other researchers have also found: that racism-related stress results in lower health outcomes for Black women in general, including during pregnancy and childbirth. Cole notes that Black women, as women who have been systematically oppressed for decades in this country, are particularly at risk; she points to the "Hispanic paradox" in maternal mortality research, the term for the so-far-unexplained phenomenon that Latinx women, who ostensibly also face daily racism, generally have good health outcomes for mothers and children. "What you see when you dig into the data, though, is that they have worse outcomes for every generation they get away from immigration," Cole says. "So the theory is that as racism becomes more understood, and more of an expected reality, that stress increases and their outcomes decline."

Tennis legend Serena Williams wrote movingly about her near-death experience during childbirth, underscoring the fact that this is not just a problem for low-income Black women.

Disrupting Maternal Traditions

Paradoxically, as we moved into the twentieth century and mothers were expected to become more knowledgeable about all aspects of mothering, from child psychology to nutrition to development, their access to information about reproduction and contraception was being restricted. And while mothers were expected to pay attention to things like development milestones (first presented to the general public by Dr. Arnold Gesell in 1920) and optimized feeding and sleep schedules, they were at the same time consistently cast as dimwits who relied on male experts for any and all advice in child-rearing. Jodi Vandenberg-Daves describes the period as being hugely disruptive to "female traditions of maternal advice sharing."

It's hard to imagine that mothers took Watson's no-emotion advice seriously, but many did. Just to give you a sense of his style, consider one of the opening lines of his best-selling child-rearing advice book, *Psychological Care of Infant and Child*, published in 1928: "It is a serious question in my mind whether there should be individual homes for children—or even whether children should know their own parents."

The more involved male doctors became, the less control women had over both the birthing process and their reproductive systems in general, and then over child-rearing as well. Even the sanctity of "mother love" and maternal instinct were questioned during this period, as doctors opined that such sentiment might be detrimental to the rearing of modern children.

Doctors were driven at least as much by professional ambition and greed as sexism. In the emergent fields of gynecology and pediatrics, both of which were routinely mocked at the outset (it wouldn't have been easy in the 1920s for a young man to tell his parents that he wanted to become either a "male midwife," as obstetrician-gynecologists were called at the time, or a "baby doctor," as pediatricians were called), they had to establish both credibility and demand for their services. They had to make the case for their presence in a formerly all-female space, and they did so not only by insinuating that midwives were partly responsible for the high rates of maternal and infant mortality at the time (they weren't—these outcomes did not improve with the replacement of female midwives by male doctors), but also by restricting access to information and medicines so that patients had to come to them.

The rise of obstetrics and gynecology as a legitimate medical field coincided with a resurgence of Puritan morality, as evidenced by the Comstock Laws (passed in 1873 and in place through the 1920s), which labeled as "obscene" everything from contraceptives themselves to any published information about contraception. Gone were the shelves full of "menstrual regulators," and in 1936 the US Court of Appeals for the Second Circuit ruled that doctors alone could have access to contraceptive information and devices. Ironically, that decision was considered a win by women's rights advocates at the time. Margaret Sanger, who had been fighting the Comstock Laws for decades by this point, planned the case—which centered on an unusual Japanese diaphragm—to create a legal challenge to the Comstock laws. It did just that, effectively ending the laws and legalizing doctor-prescribed contraception. At the time, Sanger and her allies didn't realize that handing the power of contraception over to male doctors would be another obstacle to reproductive justice.

In the late 1860s and early 1870s the American Medical Association (AMA), at the time comprising only men, began campaigning to criminalize abortion via various state laws. Many doctors vilified abortion simply as a way to stick the final nail in the coffin of their main competitors: midwives. But some felt a moral and gender superiority to women and saw abortion as a shirking of a woman's duties to her husband, her country, and her race.

The Link Between Eugenics and Reproductive Rights

It's no accident that the push to criminalize abortion coincided with a decline in birth rates for white women. Much as they are today, many white men in power were very worried at the thought of immigrants and people of color taking over America. During a speech in 1905, Teddy Roosevelt referred to women who avoided having children as "criminals against the race." It was the early twentieth-century equivalent of today's "white genocide" or "demographic winter."

Men like Roosevelt wanted to encourage more "fit" white mothers to have more children, while at the same time discouraging "other" women from having too many (or in some cases any) children. This was accomplished by putting the control of not only contraception and abortion, but also sterilization, in the hands of a few powerful institutions and the men who led them.

It was precisely this increasingly prevalent belief that some people ought to breed more than others that ultimately enabled Margaret Sanger to spread her birth control clinics (precursors to Planned Parenthood clinics) throughout the country. Sanger is a complex character. Her early writings in the short-lived magazine *Woman Rebel* were radical and unequivocal, arguing for equality among the sexes, races, and classes and advocating a sort of "burn it all down" approach to capitalism and systemic sexism, classism, and racism. But that approach won her virtually no battles in the quest to make birth control accessible to American women. After fleeing to Europe to avoid obscenity charges for printing information about contraception, Sanger observed in the UK and western Europe that reproductive-rights advocates were having quite a bit of luck when they tied their initiatives to eugenics as well as to Malthusian ideas (similar to Paul Ehrlich's later writing in *The Population Bomb*, English philosopher Thomas Malthus had argued that human populations would outstrip the available food supply if reproduction were not kept in check). There was a clear shift in Sanger's approach when she returned to America, and a strategic one, which seems to have been executed as part of a conscious decision to sacrifice everything on the altar of access to contraception for all.

The message of population control as one way to deal with resource scarcity played particularly well during the Great Depression, which brought with it a lessening of cultural concerns around contraception. Forced or coerced sterilization and questionable contraception strategies flourished during this time. In one high-profile example, Clarence J. Gamble (of Procter and Gamble) convinced the state of North Carolina to let him use their public health clinics to try out various birth control techniques on low-income women the state wanted to keep from reproducing anyway. Gamble was a big fan of eugenic sterilization as well, to keep all manner of people, and especially the poor, from reproducing. To encourage "fit" couples to breed, Gamble offered cash prizes to Harvard grads who had big families.

But Gamble was far from the only one. From 1900 to 1970, more than 60,000 Americans were surgically sterilized, 61 percent of whom were women. These sterilizations were largely not the patient's idea, but rather were ordered by doctors either at institutions or at various state agencies. Eugenics took root in the United States in the early 1900s and was promoted by intellectuals and other elites. The American Breeder's Association (ABA), established in 1906, was the first formal US eugenics organization; its members included Alexander Graham Bell, botanist Luther Burbank, and Stanford University president David Starr Jordan. Four years later the ABA launched the Eugenics Records Office (ERO), the mission of which was to integrate eugenicist science into policy and legislation. Like the ABA, the Eugenics Records Office was not an obscure fringe group; its leadership included the president of the AMA and a Nobel Prize–winning geneticist, among other luminaries from Harvard, Yale, and the like. The ERO began as an attempt to root out criminality by preventing delinquent men from procreating, but gradually shifted to focus on "unfit" mothers. In the 1920s and 1930s, as Americans were coming around to the idea of contraception, they were also embracing the idea of forced or coerced sterilization as part of an overall pragmatic approach to not just population control but population curation. So, while middle- and upper-class white women could increasingly control their own reproduction (although they were still discouraged from abortion in the name of perpetuating the "superior" race), women of color, low-income women, and the disabled increasingly had their reproduction controlled for them.

The Evolution of Women's Rights

Women began pushing for the right to vote in the mid-nineteenth century, but the Nineteenth Amendment was not passed until 1920. In order to get it passed, women paradoxically had to let go of various rights, one of which was reproductive control. Even the most radical feminists of the time, many of whom advocated a boycott of marriage until such time as women had equal rights, stopped short of acknowledging female sexuality.

To the extent that they promoted birth control, women's rights activists saw it as merely a tool for married women to minimize the harmful health impacts of closely spaced pregnancies, largely because the primary opponents to birth control and abortion fell into one of two camps. Either they were concerned that access to sex without pregnancy would make for legions of promiscuous women who saw no point in getting married or letting any man control them (yes, please), or they worried that women would have so few babies that birth rates would decline (that actually did happen but birth control was not the only driver).

One way in which feminists of the day did take back control of their reproductive lives was to opt to remain single. The nineteenth century gave rise to the largest generations of single women in US history. For the first time, white women had access to a limited number of "respectable," albeit still low-paid, jobs—generally as seamstresses, secretaries, or teachers—and thus a means to remain single should they choose.

A large number of these so-called bachelor maids also remained single because they just couldn't find a suitable mate; in many eastern cities, women outnumbered men three to one. Whatever the reasons behind any one woman's bachelorhood, single adult women living their best lives became a thing that white women could do in the nineteenth century.

Some of the most visible public women were single, including Frances Willard, president of the Woman's Christian Temperance Union, and Susan B. Anthony, a leader in the suffrage movement. Anthony saw singlehood as a necessary step for many women until the institution of marriage was transformed into a more egalitarian union. In her now-famous "Homes of Single Women" speech, Anthony said: "In woman's transition from the position of subject to sovereign, there must needs be an era of self-sustained self-supported homes, where her freedom and equality shall be unquestioned."

Anthony believed her generation and the one after would redefine spinsterhood, but the Great Depression had other ideas. In her excellent book *All the Single Ladies*, Rebecca Traister makes a solid argument for defining the era we're living in today as Anthony's predicted "epoch of single women," a few decades later than Anthony would have hoped, but here all the same. In 2012, one in five adults age twenty-five and older (about 42 million people, or 20 percent of the population) had never been married, according to Pew Research Center analysis of census data. In 1960, only about one in ten adults (9 percent) in that age range had never been married. "This is a radical shift in how we conceive of adult life for American women," Traister writes, describing "an entirely new population: adult women who are no longer economically, socially, sexually, or reproductively dependent on or defined by the men they marry."

Although the glorification of singlehood for women didn't quite stick in Anthony's day, it did hang around long enough to influence how women were thinking about marriage roles. In 1907, the *Washington Herald* began publishing a column called "Bachelor Girl Chat," an ongoing conversation between "bachelor girl" columnist Helen Rowland and the "mere man" (ostensibly also written by Rowland) constantly trying to marry and domesticate our bachelor heroine. As a testament to both the rise of the bachelor girl and the success of the column, "Bachelor Girl Chat" was soon syndicated by papers nationwide. In one column, Rowland complains about laws barring women from smoking: "The moment you find anything amusing, you discover that it's unladylike. Her reputation is the white woman's burden. It takes all the fun out of life to have a good reputation."

Black women, although no longer enslaved beginning in 1865, were still largely confined to sharecropping and domestic work. (A small Black middle class did begin to emerge in the North.) That fact, combined with the fact that recently freed Black women were looking for and reuniting with their families, made the fancy-free single life incongruent with Black women's experience.

This marks another key divergence between the formation of Black and white motherhood ideals in America. While white women were experimenting with single living, reduced family size, and occasional forays into public life, all often under the mantle of "freedom," many Black women had only recently left literal slavery, only to come into abject poverty. Their economic burdens often meant that they had to work away from home, helping to raise another family's children, and that their own children had to be put to work as well. But many found solace in the ability to keep their families together and, finally, mother their children. As historian Jacqueline Jones puts it, "Freedwomen derived emotional fulfillment and a newfound sense of pride from their roles as wives and mothers. Only at home could they exercise a measure of control over their own lives and those of their husbands and children and impose a semblance of order on the physical world."

The Great Depression

As women were gaining independence in the early twentieth century, creating public lives for themselves, advocating for and eventually winning the vote, and taking more control of their reproductive lives, a social and economic backlash ensued to force women back into the roles that men felt most comfortable with them inhabiting. First, as discussed in Chapter 4, the emergence of the family wage and protective labor laws for women combined to drive down the economic value of women's labor, making their jobs supplementary at best. This gave an economic incentive for marriage to all but the wealthiest of women.

Then, the combination of conservative religious opinion, eugenics, and physician-controlled birth control and abortion successfully undermined what had once been a glimmer of real reproductive freedom for women. It was not okay to have sex outside marriage, nor to artificially limit the number of children they might have. Access to birth control was limited and access to abortion became almost nonexistent as laws criminalizing abortion spread across the country. This gave still more incentives for marriage; a woman on her own had been perceived as a dangerous thing by many men and the dominant society, and they successfully created circumstances in which it became truly dangerous for women.

The Great Depression was the nail in the coffin for women's rights as envisioned by the Progressives of the late nineteenth and early twentieth centuries. "In the last major economic crisis, the 1930s, the vast unemployment was partially dealt with by excluding women from all kinds of jobs—one wage job per family, and that job was the man's," Hartmann wrote in 1979. "Capitalism and patriarchy recovered strengthened from the crisis. Just as economic crises serve a restorative function for capitalism by correcting imbalances, so they might serve patriarchy. The thirties put women back in their place."

Cultural Fix: Moving Beyond Birth Control to Family Plans

I have several friends who have chosen not to have children, and I'm often struck by how frequently and how convincingly they must "defend" this choice to everyone from close family members to total strangers. We would do well to encourage that level of planning and thoughtfulness in those who do decide to have children. And, in fact, to strip the word "family" from the institution of marriage and encourage all people to think carefully about the type of household they want to live in as adults.

There are examples of American families that do not revolve around the nuclear family ideal, if we look closely enough. I've already mentioned the norm of extended family networks in both the Black and Native American communities. In Latinx and Asian American families, it's extremely common for extended family members to live together in the same home. According to the most recent Pew Research Center study on multigenerational households in the United States, Hispanics (22 percent), blacks (23 percent) and Asians (25 percent) are all significantly more likely than whites (13 percent) to live in a multigenerational family household. However, this arrangement is increasingly common across racial demographics, particularly as aging Boomers opt to live with their children (or are required to, either because they have no retirement savings or because no one in the family can afford to outsource elder care) and Millennials, who graduated with record amounts of student debt into a deep and extended recession, live with their parents for longer than previous generations did.

European immigrants, of course, also initially lived in extended-family arrangements when they first arrived in the United States. Ashley Aarti Cooper, who works with a community foundation in Northern California, speaks fondly of growing up first with her single mother, whose parents moved in and helped out, and then when her mother remarried, in a larger working-class Italian family with grandparents living next door and down the street, and aunts, uncles, and tons of cousins all within a few blocks. "Now that I look back on it, it's the only way my parents' lives really worked—and it was so helpful for me growing up too," she says. "Many of us cousins went to the same middle school and high school, a lot of them to the same college. It was so unique and special to have so many people close to you who had your back. We were constantly at each other's houses, and our paternal grandparents lived up the road. When we were young and irritated with our own parents, we'd just walk over to Nana and Papa's."

Prior to the passage of equal marriage laws at the state level, the gay community was coming up with a variety of family types as well. "I was raised, as were a lot of gay people of a certain age, to think that you were either a gay person or a family person, that you couldn't have a family if you were gay," says Kera Bolonik, who's forty-seven and now lives with her wife and their adopted son in Brooklyn. "Then I started seeing people a little older than me or around my age who were having kids and it was this very cool and really radical act. You could have whatever kind of family configuration, you know?"

When the Supreme Court recognized gay marriage, in a way, the legal, social, and economic structures of society forced gay people to conform to the institution of marriage in order to be able to do very practical things like access their partner's health insurance, leave money to a partner, or visit a partner in the hospital. While opening up access to those legal tools was necessary and helpful, forcing the queer community into the nuclear family box effectively ended much of its exploration of new types of family arrangements. Other alternative family forms have emerged in recent years, from polyamorous couples cohabiting and raising children together to divorcées rooming together in order to share household and childcare duties, but these are still considered far outside the norm and are given no official support in the form of economic or legal structures.

By encouraging young women and men to really think through what family means to them, and offering more than one institutional family structure, we might reduce the number of people of all genders who wind up stuck in a situation that doesn't work. "I really wish someone had talked to me about what careers work well with parenthood when I was young," says John Eden, a tech and law consultant who works with various Silicon Valley start-ups.

> We talk to women about it a little bit—although in a lot of problematic ways—but we don't really talk to men about it. For example, if you know you want to have kids, going into a job that requires sixty to seventy hours a week—investment banking, for example—could be the wrong path if you see yourself as the kind of father who wants to be around your children during their formative years. We never talk to men about that kind of thing at all. And I think the implication of this, at least in terms of what it communicates to men, is that their participation in the lives of their children isn't valued by the social fabric. And this is a key problem to think more deeply about: When a society values X or Y, it applies pressure to its members to do X or Y. Where is that pressure when it comes to being a present and engaged father? It's really not there to the degree that it needs to be.

Also barely talked about or understood is the impact unplanned pregnancy has on women who find themselves mothers not through sexual mishap but because they simply haven't thought through the question of whether to have kids. Again, we're not really encouraged to do that unless we plan not to have children.

In 2015, I produced a series for *The Guardian* on the intersection between environmental concerns and population. From Thomas Malthus in the 1800s to Paul Ehrlich in the 1970s to at least half of the climate movement today, there have always been scholars, philosophers, and activists pointing out that human reproduction is killing the planet, which will in turn eventually kill humans. My sense was that people have a complex system of inputs into their reproductive decisions, and before we could really have policy conversations about population, we needed to better understand this decision-making process. To that end, I surveyed more than 200 people all over the world and received plenty of the expected answers: Access to birth control is obviously a huge deal, as are cultural and religious attitudes around sex and marriage, family history, income and education level, and so forth. Several people said they worried that children born today would be literally killed by climate change in the future, others said they didn't want to give birth to humans who would exacerbate climate change, and still others said concerns about climate change gave them noble cover for a personal decision they felt people would otherwise consider selfish. What I hadn't expected were letters like this one, from a mother of three (although there were others like it—ten in total, a not-insignificant 5 percent of those surveyed):

> In retrospect, I wish I had remained child-free. I was influenced by ideological factors (religion, culture, class) that it was "natural" and "normal" for a woman to have—and want—children; therefore unnatural and abnormal to not want them. Though I have never harmed and always provided for my children, I realize now I am not and have never been maternal; it would have been far better for me to have remained childless. But where are the role models in society to show that as a genuine, "acceptable," and

normal alternative? Will it ever be truly ideologically per-
missible for women to say, "I don't want children, don't feel
maternal, and feel great about it"?

It was a hard letter to read. We can and should do better.
Many radical feminists today—Jessa Crispin most vocally, but
plenty of others too—have returned to (or never left) the idea
of abolishing marriage as a fundamentally patriarchal structure that is of little use today except to limit people's choices
and perpetuate systems in which women are dominated. To
wit, society at large still makes things difficult for a woman
with a different name from her children, a holdover from the
days when that would mark her as a single mother. Day cares,
schools, and doctors made this such a giant pain in my ass,
for example, that I eventually gave up and changed my name
legally, although I still use my given name in all professional
and public arenas. Immigration is also hugely tied up with
marriage (and motherhood, for that matter), and the patriarchal side of marriage still emerges in myriad ways, particularly in the health care system, where husbands are afforded
a surprising amount of influence over their wives' decisions.

These are just a few examples of many. Where children are
concerned, the emphasis on marriage as the sole institution
of support for them is exceedingly problematic, particularly
given that more than 30 percent of US households are single-
parent homes and that many people of all genders and colors
want to have children but simply can't find a marriage partner. Moreover, for all the legal, social, and economic efforts
to impose marriage, it seems to be a uniquely dysfunctional
institution in the United States. We have higher divorce rates
and higher marriage churn rates (people who divorce and
remarry multiple times) than other rich countries, many of
which have moved past the idea of everyone needing to be
married. But our unmarried couples aren't faring any better, with frequent breakups that leave single mothers raising

children from different fathers, either on their own or with men who cycle in and out of their lives.

Kathryn Edin and Maria Kefalas document this trend in their book *Promises I Can Keep: Why Poor Women Put Motherhood Before Marriage*, for which the pair conducted extensive interviews with 162 single mothers in Philadelphia, Pennsylvania, and Camden, New Jersey. Edin and Kefalas note that most children born to "single mothers" are actually being born to unmarried couples, and that they "may see a series of mother and father figures entering their lives, along with half-siblings, step siblings, and other kin." This family complexity is most often experienced in the context of poverty and racial discrimination as well, the sociologists note, creating daunting challenges. One of the many insights of Edin and Kefalas's work is the extent to which the one social institution we've hung familial stability on forever—marriage—is failing, and no alternatives have appeared to offer equally or more stable options, leaving many families in free fall.

Communal housing has been picking up steam as many American communities struggle with skyrocketing housing prices, and is one way we might create more resilient support systems for those without "traditional" families. In my small California mountain town, there's both a new proposal for a communal housing development and a number of people creating these arrangements among themselves. "We did it for convenience and to save money initially," Marlena Johns, a restaurant owner, told me of her and her husband's decision to live with another couple. "But now we want to find a way to make it permanent because we've realized that it makes all of our lives so much easier to have two other adults helping to run a household—we cook each other dinner, walk each other's dogs...a situation that we thought might get annoying has been really great."

Amid advocacy efforts for legal marriage for all those who desire it, we've almost entirely forgotten to question whether marriage is the institution best suited to supporting the American public as it exists today. As LGBTQ activist and writer Fenton Johnson noted in his 2018 "Future of Queer" manifesto in *Harper's*, legalizing gay marriage effectively put an end to the work queer culture had been doing to redefine family, community, and romantic relationships. As much as some conservatives might have hated (and continue to hate) the idea of gay marriage, it was still more palatable than the gender-bending, norm-pushing, countercultural verve of all things queer. "What we met and worked and marched and wrote and died for was radical transformation," Johnson writes of queer activism during the AIDS epidemic of the 1980s. "What we settled for was marriage."

Marriage is what we've all settled for. But surely in a nation as diverse as America, with as many familial combinations as there are languages spoken, we can come up with a few more ideas about family, a few more ways for people to come together in supportive communities?

Although children are resilient and adaptable, they also need a certain amount of predictability to feel safe and to thrive. We need to find ways to provide that stability, ways that move beyond continued efforts to "save" marriage and provide viable, functional alternatives.

The growing ranks of single mothers by choice are finding that they can only really pull it off if they have money or extended-family support, and even then, it's still really hard. "You know, people will offer to do things here and there—I had people bringing me meals when my son was first born, things like that—but at the end of the day, it's just you and you alone," says Erika, who became a single mom by choice in her late thirties. "There's no one else to help out if your kid is suddenly sick and needs to stay home, no one to talk to about whether this or that option is best for him. It's really, really hard." Erika has none of the financial, racial, or educational challenges of the women in Edin and Kefalas's book, but she has still found single parenthood incredibly difficult.

"I mean, it wasn't really by choice," she says. "My choice would have been to have him with a partner, but the partner I was with at the time didn't want kids and I really did, and I was running out of time."

All of which is to say, it's probably well past time to expand our notions of family to include structures that might support single parents, and go beyond the nuclear family. We could all use a little more support. As a married person myself, I can understand that the idea of abolishing marriage or even expanding marriage freaks some people out or makes them feel defensive about the choices they've made or the home life they've created, so let me offer another idea: What if you get to keep your marriage, but we also open up more ways for people to define family and the relationships they have with other adults? Ways that go beyond just the sexual freedom that polyamory promises and acknowledges that humans probably need more than one person to meet all of their emotional, physical, and familial needs, particularly if we are going to continue to live in a country that provides no government support for families. As Kurt Vonnegut once put it, "Most arguments in a marriage boil down to one thing: you're not enough people." Happily married himself for years, Vonnegut was a frequent critic of marriage and often promoted the idea that people would be better off living in tight-knit groups.

Policy Fix: Modernize Sex Education

One way in which men and women with same-sex partners have one up on hetero couples is in the area of family planning: They generally don't become parents by accident. In the United States today, nearly 60 percent of pregnancies are unplanned, and half of those unplanned pregnancies are unwanted. For a country that likes to bang the drum of "family values" an awful lot, we do a terrible job of actually helping people plan families. Sex education is not guaranteed in school, and when it is offered is often sorely lacking. Access to birth control is limited to condoms for most young people. Other forms of birth control, even when covered by insurance, can be too expensive, never mind that by all accounts what we should be offering young people, if we really want to get at the unwanted pregnancy problem, is long-acting reversible contraceptives (LARCs, like intrauterine devices, or IUDs). A Washington University study of nearly 10,000 women in St. Louis found that among those offered free contraception along with solid information about which methods were most effective, 75 percent chose a LARC option, and there was "an 80 percent reduction in teen births and a 75 percent reduction in abortions among women in the cohort compared to national statistics." With these contraceptive devices, the only decision women have to make once they have the device implanted is to have it removed if and when they make a conscious decision to become a parent. The up-front cost of these devices—$1,000—is cheaper than a lifetime of birth control and also saves on health care and child-support costs in the long run.

But providing appropriate birth control is just one part of getting at the family planning problem. After all, as Native American public health researcher Janelle Palacios points out, in some cultures (many Native American tribes, as well as some African and Latinx communities) teen pregnancy is not necessarily the taboo that it is in the white American mainstream. Provided a woman has the support she needs, there's nothing inherently wrong with having a child very young. The object here is informed choice, and allowing women in particular to create the sorts of living situations that work for them. Even polygamy, although in current practice very patriarchal, could become quite a matriarchal option, with gender-equal groups that divvy up parenting, breadwinning, and household duties. Point being, we need to both explore new structures beyond the nuclear family and do a better job of talking to kids about more than just sex.

"In Sweden we go very in-depth about all the different outcomes of reproduction so you know what you're getting into when you make a decision," my friend Lina Fisher, a Swedish expat, tells me. "We leave high school knowing as much as possible about what pregnancy is actually like, what it's like to have a newborn, all of that. I feel like that's a big reason we don't have so many teen pregnancies!"

Irrespective of their views on abortion, most people agree that the high rate of unintended pregnancy in the United States is a problem. In addition to the impact unwanted pregnancy has on women, it also negatively impacts the resultant unintended children. According to the nonprofit Guttmacher Institute, births resulting from unintended or closely spaced pregnancies are associated with adverse maternal and child health outcomes, such as delayed prenatal care, premature birth, and negative physical and mental health effects for children. The Brookings Institution has found that unplanned births affect children's development, including their chances of graduating from college and earning a middle-class income.

We could expand the definition of family, offer effective birth control, and provide clear information on family planning via the home economics courses mentioned in Chapter 4. That would avoid this entire endeavor being seen as a plot to end the American family and help us move beyond the nuclear family to a society that nourishes both adults and children.

6

From Rosie the Riveter to the 1950s Housewife

"I grew up with a refugee mom who wanted nothing more than to provide a better life for her kids, so she was a workaholic," says Anh Nguyen Gray, a Vietnamese American mother of three who works part-time as a producer at the National Public Radio station in Reno, Nevada. Gray had planned to go back to work shortly after she had her first child. "You know, I grew up in an Asian household so it was all about you go to school, you do well, and you get a good job," she says. "I had two masters degrees, one from an Ivy League school, so the expectation was that I would have a career."

Despite that, Gray says she wound up really wanting to stay at home with her kids for a while, in part because of how much she had missed her own mom as a kid. "When I grew up, my parents worked seven days a week, both of them. Usually on all major holidays too. In a lot of ways, I really think my mom worked herself to death. I mean, you can never find any one thing to blame for cancer, but she didn't take care of herself, she worked all the time, and then she died young."

"That definitely played into it when I had kids," Gray says. "I wanted to be there with my kids. Because I was always longing for my mom as a child. And I respected her work ethic and self-sacrifice tremendously, but I wanted my kids to not feel that sense of longing. I wanted them to have as much access to me as possible."

After World War II, in which tens of millions of men and women sacrificed their lives, or at least their livelihoods, for their country, the economy and the country once again needed women's roles to change.

Women were used to being called upon to work and then promptly let go depending on what the labor market needed of them; working women had been scuttled out of the labor market to protect men's jobs after World War I and again when the Depression hit. Then World War II came along and women were once again a highly desirable labor segment. Many US companies already had contracts to produce war equipment for the Allies. Suddenly they had to dramatically increase their capacity to supply American troops as well. Auto factories were converted to build airplanes, shipyards were expanded, new factories were built, and all these facilities needed workers. Men were being mobilized for war, leaving companies with no option but to think about hiring women for traditionally male jobs.

As the war continued and the labor shortage deepened, attitudes shifted and soon the US government was launching a propaganda campaign aimed at getting women into the workplace. Initially, women with children under fourteen were discouraged from taking part; the government feared that an increase in working mothers would lead to a rise in juvenile delinquency. At the time, the War Manpower Commission stated: "The first responsibility of women with young children, in war as in peace, is to give suitable care in their own homes to their children."

Eventually, the demands of the labor market were so severe that the need for workers outweighed the fear of any repercussions that might result from mothers working (although, of course, any jump in juvenile crime statistics would still be pinned on working moms). Millions of women, including mothers of young children, were entering the workplace, driven either by patriotism or by economic need. According to the Congressional Research Office, about 13 million American women were in the workforce in 1940, a number that rose to 19 million by July 1944. It was also the first time in US history that married women outnumbered single women in the workforce.

As employers began complaining about women not showing up to work because they couldn't find anyone to watch their kids, the US government for the first, and still only time in history, saw fit to subsidize childcare for working mothers. Authorizing $52 million for childcare under the 1941 Defense Public Works Law (known as the Lanham Act), from August 1943 through February 1946, the government partnered with various municipalities and community organizations, which kicked in an additional $26 million, to create a nationwide childcare system. At its peak in July 1944, the system boasted more than 3,000 centers looking after some 130,000 children. The government provided indirect support of onsite day care at some private companies as well, most notably Kaiser Shipyards on the West Coast. Kaiser's day care centers were built by the US Maritime Commission and largely funded through the company's defense contracts.

A smaller network of centers (about 1,900) had been set up during the Depression, not to help mothers, who were mostly discouraged from working lest they take a job from a man, but to employ out-of-work teachers. These centers received renewed funding as part of the Lanham Act and a new mandate, to reserve the majority of their spaces for the children of working mothers. The Children's Bureau, which had been set up to provide federal funding and oversight of child welfare in 1912, was asked to provide some amount of oversight of the federal childcare program, but the bureau was strongly opposed to the idea of mothers with young children working and often sabotaged projects aimed specifically at caring for infants or toddlers.

The End of an Era

In mid-August 1945, once victory in Japan was assured, the government announced the end of Lanham Act funding of childcare centers as soon as possible, and no later than the end of October 1945. A month later, the Federal Works Administration (FWA) reported it had heard from twenty-six states and the District of Columbia (1,155 letters, 318 wires, and 794 postcards and petitions signed by 3,647 individuals, according to the Congressional Research Office), urging continuation of the program and citing the need of servicemen's wives to continue employment until their husbands returned, the ongoing need of mothers who were the sole support of their children, and the lack or inadequacy of other forms of care in the community. The state of California protested loudest—it was home to about 25 percent of federally funded day care kids—and its lobbyists eventually helped to secure an additional $7 million that allowed the program to continue until February 1946. By July 1946, less than 1,000 of the more than 3,000 wartime childcare centers continued to operate. The FWA director of childcare grants once again asserted that mothers of small children served the nation best by remaining home to personally rear their children. A 1960

Children's Bureau survey found just 376 childcare centers operating with any kind of public funding.

Despite the government's assertion that mothers belonged at home, the reality was that, with the industrial sector bloated far beyond its previous size and many men not returning home from the war, their presence was still needed in the labor force. Employment data from the postwar era backs this up: After a brief dip in employment in 1946, women's involvement in the workforce resumed an upward trend in 1947.

Mothers of school-age children often had part-time jobs (in fact, the addition of a second income, no matter how small, was a big part of what built and grew the emergent middle class). From 1948 to 1958 there was close to an 80 percent increase in the number of married women with children under eighteen who worked. That did not equate, however, to any extension of federal subsidies for day care, nor did it aid the efforts of the handful of women's worker unions advocating for maternity leave at the time. Then, as now, as always in America, balancing work and family was considered a private concern, one best solved by the people involved with no outside support.

At the same time, more socialist attitudes of communal support persisted in low-income and racial-ethnic minority communities, and as before, mothers of color were often working because their families needed the money—not for extras, but to survive. This need was driven in part by the fact that the Aid to Dependent Children program continued to discriminate against women of color. In the early 1950s, more than 30 percent of married Black mothers with children between the ages of six and seventeen worked for wages (more than twice the percentage of all married mothers). About 30 percent of all mothers (married or not) worked, but more than 50 percent of Black mothers (irrespective of marital status) worked.

Low-income white mothers, as well as thousands of African American and Puerto Rican mothers, flooded into postwar public housing projects in the 1940s and 1950s. In addition to casual childcare arrangements with family and neighbors, these mothers formed communal policing organizations like Los Vigilantes, an anticrime organization of mothers in Lexington House, a 448-unit public housing complex in East Harlem.

In the 1940s, racial-ethnic minority groups in the United States begun to push back against infringements on their rights; toward the end of the decade, the efforts of those who had just returned from fighting injustice in Europe were particularly powerful. Under the leadership of future Supreme Court justice Thurgood Marshall, the National Association for the Advancement of Colored People (NAACP) brought suits over discrimination in employment, housing, transportation, education, and voting rights, and accused the courts themselves of denying people of color fair trials. These early civil rights battles often intersected with the push for reproductive rights. In 1942, the Supreme Court reversed its previous decisions on forced sterilization, for example, in the case of *Skinner v. Oklahoma*, defining sterilization as "an encroachment on basic liberty."

Eugenicist ideas would persist, however, driven in part by Sanger's organization, which by this point had been renamed Planned Parenthood. In 1948, future Planned Parenthood director William Vogt suggested in his and coauthor Bernard Baruch's best-selling book, *Road to Survival*, that the government ought to give poor people incentives to stop reproducing.

Japanese Internment

While women found themselves suddenly pushed back home at the close of World War II to make way for men in the labor force, other Americans were returning to their homes under far darker conditions. Japanese Americans were the one group of laborers who had been forced out of the workplace during World War II, despite the need for workers. Shortly after the bombing of Pearl Harbor in 1941, some 120,000 Japanese Americans were forcibly removed from their homes and businesses, most of which were on the West Coast, and detained indefinitely in ten internment camps scattered throughout the country. Many mothers whose husbands were fighting for the US Army found themselves detained with their children in what amounted to prisons.

The camps, opened in 1942, did not shut down until 1946, nearly a year after the war's end, at which point families were allowed to return home but often found they had little to return to. Many lost businesses, homes, and possessions, and found hometowns that were now deeply and unapologetically racist, with signs like "No Japs Here" or "Japs Not Welcome. Never Again" common.

In addition to all of the obvious impacts of internment, there were subtle impacts on Japanese families as well. The traditional respect afforded to elders was upended by the camps, where only American-born children had any rights at all.

The Baby Boom

Many women did continue to work after World War II ended, but society at large did not seem to like the idea one bit. The 1950s brought a major push back to more traditional gender roles, and a nationwide yearning for stability also fed into a baby-making session the likes of which this country hasn't seen since. Birth rates jumped from an average of 2.3 children to an average of 3.2 children per family. Childlessness dropped dramatically, couples adopted in record numbers, and the average marrying age dropped to a twentieth-century low of 20.3 for women. To not be married and a parent during this moment in US history equated to being locked in a sort of permanent state of adolescence. According to surveys conducted in the early postwar years and throughout the 1950s, the vast majority of Americans believed you could not be happy if you were single. Historian Elaine Tyler May notes that for men, fatherhood became a sort of "badge of masculinity" during this time period.

Although the post–World War II baby boom was long attributed to the usual postwar drive to make babies, May found after decades of research that there was more to it; previous periods of postwar prosperity had not led to such a significant spike in marriage and childbearing. What was happening in America at this time was a convergence of factors: people had weathered the Depression and World War II and were now facing the possibility of nuclear attacks as a result of the Cold War. "Americans turned to the family as a bastion of safety in an insecure world," May concluded. "Cold War ideology and the domestic revival were two sides of the same coin."

Other historians have also noted the shift in American sex lives at the time. To wit: Access to birth control was as restricted as ever for unmarried women (although the public largely supported access—a Gallup poll in the 1940s found that 77 percent of Americans approved of public-health clinics distributing contraceptives), and abortion was still criminalized. Despite that fact, Americans were having sex at younger ages than ever, thanks in large part to the privacy afforded by the personal automobile. By the 1950s, 39 percent of unmarried women had "gone all the way" by the time they were twenty years old. Surprise pregnancies were common and tended to be dealt with either via adoption or via a shotgun wedding.

White teenage girls who got pregnant out of wedlock were told that their only option was to have the baby—usually at a home for unwed mothers, far enough away that no one would know—and they could put the baby up for adoption and return a few months later with a story about caring for a sick relative.

From 1945 to 1973 (when *Roe v. Wade* decriminalized abortion), 1.5 million babies were placed for adoption. But while anti-abortion activists have often pointed to this as the number of babies "saved," in a large number of cases, these mothers would have quite liked to have kept their babies. Also worth noting: At the time, much like today, parents—particularly those most likely to identify as religious, conservative, and anti-abortion—feared that sex education would promote or encourage sexual relations and teen pregnancy and therefore thought it best to leave young people uninformed. What happened then, as always tends to happen whenever horny teenagers are not properly educated in sex and reproduction, was a spike in teen pregnancy.

"Just about everyone who lived through this era has a memory of a girl from their high school, college, or neighborhood who disappeared," Ann Fessler writes in her excellent 2006 book, *The Girls Who Went Away*. "If she returned, she most likely did not come back with her baby, but with a story of a sick aunt or an illness that had kept her out of school. If her peers doubted her story, they probably did not challenge her directly. They simply distanced themselves. According to the prevailing double standard, the young man who was equally responsible for the pregnancy was not condemned for his actions. It was her fault, not their fault, that she got pregnant."

There was an incredible amount of secrecy surrounding these pregnancies, but thanks to the work of some dogged historians, there are now entire books filled with story after tragic story of women being railroaded into giving up their children in order to clear the path for a "proper" life that would include marriage and "legitimate" children. Fessler interviewed hundreds of these women, many of whom were given little choice in the matter of whether to keep their babies, and all of whom still agonized over the decision decades later.

"Chances are the baby wasn't unwanted," Fessler quotes one woman, Glory, as saying. "It was a baby unwanted by society, not by mom. You couldn't be an unwed mother. Motherhood was synonymous with marriage. If you weren't married, your child was a bastard and those terms were used. I think I'm like many other women who thought, 'It may kill me to do this, but my baby is going to have what everybody keeps saying is best for him.' It's not because the child wasn't wanted. There would have been nothing more wonderful than to come home with my baby."

The impact of this coerced or, in some cases, forced adoption was poorly understood at the time; parents of these girls often believed they were giving their daughters their best shot at happiness. The general sense was that they could go away, get rid of this "problem," forget about it, and move on to have a proper life. "In truth, none of the mothers I interviewed was able to forget," Fessler writes. "Rather, they describe the surrender of their child as the most significant and defining event of their lives."

Of the approximately 1.5 million women mentioned above who were sent to homes for unwed mothers, where they gave birth to children they would never see again, most were white. In her book *Beggars and Choosers*, historian Rickie Solinger writes, "Black single mothers were expected to keep their babies as most unwed mothers, black and white, had done throughout American history. Unmarried white mothers, for the first time in American history, were expected to put their babies up for adoption."

Solinger notes that underlying this notion was the persistent and insidiously racist idea that Black women were highly sexed, an idea that had been invented by white slave owners eager to justify the rape of enslaved Black women. At the same time, Black mothers were also being deemed

unworthy of raising American citizens. "Angry about developments such as federal legislation that lifted race-based qual-
ifications for immigration in 1952, and the Supreme Court's
Brown decision in 1954, many whites claimed that children of
newly entitled immigrants and the children of African Americans could not be molded into American citizens," Solinger
writes in *Pregnancy and Power.* "Surely, they claimed, the
mothers of these children were not equal to the task of training them for citizenship." A decade later, Department of Labor
sociologist Daniel Patrick Moynihan would point to the single
mothers in Black communities as evidence of the moral decay
of the Negro family in a report that would justify many more
decades of discrimination against mothers of color and Black
mothers in particular.

As birth control gradually became more accessible, thanks
in part to the expansion of Sanger's clinics throughout the
country, the tendency for family planning to turn into eugenic
population control made it controversial for a different reason
in African American communities than white communities,
where the general consensus was that giving unmarried people birth control would lead to promiscuous sex and the ruin
of the American family. In the African American community,
there were two schools of thought on birth control, Solinger
explains: It was either perceived as something that would give
Black families more financial stability, or as a racist tool of
"Black genocide." Solinger writes that African American physician Julian Lewis, a proponent of the latter perspective,
"urged Blacks to work for the kinds of economic, medical, and
educational reforms that would lower the Black death rate. He
counseled that African Americans should 'look askance at any
proposals that threatened to reduce their birth rate.'"

As had been the case through all of American history up
to this point, society's tensions—in this case over both gender
roles and civil rights—often played out in discussions over
how to control women's fertility and reproduction. Give the

women too much control, and you have a liberated woman on your hands; enable the fertility of women of color, and you have too many racial ethnic minorities demanding rights. "It would be hard to hold back change in a society where many women and minorities were defining entitlements and rights for themselves and against tradition," Solinger writes. "But the state at various levels (federal, state, local), in partnership with a range of religious and voluntary organizations, did step in, aiming to forestall or even reverse this revolution in rights and relationships, in part by restraining female reproductive decision making."

Society, TV, and the Working Mom

Mothers who did remain in the workforce in the postwar era (and again, there were a lot of them!) were expected to take part-time or low-level roles so as not to compete with male workers for high-paying jobs. In *More Work for Mother*, Ruth Schwartz Cowan describes how women who wished to pursue a career during this time were referred to by pundits and social commentators of the day as "unlovely women" who were "lost," "suffering from penis envy," "ridden with guilt complexes," or just plain "man-hating."

It was also assumed that women were married and that their husbands were the primary earners, which, in combination with lingering notions about the "family wage" in general, helped companies to justify paying women less. They were only spending their wages on "extras," after all, shopping for shoes or Christmas presents.

Further fueling the idea that there was something inherently wrong with mothers working outside the home were the rise of two new propaganda distribution mechanisms: television and pop psychology. The first sitcom to air on American broadcast television, in 1947, was *Mary Kay and Johnny*, which starred real-life married couple Mary Kay and Johnny Stearns. Mary Kay played the hot, zany wife to Johnny's bank employee as the couple traversed everything from the early days of marriage to pregnancy and child-rearing. Setting the stage for the many women who would follow her onto the small screen, Mary Kay was a wife and mother. Women were always married on TV, and usually mothers, up until a divorced Lucille Ball convinced networks to take a risk on *The Lucy Show*, which featured Ball as a widow (the character was originally intended to be a divorcée, but the network thought that was too risqué).

We didn't get our first never-married woman on TV until Marlo Thomas took on the role of struggling actress Ann Marie in *That Girl* in 1966, followed a few years later by Mary Tyler Moore, who went from playing Laura Petrie, wife and mother, on *The Dick Van Dyke Show* (1961–1966) to playing single working woman Mary Richards on *The Mary Tyler Moore Show* in 1970. For twenty years, then, American homes were filled with the same model woman on TV—she was a wife, often a mother, and she was at home and available to meet your needs 24/7. It differed from the eighteenth- and nineteenth-century notions of "true womanhood" and the "cult of domesticity" in exactly one way: Women were now also supposed to be sexy, but only within the confines of marriage, of course.

The Pop Psychology and Parenting Advice Boom

Popular psychology, which was largely designed to explain to women exactly what was wrong with them and why they were failing to be adequate wives and mothers, first appeared in the late nineteenth and early twentieth centuries and exploded in postwar America. In his decade-long monthly column for *Ladies' Home Journal*, "Can This Marriage Be

Saved?," eugenicist, self-appointed marriage guru, and pro-totypical bro Paul Popenoe wrote, "Children are especially needed by the wife for her own health and mental hygiene.... A woman's body is made for childbearing and is not function-ing normally unless it bears children."

In a return to nineteenth-century ideas about the neg-ative impact of book learning on baby making, books and magazines of the day cautioned against too much education for women. The one exception to the maternalist tone of the day lay in the expectation that women be as good or better wives as they were mothers. Nurturing their husbands—by keeping themselves thin, beautiful, and impeccably dressed; by being always available for and interested in sex; by tend-ing to his every basic need, meeting him at the door with a cocktail upon his arrival home from work—was the primary duty of every wife. She was encouraged to keep the chil-dren occupied for at least thirty minutes when their father returned home so as not to overly burden him with family pressures as soon as he walked through the door. And nu-merous advice columns and books tackled the thorny issue of whether you could be a good mother without slacking on your wifely duties.

When popular psychology books weren't teaching women how to be better wives and mothers, and thus better women, period, they were busy blaming mothers for every societal ill. In books like *Generation of Vipers*, published in 1942, we see a return to the early twentieth-century backlash against mother-love and all its overbearing, self-absorbed neediness. Channeling John B. Watson, *Vipers* author Philip Wylie used "mom" as a pejorative for the first time and laid into American mothers, accusing them of robbing their sons of masculin-ity via their suffocating and monstrous mother-love. Wylie's theory was that the conveniences of modern appliances had opened up more time in mom's schedule, creating the ideal conditions for pathologizing mother-love into an obsession with meddling in the lives of her children and a need for all-encompassing obedience from them.

To be fair, Wylie rails against all aspects of American society at the time; the subtitle of his book is: "in which the author rails against Congress, the President, professors, motherhood, businessmen & other matters American." But his critiques of the education system and bankers are rooted in a sort of democratic socialist desire for equality, while his rips on motherhood are laden with misogyny. He uses the word "mom" to describe the mothers who displease him and to distance them from "mothers," whom he claims to hold in high regard. "Never before has a great nation of brave and dreaming men absent-mindedly created a huge class of idle, middle-aged women," he writes. "Satan himself has been taxed to dig up enterprises enough for them. But the field is so rich, so profligate, so perfectly to his taste, that his first effort, obviously, has been to make it self-enlarging and self-perpetuating. This he has done by whispering into the ears of girls that the only way they can cushion the shock destined to follow the rude disillusionment over the fact that they are not really Cinderella is to institute mom-worship."

In the introduction accompanying the 1954 printing of *Generation of Vipers* (the book's twentieth printing), Wylie is clearly bothered by the fact that he has been labeled a misogynist by those who, according to him, have missed the point entirely. He had been pointing out the problem with a particular type of mom, see, one who ruins it for the rest of us, including other mothers and women in general. Then he proceeds to write things like: "Today, while decent men struggle for seats in government with the hope of saving our Republic, mom makes a condition of their decision the legalizing of Bingo. What will she want tomorrow when the world needs saving even more urgently?"

If you're tempted to write Wylie off as a fringe crank, consider that his publisher had just 4,000 copies printed, which

Wylie and his editor considered somewhat high for this book, but by 1954 it had sold more than 180,000 copies. And today, the book still has multiple five-star reviews on sites like Amazon and GoodReads, with most readers commenting along the lines of one review, which notes that "his thoughts on women probably have more kernels of truth to them than is fashionable to admit nowadays."

A best-seller in his time and a persistent favorite today, *Generation of Vipers* also coined a new word, "momism," defined by the Oxford English Dictionary as "an excessive attachment to, or domination by, the mother." Wylie also opened the floodgates for various other critics. Books like *Their Mother's Sons, Modern Woman: The Lost Sex,* and *Maternal Overprotection* blamed the nation's mothers for everything from neurosis to rape.

At the other end of the spectrum, still more popular psychology books argued that cold mothers who either had too little love for their children or did a poor job of expressing their love were responsible for autism, schizophrenia, and various other mental illnesses. The "refrigerator mother" theory, believed by most psychologists and pediatricians from 1950 to 1970, held that autism and schizophrenia in particular (in part because at the time these were not diagnosed until later in childhood) were the result of deficient mother-love. It was truly a damned-if-you-do, damned-if-you-don't scenario for mothers of the 1950s, expected to toe an impossible Goldilocks line, doling out just the right amount of love to their offspring.

Psychologists also wrote frequently and vehemently about the connection between absent (or in reality, working) mothers and criminal activity. J. Edgar Hoover, in a 1944 *Woman's Home Companion* article entitled "Mothers…Our Only Hope," lays what he calls the country's rising problem of juvenile delinquency at the feet of working mothers: "What we are up against—what the whole country is up against—is not juvenile delinquency but adult delinquency," he writes, noting that attempts to pin juvenile delinquency on the war are misplaced. "If the drift of normal youth toward moral decay is to be stopped, it is mothers who must do the stopping," he continues. And how might mothers do this?

In the first place, unless family finances absolutely demand it, the mother of young children should not be a warworker mother, when to do so requires the hiring of another woman to come in and take care of her children. Motherhood has not yet been classed as a nonessential industry! There is small chance that it ever will be. The mother of small children does not need to put on overalls to prove her patriotism. She already has her war job. Her patriotism consists in not letting quite understandable desires to escape for a few months from a household routine or to get a little money of her own tempt her to quit it. **There must be no absenteeism among mothers.** *[emphasis Hoover's].*

After the war, British psychologist John Bowlby picked up where Hoover left off. Having studied European children left homeless by the war, and how losing one or both parents had affected them, Bowlby developed his theory of childhood attachment, the need that children have to be attached to a trusted adult. Subsequent parenting "experts" have extrapolated his findings to equate what those orphaned and homeless children experienced to what American children experience when their mothers leave the home for work. Just in case you were wondering where mom guilt started, here's where it really kicked in. Bowlby posited that a mother's daily absence might be perceived by her children as a lack of love, and thus instill in them "acute anxiety, excessive need for love, powerful feelings of revenge and, arriving from these last, guilt and depression." Bowlby's attachment theory is still quite popular today.

Historian Jodi Vandenberg-Daves notes that while attitudes toward working mothers were more mixed during the 1950s than these writings might suggest, the prevalence of criticism reinforced certain cultural norms: "Widespread circulation of such ideas, however, regularly drove home a key point: domestic women were 'normal' women; ambition was unfeminine, and unfeminine women were a menace to society because being both wife and mother required deference, subordination, and 'acceptance' of a role."

In *Modern Woman: The Lost Sex*, written by Ferdinand Lundberg and Marynia F. Farnham and published in 1947, the authors define the only adequate mother as the "feminine mother" who accepts her role as wife and mother, accepts her dependency on men, and holds no "fantasy in her mind about being an 'independent woman.'" Farnham was early in a long line of professional women who, ironically, made a career out of telling other women they shouldn't have careers. A 1950 newsreel about the book is introduced with a doom-and-gloom voiceover about how women working outside the home are ruining marriage, leaving unsupervised children to get up to no good, and making it far too easy for women to leave their marriages, none of which is actually leaving women better off. In introducing Farnham, the narrator says, "Strongly against careers for women is Dr. Marynia Farnham, noted physician and coauthor of the bestseller *Modern Woman: The Lost Sex*." With this unapologetic, obliviously hypocritical introduction, Farnham goes on to say (from her own psychiatry clinic in New York City, mind you):

Catastrophic social forces have propelled American women away from femininity and into careers at terrific cost to themselves and society. Abandoning their feminine role has made women unhappy because it has made them frustrated. It has made children unhappy because they do not have maternal love, and it has made their husbands

unhappy because they do not have real women as partners.
Instead, their wives have become their rivals.

It's no wonder that amid all the experts telling mothers the myriad ways in which they were ruining their children and the world, Dr. Benjamin Spock's *The Common Sense Book of Baby and Child Care,* which opened with the line "Trust yourself. You know more than you think you do," flew off shelves like no other child-rearing book had (over a million copies in its first three years). Although he was also an elite male expert, Spock was one of the first to incorporate mothers' opinions and advice into his books and columns, and the first to open up space to discuss some of the less pleasant aspects of child-rearing, like the "baby blues." He also moved sharply away from the trend of blaming mothers for everything, allowing them to be imperfect humans who sometimes make mistakes; and he moved away from the Freudian- and behaviorist-dominated ideas of the early twentieth century that had attributed things like babies sucking their thumbs or exploring their genitals to dark psychosexual sources. While John B. Watson cautioned mothers against allowing their children to touch themselves, lest they become excessive masturbators and sexual deviants later in life, Spock encouraged mothers not to worry about it.

Still, some mothers complained that his emphasis on children being essentially good implied that any bad behavior was the fault of their parents. His child-centered approach was also considered by many to be too fawning over the child and generally too permissive. And of course, this debate between child-centered or parent-centered parenting continues to dominate parenting discussions even today. As Ann Hulbert points out about the twentieth century in *Raising America,* her comprehensive look at the parenting advice industry, "Again and again the advisers' careers and their conflicting

counsel reflected American confusions about children's na-
tures and futures, and about mothers' missions, during a dis-
orienting century."

Maternal Migration

Internal migration was common in the United States after
World War II. While middle-class white families moved in
droves to the suburbs, where they could have yards and cars
and ranch homes, Black families that could afford to escaped
the Jim Crow South for more hospitable cities in the North
or West. In her book *Storming Caesar's Palace: How Black
Mothers Fought Their Own War on Poverty*, historian Annelise
Orleck writes, "Like the war refugees from Europe and Asia
who would arrive in American cities in the 1950s, many Black
migrants of the postwar generation suffered from what would
now be called post-traumatic stress disorder."

Their new homes were not much better, with intense segregation and limits on where Black people could live, work,
eat, or go to school. In states like New Mexico and Arizona,
southwestern Jim Crow laws limited the social and economic
mobility of Mexicans, Native Americans, and Asian immigrants at the time as well. Restrictive housing covenants created racialized ghettos that are still in place today.

Various policies of the day also conspired to push African
American women into single motherhood. Orleck writes of
Ruby Duncan, one of the women profiled in her book, that in
1959, "at twenty-seven she was a striking young woman with
a steady job and a host of suitors, including a Nellis Air Force
Base airman who wanted to marry her. Duncan was also a
single mother, supporting six children on her wages as a Fla-
mingo hotel maid. That's not how she had envisioned her future when she left the Ivory Plantation. But trauma, romance,

and limited access to contraception had left Duncan—like one in four Black women of her generation—with a burgeoning family and no partner with whom to raise them."

A growing middle class of Black women began emerging in northern cities at this time as well. But unlike their middle-class white counterparts, the majority of these women worked, and not just because they had to, but because work was seen as a way they could contribute to society and as a way that Black women avoid being dependent on anyone. "White women raised in the 1950s often reported that their mothers and grandmothers criticized them when they later chose to combine motherhood with paid employment," historian Stephanie Coontz writes in *The Way We Never Were*. "But Black women raised in that era often faced the opposite reaction when they or their friends considered becoming stay-at-home mothers in later decades. Their mothers and grandmothers made disapproving comments such as 'I didn't raise you to be dependent' or 'You'll never get any respect by just staying home.'"

By 1960, close to 60 percent of Black middle-class families were two-earner households, while less than 40 percent of white middle-class families were. The idea of work having value for women beyond economic necessity had not yet entered into white consciousness but had already become a key value in the minds of Black middle-class women, and remains so today. Researcher Dawn Dow says it's one key difference between how ideal motherhood is defined in Black society and in white society. "The [Black middle-class] mothers in my research think of work as part of the duty of motherhood, in part because of necessity but also because it's their preference, and the fact that both are present doesn't mean that we should focus on one over the other or that one trumps the other," she says. "The cultural expectation in the Black community is that you should be economically self-reliant. That expectation is very present among middle- and upper-middle-class Black moms and the families they grew up in."

That insistence on self-reliance can sometimes create other problems for Black mothers, in the form of the "strong Black woman" trope, under which Black mothers are expected to handle everything and never need or ask for help. What that looked like in the 1950s was a tendency for middle-class Black women to work, just as their husbands did.

Meanwhile, as low-income Black women were being pushed—by racist housing codes, lack of access to birth control, and lack of economic opportunities—into ghettos, white middle-class women found themselves trapped in a prison of their own making: suburbia. Ninety percent of married suburban women did not work during this time period. These were the women many authors had in mind when penning books or articles about the ideal wife and mother, and they were the women targeted by the makers of everything from dishwashers to TV dinners.

Although many would eventually suffer from the malaise Betty Friedan would call "the problem that dare not speak its name," in the early postwar years and through most of the 1950s these suburban moms led something of a return to early nineteenth-century ideals of republican motherhood. In part because of their experiences during the Depression and World War II, these women seem to have been content to line their nests and raise a new generation of Americans. The large yards, cars, and homes, coupled with dozens of futuristic new items available for purchase every year, created peace and abundance in these homes, a sense that things had finally returned to "normal."

Cultural Fix: Assign Value to Caregiving

There are various ways in which American culture systematically signals its low regard for the carework required to maintain our human society. Lingering devotion to the idea of men as primary breadwinners and women as unpaid care-givers continues to depress both wages and job prospects for women and, in particular, mothers, but the biggest cultural issue underlying the persistent devaluation of mothers' labor is the simultaneous overvaluation of independent success and competition and the undervaluation of caregiving and collaboration in American society. The American economy has long valued logic and productivity (traits typically as-sociated with men) over relationships and communication (which women often prioritize), creating a gendered lens through which sociologists and psychologists have justified both evaluating women as less logical and more emotional or neurotic, and defining these traits as undesirable. This in turn has translated to widespread cultural understanding of "emotional" as a pejorative, a weakness, something that is not only not rewarded but actively penalized, despite the fact that it is indisputably valuable to the health and survival of the human race.

In her anthropological work, Sarah Hrdy notes that the capacity to care about strangers is uniquely human: "Along with language and symbolic thought this capacity for com-passion is quintessentially human. It is what...defines us as human."

Anne-Marie Slaughter noted this problem more recently, in her 2015 book *Unfinished Business*:

> *In looking at the stark facts of women at the top and at the bottom, a common pattern in their seemingly dispa-rate experiences begins to emerge.... The key to that pattern lies in two complementary human drives: competition, the impulse to pursue our self-interest in a world in which oth-ers are pursuing theirs, and care, the impulse to put others first. These are the two great motivators of men and women alike.... Suppose then that what unites all women is the*

struggle to combine competition and care in a system that rewards one and penalizes the other?

A system that rewards one and penalizes the other is precisely right: Those who take on the responsibility of care are not only not rewarded but are penalized—paid less, valued less, driven into poverty more often (as of 2016, women age eighteen to sixty-five are 38 percent more likely to live in poverty than men in the same age range).

As feminist writer Frigga Haug put it: "What look like female values are regulations of society at large: to protect, conserve, love and rescue life. It is because these are demanded as actions and attitudes from individual women and not from a social structure that women are oppressed."

The key then, is to lift both the stigma and the gender connotations surrounding care. Many have written about the need to encourage men to take on more caring roles, and while I don't disagree with that sentiment, I do think it skips a key step: First we have to attribute value to care, which is to say we need to attribute value to traits historically and traditionally associated with women. It's here that I see the "unfinished business" of feminism. In the same way that it has been problematic to encourage women to simply ape men in their attempt to gain status in competitive realms, encouraging men to just "do women's work" isn't likely to be an effective solution. Instead, we need to redefine success so that, for any and all people, irrespective of gender, there is a social and economic value placed on caring.

We could do that by combining a reevaluation of media (shifting the norms portrayed on TV and in film and various other media) with economic change (fixing tax codes that penalize married women for working, paying caregivers more and establishing parity pay and benefits for part-time workers, and adding unpaid household labor to the GDP) and revisions to the same private ways in which we've reinforced the status quo for years. We raise our children to appreciate the value of domestic labor instead of just silently shouldering the burden, and we divvy chores up equally among genders.

Policy Fix: Subsidize Day Care

As you've now read, the United States has a long history of seeing subsidized day care as something that just makes it easier to be an absentee, bad mother. This country has pathologized day care from the opening of the very first government nurseries to modern-day news stories that have created various unfounded panics about both working mothers and day care. The result has not been more mothers either choosing or being able to afford to stay home with their children, but rather overpriced day care that is not quality controlled, plus a huge helping of guilt that American mothers just don't need.

Here's the infuriating thing: The government *does* subsidize day care for many federal employees. Thirty-three federal agencies offer a childcare subsidy to their employees. The military and the Pentagon have famously great childcare centers for the children of enlisted military and Department of Defense workers. Various studies have shown that providing this service improves efficiency and productivity in workers, and stability in military families. Much like the health care provided to Congress but not the rest of the country, it's hard to find a logical reason why what's good for the gander isn't also good for the goose.

We also have a small number of programs in place that could provide a model for universal childcare, in addition to the comprehensive policy that passed in the 1970s, only to then be vetoed by Nixon (more on that in Chapter 7). The Head Start program, although chronically underfunded, provides a comprehensive early learning program for preschool-age children of families in poverty. Designed to meet children's emotional, social, health, nutritional, and psychological needs, the program serves more than 929,000 children.

Most other developed countries provide some amount of government-subsidized day care. The French system offers both a crèche for infants and nurseries for toddlers, all of which include healthy food and myriad scheduling options to support moms who are working or not, breastfeeding or not, rich, poor, or working class. In *Overwhelmed*, Brigid Schulte points out that if you add the amount of money individual citizens pay into things like health care and childcare, which in other developed countries the government pays for, spending on these services is about the same in the United States as it is in places like Sweden and Denmark. "It's just that in the U.S., individual citizens are paying out-of-pocket," she writes, adding that parents who have to take off work to take care of sick kids or otherwise deal with childcare issues cost American businesses $3 billion a year.

Subsidized day care has been an important policy in Japan, but the system there also showcases the need to get implementation right. Demand far outpaces supply for the government day care system, often pushing moms out of the workforce or into the high-priced private day care system (prices there are still slightly less than the privatized American day care system, which is the only option available). A viral blog post written by one irate mother last year galvanized the country's working mothers behind a push for more day care centers with more, and better-paid, staff. It won't happen overnight, but the government is working to certify more day care staff, increase wages, and find ways to either build new centers or increase the capacity of existing ones.

Creating a subsidized child-care system in the United States wouldn't necessarily require the building of day care centers so much as a system to standardize, certify, and re-imburse the existing ones. It could, and should, include smaller in-home day cares as well as onsite day care centers at companies.

The latter idea is a good one for companies, and one that is already supported by the government. The federal government grants companies with a qualified child-care program a yearly tax credit of $150,000. In addition, the government allows a company to deduct 35 percent of unrecovered costs from running such a program. Patagonia, the company that pioneered onsite day care (random coincidence: My cousin ran the company's first experiment with this, at its headquarters in Ventura, California), has opened up the books on its day care program to show other companies how much financial sense it makes. Patagonia charges its employees tuition that is below market rates, with income-restricted subsidies available, for its child development centers (one at its headquarters in Ventura and one at its distribution and repair center in Reno, Nevada). After accounting for that tuition, the cost of running the centers is approximately $1 million. With a yearly tax deduction of $150,000 and a second deduction of 35 percent of costs (35 percent of $1 million = $350,000), that's a total of $500,000 in costs recouped, or 50 percent.

Patagonia also recoups what it spends on providing childcare with gains in employee recruitment and retention. Turnover costs include lost productivity while the position is vacant, plus recruitment, relocation, and training time, which can range from 35 percent of annual salary for a nonmanagerial employee, to 125 percent of salary for a manager, to a couple of years' pay for a director or vice president. For the past five years, turnover among Patagonia employees who use its childcare program was 25 percent lower than among its overall workforce. The company sees 100 percent of its moms return after maternity leave. To put that in context, in the United States, 20–35 percent of working mothers who give birth never return to their previous job. Patagonia estimates that what it saves in turnover costs helps the company recoup

30 percent of the cost of running its childcare program. The company also estimates an 11 percent return in the form of employee engagement and increased productivity, for a total quantifiable recoup of 91 percent of the cost of its childcare program. That number actually looks bad when compared to some others. JPMorgan Chase Bank has estimated returns of 115 percent for its childcare program; global business consulting firm KPMG found that its clients earned a return on investment (ROI) of 125 percent for onsite childcare programs. Patagonia execs say when they factor in intangible benefits like the increased number of women in leadership, the loyalty of its workplace, and the culture of trust the company has created by really supporting its employees, the ROI is probably closer to 115 to 125 percent for them, too.

Were the federal government to take the fairly minor step of simply touting the corporate tax break for onsite childcare, that might instantly improve the lot of many working moms. It would, however, greatly disadvantage working-class and low-wage-earning mothers, whose employers are historically less likely to implement these programs or to care overly much about turnover costs or talent recruitment. To create an egalitarian system, we would need a government program to fill in the gaps. One of the oft-repeated mistakes of feminism has been to help one class of women while either ignoring other groups of women or outsourcing work deemed demeaning to those other groups of women; to truly shift the culture toward a more caring center, we have to think about the daily realities of all mothers, not just an exceptional few.

7

Second-Wave Feminism

"I was raised, as were a lot of gay people of a certain age, to think that you were either a gay person or a family person, that you couldn't have a family if you were gay," says Kera Bolonik, a magazine editor in Brooklyn, who's now forty-seven, married, and a mother. "Then I started seeing people a little older than me or my age who were having kids and having these sort of what was considered then as unconventional families, and it was this very cool and really radical act. You could have whatever kind of family configuration, you know? Maybe the birth father became part of the family or you had an anonymous donor or there was an ex involved—people grouped up in a lot of different ways—and there was almost always more than two people involved so you literally had a village."

In 1990, Bolonik met the first same-sex couple with kids she'd ever known. "It opened a door of possibilities for my life. I came out in high school to myself and my parents and a couple of friends, but at that point I didn't even know that same-sex desire could be consummated! I didn't really know until I went to college and got some sense of things. More than a few of my lesbian friends ended up kind of getting together with men or even marrying men for a while because they thought it would be easier to have kids that way. People defined themselves a little more on the binary then too."

But that was not a path Bolonik could imagine herself taking. "I just knew that wasn't gonna fly for me. There was a big part of me that thought I might not be able to have kids if I don't find a partner who is willing to do this with me, although I wasn't really that interested until I was in my mid-twenties. By the time I was thirty I was really determined to figure out a way to eventually become a parent and that's when I started dating my wife. This is such a lesbian cliché but on our first date we both talked about the fact that we wanted kids."

That was April 2001 and same-sex marriage hadn't yet been legalized. "Legal gay marriage wasn't something we thought we'd see in our lifetime," Bolonik says. "But parenthood was. So we talked about that, just in the abstract. I kind of wanted to know if that was an option for her because I'd dated women who would say, 'No way, I'd never want kids,' and I felt like I was in my thirties so had to start thinking about these things."

In their mid-thirties Kera and her partner (now wife) Meredith started the process of trying to adopt a baby. "It was a long path—I wouldn't say it was an easy one but I'm glad it took us as long as it did. We were so ready for our son, whom we adopted—he is an amazing kid—we're so lucky to have him in our lives."

He's six now, and Bolonik says there's really not much difference between her family and the hetero families she knows. "I never knew that having a family with a same-sex partner would become as banal as anyone else's version!"

In her 1963 book *The Feminine Mystique*, Betty Friedan wrote: "The feminine mystique says that the highest value and the only commitment for women is the fulfillment of their own femininity...women by merely being women and bearing children will earn the same respect accorded men for their creative achievements."

What Friedan was calling out, of course, was the age-old American sport of telling women that motherhood and housekeeping were of equal value to paid work, but continuing to behave as though they were of distinctly less value. It wasn't just men who had been beating this drum in the lead-up to Friedan's bomb drop; it was women too. In fact Friedan's book was in many ways a response to the book *Modern Woman: The Lost Sex*, a best seller in Friedan's youth that had influenced not only sociology and psychology researchers but also American culture in general. Although criticized for its rants against feminism, disorganized thinking, and lack of data, the book was widely acclaimed, and even those social scientists who critiqued the book (anthropologist Margaret Mead among them) tended to agree with its primary thesis, that women of the day were unhappy because they were not embracing the roles bestowed upon them by both Nature and Western society. Like so many before her and since, the book's coauthor, Dr. Marynia Farnham, was a career woman who made a name for herself by warning other women against having careers. Farnham was primarily concerned with two things: the declining birth rate of white babies, and the increasing frequency with which she saw people coming to her with neuroses, a fact she figured could only be driven by the biggest change she saw in the society around her—so many women, and particularly mothers, working. (It couldn't possibly be, say, the explosion of advertising constantly telling women they needed to be prettier, thinner, or better cooks; the general lack of options for women outside marriage, motherhood, and, maybe, a low-wage job; or the wave of consumerism sweeping the country and convincing most people that they couldn't be happy unless they could afford a certain amount of stuff.)

Farnham saw an inherent tension in women as the root of these neuroses; it simply wasn't natural for them to be pursuing more "manly" pursuits, and thus they were not only harming their families but also making themselves miserable. Embracing what Friedan later termed the "feminine mystique" would sort them right out. As psychologist Elaine Heffner wrote in her 1978 book *The Emotional Experience of Motherhood After Freud and Feminism*: "The dilemma was that while society had made many of her traditional functions obsolete, thereby leaving her with a less than satisfying role, society needed a contented mother in order to ensure the happiness of those around her. The solution was to persuade women that motherhood was not only their social obligation but also the source of their own happiness. Thus, the feminine mystique added the illusion of complete personal fulfillment as sugar coating to make the pill of social responsibility more palatable."

By contrast, second-wave feminism sought to burn down all previously conceived notions about what was and wasn't female. To hell with Freud and his assumptions that biology determined feminine traits—all characteristics and behaviors understood as "female" were the result of cultural expectations placed on women, the end.

As Adrienne Rich put it in her perspective-changing 1976 book on motherhood, *Of Woman Born*, "The new scholars of women's history have begun to discover that, in any case, the social institutions and prescriptions for behavior created by men have not necessarily accounted for the real lives of women."

It was a liberating time for many women and one that saw some real gains in terms of access to skilled jobs and better pay, broad access to birth control, the decriminalization of abortion, and a general softening of cultural norms that allowed for a new comfort, at least in some circles, with expanded ideas of sexuality and what it meant to be an adult.

Radical feminists, although too extreme for many of the mainstream feminists (and certainly for women who didn't identify as feminists) inspired the movement to think big and blast through limits.

Over time, of course, rifts began to emerge. With its emphasis on winning women more rights within the existing patriarchal structures of marriage and motherhood, the National Organization for Women (headed by Friedan) was seen by radical feminists as too establishment, sellouts who were too bought-in to their own oppression. For some, women who got married and had children were buying into the patriarchy and preventing feminist progress. In her searing book *The Dialectic of Sex*, written when she was just twenty-five, Shulamith Firestone, one of the best-known radical feminists of the time, suggested that women would never be truly free until they were free of motherhood. Firestone dreamed of a day when technological advances would make extra-uterine pregnancies possible and thus free women from their reproductive shackles.

Much as Susan B. Anthony had envisioned an epoch of single women to, in effect, reset society and put it on a more gender-balanced path before bringing the sexes back together again, radical feminists saw the need for a break from marriage and motherhood to enable women to live their lives free of the two roles that had always been prescribed to them. It was a stance that not only created a wedge between radical and "establishment" feminists but also between white feminists and women of color, who largely saw institutional racism as a far bigger source of their oppression than their children.

As in the suffragist and abolitionist movements, in the early days of second-wave feminism, activists fought for women's rights and civil rights together (and often joined antiwar protests as well). In her famous 1970 "Living the Revolution" speech at Vassar, Gloria Steinem—perhaps the most enduring leader of the feminist movement—said, "Women's Liberation is a bridge between Black and white women, but also between the construction workers and the suburbanites, between Nixon's Silent Majority and the young people they hate and fear. Indeed, there's much more injustice and rage among working-class women than among the much-publicized white radicals."

But as time went on, and women felt the need to choose some issues over others, women of color and their concerns were often left out of the decision-making process. Meanwhile, some white feminists saw misogyny within the civil rights movement and couldn't understand why their Black sisters would put up with it—many struggled to see the need Black women had to fight racism, which was physically harming them and their families, at least as much or more than sexism. Women of color, who had always balanced work and motherhood, also found it grating that white feminists not only seemed to be oblivious to this fact but also took to blaming motherhood and home life as the source of all oppression.

Most Black feminists of the time did not see motherhood as their key oppressor; in fact, motherhood was something that their actual oppressors—white people, not just the men, but also the white women who were complicit in their behavior, particularly the routine sexual assault of enslaved women—had taken from them. When Black women were released from slavery into the prison of poverty, the one bright spot was often their ability to keep their children. To have white women tell them less than a century later that those children were part of their oppression was galling.

As bell hooks put it in her essay "Revolutionary Parenting":

Although early feminists demanded respect and acknowledgment for housework and child care, they did not attribute enough significance and value to female parenting, to motherhood. It is a gesture that should have been made at the onset of the feminist movement. Early feminist attacks on motherhood alienated masses of women from the movement, especially poor and/or non-white women, who find parenting one of the few interpersonal relationships where they are affirmed and appreciated.

Alice Walker, who coined the term "womanism" as a label that could be broader than feminism and more inclusive of women of color, described her feelings on the topic as well, echoing a widespread sentiment among Black women: "It is not my child who tells me: I have no femaleness white women must affirm. Not my child who says: I have no rights Black men must respect. It is not my child who has purged my face from history and herstory, and left mystory just that, a mystery; my child loves my face and would have it on every page if she could, as I have loved my own parents' faces above all others.... We are together, my child and I. Mother and child, yes, but sisters really, against whatever denies us all that we are."

Philosopher Marjorie Jolles describes how this rift widened as some radical feminists took to tearing down anything that society had labeled as feminine, and how it persists even today: "There are feminists who think it's anti-feminist to have children," she says. "Of course, there is no one feminism, but for some of feminism's history, anything that was traditionally feminine and that had a clear link to women's un-freedom in the past was sort of thought to be an engine of oppression, a tool of the patriarchy to be rejected. So motherhood, heterosexual sex, marriage, high heels. A whole slew of feminine norms that came under intense feminist scrutiny."

Much of that scrutiny led to productive debates within the women's movement, Jolles says. "And then a competing feminist ethic emerged that said rather than rejecting those things that are distinctive to female experience—because really it's kind of male doing that, it says that the only truly free experience is the male experience—we say no, women have a distinctive culture and experience and trashing it is not the thing. Instead, maybe we assign it new value."

What these two competing threads of feminism did, no matter which camp you were in, was open up ways for women to redefine motherhood themselves.

Dividing Motherhood from Mothering

It's hard to believe now, given the number of feminist texts on mothers and daughters alone, much less an entire field of study—matricentric feminism—devoted to the intersection of the two, but Adrienne Rich's *Of Woman Born*, published in 1976, was one of the first feminist books on motherhood, and was instrumental in starting a new conversation about a place for mothers in feminism, and a woman-centered rethinking of motherhood. Rich was the first to clearly separate the institution of motherhood, which she described as patriarchal and defined by men, and the practice of mothering, which was woman-centered and encompassed women's thoughts, feelings, and experiences as mothers.

Rich inspired countless other scholars and authors, and went on to become one of the first widely published contemporary feminist poets. Her book kicked off, for the first time in modern American history, a public conversation about the difference between any one woman's experience of motherhood and the societal expectations placed on mothers. Women began to closely examine the relationship any woman has between her powers of reproduction and her own feelings about children—whether she wants them or not, if so, what type of mother she might be, what she defines as being a "good" mother and how that relates to being the woman she is or hopes to be—and the centuries' old societal expectations surrounding mothers and motherhood, which in the dominant white European culture were defined and controlled by men.

"Under patriarchy, female possibility has been literally massacred on the site of motherhood," Rich writes. "Most women in history have become mothers without choice, and an even greater number have lost their lives bringing life into the world. Women are controlled by lashing us to our bodies."

Despite that setup, neither Rich nor her book were anti-motherhood. Rather she shone a light on many of the assumptions of motherhood that dominated mainstream discourse at the time (and still do today, in many ways), including "that a 'natural' mother is a person without further identity, one who can find her chief gratification in being all day with small children, living at a pace tuned to theirs; that the isolation of mothers and children together in the home must be taken for granted; that maternal love is, and should be, quite literally selfless; that children and mothers are the 'causes' of each other's suffering." By creating space for a woman-centered understanding of motherhood, Rich began to bridge the chasm that had been growing in the feminist movement between mothers and those who were anti-motherhood. She also was one of the first writers to break the taboo on maternal ambivalence, not just acknowledging its existence but describing in great detail the exquisite pain of holding both love and hate, adulation and resentment toward one's children in the same space.

While motherhood may still be oppressive, then, mothering didn't have to be. It could be empowering, spiritual, a practice known only to women and up to women to define. The understanding of motherhood that emerged during the 1970s applied not only to those who had biologically given birth, but to all those who nurtured others and saw value in doing so.

Subsequent feminist writers, psychologists, and sociologists took Rich's work and ran with it, delving into mothering and in particular the mother-daughter relationship, in great detail. These texts continue to influence our thinking on both motherhood and mother-child relationships today. Nancy Chodorow's treatise on the reproduction of gender, for example, offered a sort of counterpoint to Freud's ideas of the Oedipal complex and female "penis envy," suggesting that while boys must begin to see themselves as separate from their mothers at an early age and thus begin to develop boundaries and individuate the self from childhood on, girls see in their mothers a mirror and a model, the daughter a continuation or reproduction of the mother, a continuous line of relationship. While Chodorow saw this reproduction as the foundation of women's weakness in a patriarchal society, her research in matriarchal communities revealed that it didn't have to be.

The field of women's studies is, of course, chock-full of books about the complexities of the mother-daughter relationship, which in the twentieth and twenty-first centuries has often become a sort of microcosm of broader cultural trends and ideas about what women can or should do in the world. I've certainly found this to be the case after interviewing dozens of women about their relationships with their mothers—a mother who felt she was denied certain opportunities growing up in the 1950s might push her daughter to excel in male-dominated areas, for example, prompting the daughter to perhaps reject the idea of career entirely, or to chafe at the idea that she's not allowed to be lazy occasionally or make mistakes. Were she to have a daughter of her own in 2018, she might encourage her toward a more fluid gender identity, let's say, which the daughter might jive with or reject in favor of a more rigid identity. Point being, for women and their mothers it's often not just the parent-child dynamic but also the women of one generation and another navigating what it means to be a woman in very different contexts. None of which is to say that fathers and sons don't have such experiences—while the roles men play may not have changed quite as dramatically as the roles women are allowed to inhabit, ideas of masculinity have shifted quite a bit.

Miriam Johnson built on and expanded Chodorow's theory, focusing on the importance of daughters viewing their mothers as mothers more so than wives. By doing so, Johnson posited that children would form positive ideas about women in general (seeing them as authority figures and nurturers rather than as second-class citizens to men, which, for daughters, Johnson imagined would translate to a positive female identity). By seeing their mothers as women who inhabited a role of value and strength equal to their fathers, children and particularly girls, Johnson theorized, would grow up with fewer embedded notions about the differences between men and women.

These books began to dramatically shift the thinking around motherhood, particularly with respect to mothering girls. While the idea had once been that one must train one's daughter to follow in her footsteps as a dutiful wife and mother, second-wave feminists posited that it was the duty of mothers to not only rethink their own positions in society but also prepare their daughters to be new sorts of women. This idea worked both ways. By the end of the 1970s, daughters were writing their own books, holding their mothers responsible for either expecting too much or not enough, for living vicariously through them and being too controlling or for abandoning them in the name of fostering independence.

Black women writers, including Patricia Hill Collins, bell hooks, Angela Davis, and Alice Walker, also began writing about motherhood in the 1960s and 1970s, speaking largely to an audience of Black mothers who had felt excluded from the dominant white feminist narrative that viewed home life as oppressive and didn't seem to see or acknowledge the ways in which racist systems and institutions placed stresses on Black women.

The Evolution of the Reproductive Rights Movement

The 1970s also birthed the feminist reproductive rights movement, which, after briefly declaring victory at the *Roe v. Wade* decision in 1973, found itself facing a powerful and well-funded backlash. Reproductive justice was another area where the experiences of Black and white women diverged, and the brushing off of the concerns of women of color by white feminists served to further deepen the divide in the movement. What many white feminists didn't realize at the time was that Black women had endured several decades of eugenics-driven forced sterilizations.

Incarcerated women, for example, who were disproportionately women of color, were routinely sterilized, even in the great progressive state of California, where the practice only recently ended (in 2014). A thirty-year sterilization policy under the US Agency for International Development had resulted in the sterilization of a whopping 35 percent of Puerto Rican women of childbearing age. From 1973 to 1976, more than 3,400 American Indian women were sterilized. Indian Health Service doctors routinely performed sterilizations, paid for by the US government, and often coerced or done without consent. At one such hospital in Oklahoma one in four women admitted in 1974 were sterilized, for a total of 194 that year alone. Mexican American women were routinely sterilized in California hospitals at the time, again often without their consent or under false pretenses. By 1974, the Department of Health, Education, and Welfare (HEW) was financing 100,000 sterilizations a year through Medicaid and family-planning agencies. At the same time that institutional support for abortion was decreasing in the face of sweeping opposition from conservatives and the religious right, sterilization policies were being vehemently defended. The Hyde Amendment, introduced in 1976, prohibited the use of federal funds or Medicaid for abortion, for example, but continued to allow their use for sterilizations. A consortium of women of color activists pushed for HEW guidelines on federally funded sterilizations that would require informed consent and a thirty-day waiting period, and were met with white feminist backlash as the issues of abortion choice and sterilization were conflated and confused. White women had had to beg doctors for voluntary sterilizations (as Rich had, after having three children) and often didn't understand that theirs was not a universal experience. The National Organization for Women began fighting such things as mandatory wait times for sterilizations, believing it would erode women's reproductive rights and unaware of the fact that for many Black, Native American, and Latinx women, such policies would allow them time to actually take control of reproductive decisions that were being forced upon them.

The Moynihan Report

It's hard to imagine that a government report that wasn't even commissioned could shift the path of history, but the Moynihan report on Black families during the 1960s had just that sort of impact. Daniel Patrick Moynihan was a liberal sociologist working in the Department of Labor under President Lyndon B. Johnson when he penned his now-infamous report, entitled "The Negro Family: The Case for National Action" in 1965. The report was neither commissioned nor paid for by any organization or the government. Moynihan simply took it upon himself to educate the government about a problem he saw in then president Lyndon B. Johnson's "War on Poverty"—Moynihan felt the War on Poverty was missing what should have been its clear target: the demise of the patriarchal family. Sound familiar? Moynihan was one of the first to use the demise of the American family as a reason for implementing social policy. In addition to his specific concern about the patriarchal family, Moynihan saw another key issue threatening American society: namely, that too many families, and particularly Black families, were missing a father figure. Moynihan believed that the War on Poverty ought to be solving the problem of male unemployment, primarily, instead of focusing on what he saw as government handout programs like Head Start. He envisioned a subsidized jobs program for men and guaranteed minimum family income, which he felt the US government owed to Black families to enable them to pursue the "American dream" after more than a century spent denying it to them. Moynihan was concerned that enthusiasm over the passage of civil rights legislation was obscuring key issues in Black communities: high unemployment rates and the absence of generational wealth after having been denied access to the economy for more than a century. His intent, it seems clear from various interviews and his own writing on the subject, was to convince Johnson that civil rights legislation alone would not be enough to create racial equality in the country.

"In this new period, the expectations of the Negro Americans will go beyond civil rights," Moynihan wrote in his report.

Being Americans, they will now expect that in the near future equal opportunities for them as a group will produce roughly equal results, as compared with other groups. This is not going to happen. Nor will it happen for generations to come unless a new and special effort is made. There are two reasons. First, the racist virus in the American blood stream still afflicts us: Negroes will encounter serious personal prejudice for at least another generation. Second, three centuries of sometimes unimaginable mistreatment have taken their toll on the Negro people. That the Negro American has survived at all is extraordinary—a lesser people might simply have died out, as indeed others have... But it may not be supposed that the Negro American community has not paid a fearful price for the incredible mistreatment to which it has been subjected over the past three centuries.

Most Black families and white progressives probably would have agreed with him up to this point; it would take a whole host of other things, including changes to the economic system, reparations, a removal of restrictive housing codes, and so on to truly right some of the racial wrongs of America, but Moynihan failed to make a clear case for economic restructuring in his report, focusing instead on what he saw as the structure of the Black family, mutilated by slavery and systemic racism: "In essence, the Negro community has been forced into a matriarchal structure which, because it is so out of line with the rest of the American society, seriously retards the progress of the group as a whole, and imposes a crushing burden on the Negro male and, in consequence, on a great many Negro women as well."

Here, Moynihan fundamentally misunderstood his subject: It wasn't matriarchal structures that were destroying families; it was a history of trauma, abuse, and systemic racism, through which Black mothers had been the primary preservers of any sort of family or community structure at all. That strength Moynihan marveled at, the resilience of these people to still be standing after three centuries' worth of torture? It was the strength of Black women in particular that did that, and he was insulting them for their trouble.

This prompted the first documented use of the term "victim blaming," by William Ryan, a sharp critic of the Moynihan report. At the time, Moynihan didn't intend to blame Black families for their plight, and President Johnson seemed to get that. In a speech announcing the report at Howard University, Johnson said, "For this, most of all, white America must accept responsibility." He noted that the breakdown of families "flows from centuries of oppression and persecution of the Negro man. It flows from the long years of degradation and discrimination, which have attacked his dignity and assaulted his ability to produce for his family."

What got picked up in the media was the "breakdown of the Negro family" part, which many readers were happy to run with. Amid rising crime rates and a few high-profile cases against Black men at the time, the vast majority of Americans read newspaper reports about the high numbers of single mothers, unwed mothers, and generally "broken" homes in Black communities but could not read the Moynihan report itself, which wasn't made public, and concluded that Black communities were too far gone. As Ta-Nehisi Coates put it in his *Atlantic* story on the link between the Moynihan report and mass incarceration,

> *Moynihan's aim in writing "The Negro Family" had been to muster support for an all-out government assault on the structural social problems that held black families down. ("Family as an issue raised the possibility of enlisting the support of conservative groups for quite radical social programs," he would later write.) Instead his report was portrayed as an argument for leaving the black family to fend for itself. Moynihan himself was partly to blame for this. In its bombastic language, its omission of policy recommendations, its implication that black women were obstacles to black men's assuming their proper station, and its unnecessarily covert handling, the Moynihan Report militated against its author's aims.*

What Moynihan gave the government and the public instead of policy solutions was the perfect excuse to continue operating as though America is fundamentally a meritocracy and any individual's failings are the result of his or her own bad choices. Instead of instituting social programs that supported Black families, America opted to "support" Black men instead by offering them free shelter and three meals a day in prison. The idea that Black families, and Black men in particular, are damaged beyond repair continued throughout the ensuing decades and continues today as evidenced by the insistence of many politicians that there are more Black men in prison because Black men are simply more likely to commit crimes, or that the perpetual cycle of poverty in the Black community has more to do with the laziness of individual welfare moms looking for handouts than institutional racism, thinking that completely erases not only the impact of slavery and Jim Crow on Black families and their ability to accrue wealth but also discounts the enormous economic benefit their unpaid and low-paid labor contributed to the building of this country in the first place. The Moynihan report also helped to perpetuate the stereotypes of the oversexed Black male and promiscuous Black female, another handy device for shifting responsibility from those in power to those abused by that power and, again, create the illusion that Black families were disrupted not by centuries of slavery that ripped children from parents, or a subsequent century of economic slavery that put families under the constant strain of poverty, but by their own inability to control their hormones and commit to family life. It laid the groundwork for the Reagan-era "Welfare Queen" trope, which justified massive cuts to social welfare.

What was perhaps most damaging to Black communities about the Moynihan report was the way in which it perpetuated a sense of Black families and, in particular, Black mothers, as flawed. Patricia Hill Collins credits Moynihan with creating and perpetuating the "Black matriarch" myth. "Just as the mammy represents the 'good' Black mother, the matriarch symbolizes the 'bad' Black mother," she writes in *Black Feminist Thought*.

> *The Black matriarchy thesis argued that African-American women who failed to fulfill their traditional "womanly" duties at home contributed to social problems in Black civil*

society. Spending too much time away from home, these working mothers could not properly supervise their children and thus were a major contributing factor in their children's failure at school. As overly aggressive, unfeminine women, Black matriarchs allegedly emasculated their lovers and husbands.... From the dominant group's perspective, the matriarch represented a failed mammy, a negative stigma to be applied to African-American women who dared reject the image of the submissive, hardworking servant.

The idea that you can't be a good mother or wife if you work was eventually applied to all working mothers and is one we're still dealing with today. Moynihan concluded that slavery and poverty had destroyed communities by forcing a reversal of gender roles. In fact, it was this reversal that preserved whatever community Black people had left after slavery had decimated families, traditions, and social ties. Female-headed communities came about largely due to slavery followed by the mass incarceration of Black men. Black men had not left their families because of any misconduct from Black women; they had been forced away from their families through a combination of a history of institutional abuse, systematic economic disadvantage, and a discriminatory criminal justice system. Community- and othermothering were necessary, and strong matriarchal communities grew out of that necessity. Though Moynihan saw them as deviant, and ensured that subsequent generations would as well, these matriarchal tendencies are hugely valuable and ought to be emulated, not stigmatized.

"Black family structures are seen as being deviant because they challenge the patriarchal assumptions underpinning the traditional family ideal," Collins writes. "Moreover, the absence of Black patriarchy is used as evidence for Black cultural inferiority."

In addition to providing further justification for discriminatory practices, the Moynihan report created an image of Black women that helped to separate them from both the civil rights movement and the women's rights movement, as Collins explains. "Black women's failure to conform to the cult of true womanhood can then be identified as one fundamental source of Black cultural deficiency," she writes. "The image of Black women as dangerous, deviant, castrating mothers divided the Black community at a critical point in the Black liberation struggle. Such images fostered a similar reaction within women's political activism and created a wider gap between the worlds of Black and White women at an equally critical period in women's history."

The War on Poverty and the Welfare Queen Myth

Inspired by Michael Harrington's 1962 exposé of poverty in America, *The Other America*, Lyndon B. Johnson launched his War on Poverty, which Moynihan actually consulted on, as did the NAACP. It consisted of a set of initiatives that aimed to, as Johnson put it, "not only relieve the symptoms of poverty, but to cure it and, above all, to prevent it."

The effort included four key programs: (1) the Social Security Amendment of 1965, which created Medicare and Medicaid and expanded social security benefits; (2) the Food Stamp Act, which made the food stamp program permanent; (3) the Economic Opportunity Act of 1964, which established the Job Corps, the Volunteers in Service to America (VISTA) program, federal work-study programs, and the Office of Economic Opportunity (OEO); and (4) the Title I program, which subsidized school districts with a large share of impoverished students. The OEO implemented the War on Poverty and eventually started and ran the Head Start program.

Although the OEO became a casualty of Nixon's presidency, used as a pawn in budget negotiations and eventually shut down in 1974, many of the programs it oversaw continue to this day. And the War on Poverty worked, in some ways. Poverty rates fell from 26 percent in 1967 to 16 percent in 2012, and recent research has shown that without government intervention, poverty rates would have increased over the same amount of time.

At the same time, as more Black and Latinx mothers gained access to both the War on Poverty programs and the previously discriminatory ADC program, the number of single mothers on welfare increased. In 1959, 30 percent of single white mothers were on AFDC compared to 16 percent of single Black mothers. By the end of the 1960s, however, Black and Latinx mothers outnumbered white mothers on welfare. This fact, coupled with the findings of the Moynihan report, made it easy for politicians to target women of color and Black single mothers in particular as drains on the system, especially in the South, where the prevailing belief was that welfare simply rewarded the "loose morals" of Black women (it bears repeating that the "loose morals" myth was created during slavery in the South in part to justify white men's frequent rape of enslaved Black women). It wasn't long before politicians were accusing Black women of having children simply to collect welfare checks.

The idea of Black women in particular on welfare enraged many southern politicians who had grown up with the idea that Black people existed to provide free or cheap labor; the idea that they should be given money or benefits of any kind— even if they were the same benefits all other Americans had access to—that they should go from being profit centers to costs, chafed at these men. Echoing his slave master relatives, Louisiana senator Russell Long referred to Black mothers on welfare as "brood mares," and backed bills that would have criminalized welfare mothers having more than one child out of wedlock. These men's ancestors had spent decades harnessing Black women's fertility for their own gain; now they wanted to criminalize it for the same reason.

African American studies scholar Wahneema Lubiano defines the welfare queen trope that emerged during this period in scathing detail:

> *"Welfare queen" is a phrase that describes economic dependency—the lack of a job and/or income (which equal degeneracy in the Calvinist United States); the presence of a child or children with no father and/or husband (moral deviance); and, finally, a charge on the collective U.S. treasury—a human debit. The cumulative totality, circulation, and effect of these meanings in a time of scarce resources among the working class and lower middle class is devastatingly intense. The welfare queen represents moral aberration and an economic drain, but the figure's problematic status becomes all the more threatening once responsibility for the destruction of the American way of life is attributed to it.*

The welfare queen myth and the continuing cycle of poverty, as well as the War on Drugs, eventually led to a spike in maternal incarceration as well, which we'll look at in detail in Chapter 8.

The Toll of the "Forgotten Child" on American Indian Communities

Native American families were also left reeling as a result of both economic and social welfare systems that kept them from opportunities and inflicted enormous harm on them at the same time. As Indian boarding schools were being shut down during the 1950s due to various abusive practices, the Indian Adoption Project began funneling thousands of American Indian kids from their homes into the homes of non-Indian (usually white) parents. Beginning in 1958, the project worked with first the Child Welfare League of America and then the Adoption Resource Exchange of North America, as well as state child welfare agencies, to place American Indian children in foster homes and with adoptive parents. Often, these children were not originally in abusive or neglectful homes; the motivation was plain ignorance and racial bias: Native families that didn't fit into the white European nuclear family ideal were seen as unhealthy or deviant by white social workers who were also given financial incentives to remove children from "bad" homes. The common tribal practice of elder relatives caring for children while their parents worked, for example, was seen as "parental abandonment" by white social workers auditing American Indian reservations. The Bureau of Indian Affairs, created with the stated intention of supporting American Indian communities, often paid state governments to remove children from their parents and place them either in foster homes with white parents or in homes run by religious groups.

It wasn't until 1978 that the Indian Child Welfare Act (ICWA) stopped the practice of removing American Indian children from their homes. By then, decades of this practice, first through Indian boarding schools and then forced adoptions, had decimated families and communities, the lifeblood of Native American culture. It's hard to believe such broad and deep destruction was not intentional—what the new Americans hadn't managed to do in physical battle they accomplished via the systemic and sociopathic destruction of families.

In 1977, Congress noted that up to 35 percent of American Indian children had been removed from their homes, and in some cases American Indian children had been placed in foster care at sixteen times the rate of non-Indian children.

Some churches also had programs aimed at "saving" Indian children. In the Southwest, the Church of Jesus Christ of Latter-Day Saints' Indian Placement Program removed some 5,000 children from their homes and placed them in white Mormon homes. The Catholic Church and various Christian churches had similar programs throughout the country.

By the time the adoption project ended and the ICWA was in place, American Indian children had been forcibly removed from their families for nearly one hundred years. Tribes are still reeling from the displacement today. "We have whole generations of kids who were in a sense lost," says Native American public health researcher (and mother) Janelle Palacios. "Because if you take a kid out of their home when they're four, and you hold them hostage until they're eighteen or nineteen, and you take away their cultural environment, you take them away from their family and friends, then it's difficult to have a shared language, shared values, and then you also grow up with this indoctrination that you should strive to be different than you are, that you should hate what you look like, that you should hate your roots."

While Native American activists were reuniting children with parents, reclaiming native culture, and staging high-profile protests in the 1970s, the broader civil rights and feminist movements were dealing with a good deal of backlash. Sometimes that backlash took the form not of anger or defensiveness, but of narcissism and apathy.

Self-Actualization in the 1970s

As feminism was dealing with some growing pains, and growing rifts, the rest of the country was really getting into finding itself. With Freud losing favor and with social and sexual revolutions increasingly turning Americans toward the self, the humanist theories of Abraham Maslow began to gain in popularity in the 1960s and 1970s. Maslow's hierarchy of needs initially included five layers: physiological (the basic physical needs—food, shelter, and so forth); safety (not just physical safety but also financial stability and good health); love/belonging (friendship, family, sexual intimacy); esteem (self-esteem, the respect of others, confidence); and self-actualization (morality, creativity, spontaneity, problem-solving, lack of prejudice). In the 1970s, with anti-war protests raging, Nixon resigning, and the 1960s counterculture revolution still simmering, Americans were ready to plunge head first into self-actualizing.

A big part of this journey involved determining exactly how your mother had messed you up. The mother-blame trend, kicked off by *Generation of Vipers* in the late 1940s, continued with the publication of the bestseller *My Mother/My Self* in 1979. Where Philip Wylie was the smothered son railing at his oppressive and silly mother, author Nancy Friday subtitled her popular book: *The Daughter's Search for Identity*. Although cast as an enlightened search for the self via an in-depth investigation of the mother-daughter bond, Friday's book was really a continuation of the theories of "maternal deprivation" and attachment parenting theories proposed by John Bowlby back in the 1950s. Where Bowlby had warned mothers of following the sort of detached approach promoted by behaviorists like John B. Watson, or even the more gentle and pragmatic approach encouraged by Dr. Benjamin Spock, here came Friday nearly thirty years later to tell the story of the impact those frigid 1950s mothers had on their 1960s and 1970s daughters. As Judith Warner put it in her best seller *Perfect Madness*, "Many women began, retrospectively, to label their Spockian mothers' pragmatic parenting style as rejecting. Retrospectively, their problems in adulthood were linked back to 'abandonment issues.' Bad mothering (once again) became the catchall cause of adult suffering."

How Ronald Reagan Sparked the US Divorce Boom

Given conservative efforts to preserve the American family by stamping out feminism, it might come as a surprise that it was none other than the king of the conservatives himself, Ronald Reagan, who set this country on its path toward a 50 percent divorce rate. As governor of California in 1969, Reagan pushed through the country's first no-fault divorce bill. Prior to the passage of this bill, spouses had to show some sort of acceptable reason for filing for divorce—infidelity, physical abuse, and substance abuse were all allowable reasons. In 1948, Reagan's first wife, actress Jane Wyman, had accused the man who would go on to be the fortieth president of the United States of mental cruelty in order to obtain a divorce. Reagan felt he was wrongly accused, and figured plenty of other fellas were being dealt a raw deal by women who would make up stories to divorce them, so as governor he shepherded through California's no-fault divorce bill. Nearly every state followed suit within the decade, and the divorce rate more than doubled—from less than 20 percent in 1950 to about 50 percent by 1980 (it has since dropped to about 40 percent). Half the children born to married parents in the 1970s saw their parents divorce, compared to 11 percent of kids born in the 1950s.

During the 1970s, the trend in pop psychology toward finding oneself, and finding both sexual fulfillment and self-actualization bled into marriage as well, fueled by best-selling books such as *Everything You Always Wanted to Know About Sex (But Were Afraid to Ask)* and *I'm OK-You're OK*. Americans increasingly came to see the goal of marriage as providing emotional, spiritual, and sexual fulfillment rather than economic and social support. While the prevailing belief in the 1950s and 1960s was that parents should stick a marriage out for the sake of the children, in the 1970s that thinking turned around entirely; in 1962, more than half of American women believed couples should stay together no matter what if there were children involved, but by 1970 that number had dropped to just 20 percent.

Some churches even got behind divorce. The United Methodist Church announced in 1976:

> *In marriages where the partners are, even after thoughtful reconsideration and counsel, estranged beyond reconciliation, we recognize divorce and the right of divorced persons to remarry, and express our concern for the needs of the children of such unions. To this end we encourage an active, accepting, and enabling commitment of the Church and our society to minister to the needs of divorced persons.*

The combination of a relaxation of both social norms and laws regarding divorce, access to birth control, increased sexual freedom, and increased employment options for women all conspired to increase the average marrying age from twenty throughout the 1950s to twenty-three by the 1980s. Often this era was depicted as a time of great freedom for women, but while some women in unhappy or abusive relationships were newly able to get out of bad situations, the sword cut both ways. Newly freed of the obligation to stay in marriages that were unhappy, boring, or sexually unfulfilling, men began opting for divorce as well, leaving a lot of mothers suddenly single and—because it was still unusual at this time for a mother to have a successful career, let alone be the primary breadwinner—in poverty. Many recently divorced mothers who were white and middle class had been discouraged from working and now found themselves in charge of households with no work experience or education that would enable them to earn a high enough wage. Child support and alimony helped, when they were available, but they often weren't. By the mid-1980s, 20 percent of children were born to unwed mothers, and the child support collection system that had been set up in 1975 offered no options to them; then, as more mothers entered the workplace in the 1980s, courts found it increasingly difficult to require child support from fathers.

There's Always a Pat Buchanan

It is infuriating the extent to which the systemic lack of support for mothers in the United States can often be traced back to one person who claims to be fighting for the American family. In the case of universal childcare, that person was Pat Buchanan.

In 1971, Congress passed the Comprehensive Child Development Act, cosponsored by Minnesota Senator Walter Mondale and Indiana Representative John Brademas. It passed on a bipartisan vote and was wildly popular with the American public. The act established a network of nationally funded, locally administered, comprehensive childcare centers, which were to provide quality education, nutrition, and medical services. They would have been government-subsidized and regulated to provide quality and safety assurances to working parents, and as Mondale later explained, because he didn't want it to be seen as a "poor person's program," while the system would have been free for those at or below the poverty line, it would have charged everyone else according to a sliding fee scale. The budget authorized by Congress was equivalent to about five times what the Head Start budget is today.

Proponents of the program, and there were many, thought they had won. Nixon's administration had helped to draft the bill, and its only vocal opponents just wanted to see the budget reduced. Then, in a surprise move, Nixon vetoed it, warning that it was a "leap in the dark" that would "commit the vast moral authority of the National Government to the side of communal approaches to child rearing over against the family-centered approach."

There's that entrenched individuals-do-it-better American attitude! Nixon was listening, of course, to his adviser Pat Buchanan's fever dreams about the death of the American family, mixed with a vague concern that this program was a little too close to communism for his liking. Mondale and Brademas regrouped, introducing a bill with a dramatically reduced scope and budget in 1973 that passed the Senate but flopped in the House. The bill effectively died in 1975, a victory for the panic campaign Buchanan had launched in the South and Midwest via flyers in every church claiming that the childcare bill would force women to drop their kids off at "communal" day care and make it illegal to take them to church. Despite the absurdity of such claims, enough anti–Equal Rights Amendment women's groups believed them to kill the best shot we ever had at universal childcare.

For all his claims of expertise on family, and what American mothers should and shouldn't do, Buchanan never had children.

Cultural Fix: Integrated Mothering

Since the early 2000s, Dawn Dow has focused her research almost exclusively on Black middle-class mothers in order to present a model of motherhood that differs from the pervasive white middle-class model and illuminates how the particular history and economic realities of Black communities have inspired a unique conception of motherhood. Dow describes these women's ideology as "integrated mothering," and I see in it a solution to many of the issues women of various races and classes have long faced in balancing work and family.

Dow defines the integrated mothering ideology as one that assumes that: "(1) child care is a mother-centered, but community-supported activity, (2) working is a duty of motherhood and (3) considerations of race and racism should be consistently present in determining how to best raise children." She also points out that many Black middle-class mothers feel excluded from "white motherhood society," which she defines as "an ideology that is widespread in society and also in family and work-life scholarship," consisting of three dominant assumptions: acceptance of the intensive mothering ideology detailed in the work of feminist scholar Sharon Hays, which assumes mothers are primarily responsible for raising their children and that they should be intimately involved with every aspect of their child's development; that a mother's decision about work and family can be captured by a "competing spheres" framework in which work and family are always at odds; and that middle-class parents adopt a "concerted cultivation" approach to raising their children, in which the focus is on developing children's educational capacity and skills, and it is assumed that socioeconomic class status trumps racial/ethnic identity in its influence on how children are parented.

Dow argues that "African-American middle-class mothers have historically been structurally, culturally, and economically excluded from embracing the practices related to the theories to which these assumptions are connected." That exclusion has meant that not only do prevailing theories of motherhood tend not to speak to or reflect the experiences of African American mothers (and many other mothers from nonwhite racial and ethnic groups), but also that African American mothers have created their own interpretations of what it means to be a "good" mother, a framework that merits its own study and, in my opinion, could also provide solutions for those struggling within the dominant white, middle-class framework.

Dow's research highlights that working is intrinsically linked to what it means to be a good mother in the African

American community, a finding backed up by historian Stephanie Coontz's survey of Black women born in the 1950s as well. In addition, Dow has found that "African-American middle-class mothers have both emotional and tangible supports to work outside of the home including encouragement from family and the availability of child care from relatives."

"Some of the things that white women were fighting for in Second Wave feminism were things Black women didn't really feel the need to fight for," Dow says. "Jobs? Nah, not really. Better jobs maybe, but Black women have never had to fight for the right to work. And having to juggle family and work was not something new to Black women."

Were the broader culture to adopt more of an integrated mothering ideology, in which extended family and community are involved in child-rearing and mothers are rewarded for working—even encouraged to do so for their own independence and to contribute to the greater good of their families and communities—many of the tensions within "white motherhood society" might soften. At the same time, middle-class Black mothers have tended to report that the notion of being a stay-at-home mom carries with it much of the same stigma in the Black community as the working mom carries in the white community. A framework that allowed room for both, that opened up space in each particular community for defining "good" mothering in different ways could be quite powerful.

The third leg of Dow's integrated mothering ideology is also something white parents need to come to grips with. "Navigating race and stigmatization, how their sons are treated in both the school system and in the community, how they are often criminalized—having more money doesn't buy middle-class Black mothers out of those concerns," Dow says when I interview her. "There are certain things they can do— for example, some moms in my research knew that if they had their kid in private school there were certain things they could demand or that would be easier for them to get done than in public school, so people would take that option. If you're a poor or working-class mom, you can't really do that."

While Black mothers, and mothers from various other oppressed groups, including Asian American, Latinx, immigrant, LGBTQ communities and, in some ways, low-income white communities, have to worry about the instant judgment and stigmatization of their children and how to prepare them both to deal with that and to resist internalizing it, white middle-class parents need to take on the job of raising their children not to judge and stigmatize those who are different. Or, as Danielle Lovell-Jones frames it, "to allow everyone else to be confident and strong, too."

"It doesn't bother me if, for example, white men are loud and confident," she says. "Just allow me and my kids to be loud and confident too, you know? I would never ask someone to diminish themselves to make me feel more comfortable; I just don't want to be asked to diminish myself to make anyone else feel comfortable, either."

Policy Fix: Broaden the Variety of Work Arrangements

The rigidity of the American workplace is a problem for all workers, with or without kids. The fact that the face-time warrior who's in the office at all hours, ready to hop on a business trip or work weekends whenever needed, is still the dominant ideal, and that part-time work continues to be underpaid and generally done without benefits, perpetuates a workplace in which anyone concerned with work-life balance will suffer.

This holds particularly true for working mothers, the workers who continue to suffer the largest impacts of the gender pay gap. In a 2007 study conducted at Cornell University, researchers Shelley J. Correll, Stephen Benard, and In Paik found that mothers were both less likely to be hired and more likely to be paid less than fathers. Their research found that employed mothers faced a wage penalty of 5 percent per child, on average, and that mothers were also discriminated against in the hiring process. In an experiment, the researchers asked participants to evaluate exactly the same résumé and cover letter from fathers, mothers, and childfree men and women. The experiment found that while everyone wanted to hire the father and pay him well, mothers were last on everyone's list as a potential hire, and the salary recommended for them was some $11,000 less than that recommended for fathers. Mothers were penalized on a host of measures, including perceived competence and recommended starting salary, while fathers received no penalty and often a bonus.

University of Massachusetts at Amherst researcher Michelle Budig has also conducted extensive research of the "motherhood penalty" since 2001. In 2014, she tracked what had happened with the gender wage gap since women first began making their way into more skilled and highly paid jobs in the 1970s, and found a persistent motherhood penalty in wages as well. For certain cohorts of women—namely white, never-married women without kids—the wage gap had nearly closed. These women were even, in some cases, making more than their male counterparts. But Budig found that while the gender wage gap was closing, the parenthood wage gap was increasing. Controlling for a variety of variables that could produce a gap between fathers and non-fathers, her conclusion was that men in top career positions receive a hefty "fatherhood bonus." "Fatherhood," she concluded, "is a valued characteristic of employers, signaling perhaps greater work commitment, stability, and deservingness."

Motherhood, on the other hand? Not so much. Budig found that every child a woman has hurts her in the workplace, but that, as with the fatherhood bonus, the motherhood penalty is not evenly distributed across class lines. The motherhood penalty is virtually nonexistent for women in the highest income brackets (think Sheryl Sandberg, COO of Facebook), but the lower your income, the higher the penalty. As Budig put it, "the women who least can afford it pay the largest proportionate penalty for motherhood."

There have been numerous other studies on this gap since 2005, and researchers are consistently finding that the wage gap between mothers and fathers, and between mothers and non-mothers, is larger and more persistent than the wage gap between men and women.

In addition to all the quantitative data on the motherhood penalty, there are plenty of qualitative ways in which this setup hurts women, too. For example, many women have anecdotal tales of employers trying to suss out their family plans in interviews. A friend of mine who doesn't have or want children was once interviewed by a company where everyone had kids and it was made clear that she wouldn't fit in. In the same month, she interviewed with a potential employer who was clearly relieved that he wasn't dealing with someone who would be wanting maternity leave or needing to leave work early to pick up her kid.

Another way in which the motherhood penalty works against women in the workplace, irrespective of whether or not they actually have children, involves the unseen burden placed on childfree employees. In many ways, childfree adults are picking up the slack for the US government's refusal to institute family-friendly work policies. In offices across America there is a sort of unspoken rule that employees without children will pick up the night and weekend hours their colleagues who are parents can't take on. It's difficult to determine whether women do this more than men, but what is clear in the dozens of conversations I've had with childfree women about this, is that women feel an additional social burden to take on this extra work without complaining.

When I first joined the news team at the public radio station in Reno, for example, there was a three-month period

during which we had an all-female team: three women re-
porters and a woman news director. Of the four of us, Julia
Ritchey was the only one who didn't have kids, and she was
constantly being asked to work late or on weekends. When I
mentioned it to her, she let out a sigh of relief. "Thanks for
noticing—it really sorta sucks," she said. "Mainly just that
it's expected that I do it, and that it's never really discussed
or acknowledged." When I asked if she could sit down with
our boss and maybe work out some sort of deal whereby she
could recoup the extra hours in vacation days, for example,
or leave early during weeks when there wasn't a lot going on,
she shook her head vigorously. "Oh god, no! I feel like I would
be a bad feminist if I did that, like I would be not supporting
a working mom in the workplace, not supporting a woman
who's doing what I plan to do some day."

Several months later when I mentioned this to an editor
in New York, she let out a similar sigh of relief. "God, yes,
the problem that dare not speak its name," she said. "I've had
three employees this year go on maternity leave and the rest
of us have had to scramble to cover that—I don't begrudge
them maternity leave, of course! It just would be great if that
leave was actually supported in a way that worked for the rest
of the staff."

Single mother Erika says this impacts mothers in the workplace too. "At my work, we have this secret mom code where
we're all always covering for each other, so if one of my co-
workers' kids is sick, then I'll cover for her and vice versa," she
says. "And definitely the folks without kids in the office bear
that burden, too. It would be great if we could just sit down and
talk transparently about it and figure out a system that works."

While "flextime" has been the buzzword of the decade, the
silver bullet expected to address all working-mother woes, recent studies indicate that in situations where it is poorly implemented, it harms women. University of Connecticut researcher
Christin Munsch found that when male employees requested

flexible schedules to accommodate childcare, almost 70 percent of bosses were either likely or very likely to grant the request, but when female employees made similar requests, only around 57 percent of participating employers approved the request. Employers were also more likely to describe the men as likable and committed than the women. "In an arrangement where both partners contribute equally at home and in terms of paid labor—men, but not women, would reap workplace advantages," Munsch said in a press release that accompanied her research. "A move towards gender equality at home would perpetuate gender inequality in the workplace."

Meanwhile, a recent German study reveals the potential for flextime to actually exacerbate the gender wage gap. Using a survey of some 30,000 German employees, researchers Yvonne Lott and Heejung Chung looked at the impact of flextime on both hours worked and income. They found that men and women on flex schedules both worked more overtime than employees on fixed schedules, but men on flex schedules made considerably more money than either women on flex schedules or employees of either gender on fixed schedules. So again, flextime appears to offer a great alternative for men, but another way for women to fall behind.

Annie Dean and Anna Auerbach, cofounders of the consulting firm Werk, which helps companies craft and implement policies that attract and retain women employees, say flexibility is the number-one thing that could help support working mothers. In their research, they've found that 30 percent of the most qualified women in the workforce are dropping out one to two years after having a child; 70 percent of that group says they would still be working if they had flexibility in their work schedule."

Dean and Auerbach are careful to emphasize that they are not advocating for working moms to join the "gig economy" and get contract jobs with flexible schedules, despite the fact that at first such work situations sound ideal for working parents. "You know, when we first started we, like everyone else, thought the gig economy thing was a real boon for working moms, but the more we talked about it, especially with Anne-Marie [Slaughter, an advisor to Werk] the more we realized that it probably does more harm than good," Dean says. "Gig jobs are often targeted to women and, in particular, mothers, because they help enable work-life balance by putting people in charge of their schedules, but with that control comes lower pay, less stability, no benefits, and usually less valuable titles."

Instead, Dean encourages companies to look at offering some employees a shorter workweek (with less pay, if warranted), which Amazon is currently piloting, or a mix of flexibility options like telecommuting or unusual schedules, as Condé Nast is doing. In the Netherlands, many parents either work part-time (the Netherlands has a higher proportion of its workforce working part-time than any other developed country) or have a condensed workweek—the same number of hours (a full-time week in the Netherlands is thirty-six hours) over four days so that Dutch couples with young children can alternate their days off and need day care only three days a week. This "papadag," or "Daddy day," emerged in the Netherlands in the mid-2000s and is now incredibly common. Sociologists and public-health experts caution, however, that working more than ten hours in a day can be harmful for health, and that is where most American concerns over the idea of a condensed workweek lie: A reduction in the number of days but not the number of hours would likely result in disastrous health impacts for American workers, particularly women. American workers are far less likely to work fewer than forty hours per week, even in a flextime scenario, and they are far more likely to work unintentional overtime in a flextime scenario, which is why flextime options need to be created thoughtfully. In 2016, Allard Dembe, a public-health researcher at Ohio State University, found that women working more than sixty hours per week—twelve hours or more per day—were more than three times as likely to eventually suffer heart disease, cancer, arthritis, or diabetes, and more than twice as likely to have chronic lung disease or asthma, as women working a conventional forty-hour workweek. Working just a bit more, an average of forty-one to fifty hours per week, over many years appeared to substantially increase the long-term risk of disease. In the wake of his research, Dembe wrote several op-eds encouraging American employers to be mindful of these impacts and roll out flextime in ways that would limit overtime work.

In Japan, it's very common for working mothers to return to a part-time job after having a baby, but there, as in the United States, this means a huge cut in pay, benefits, and prestige. Moreover, the fact that many women plan to go this route has helped to reinforce the custom of putting women on either the "mommy track" or the executive track when they start working at a company, a designation that's typically set once and never adjusted. It makes for huge attrition of women from the workplace once they have kids.

"Why would they come back?" asks researcher Masako Ishii-Kuntz. "They have to struggle to find day care and if they can't get into the government ones then it's really expensive, to go back to a job where they will never advance past a certain point or make more money. The government has finally realized that part of its workforce issue could be solved by keeping women in the workforce, so they're starting to tackle that, but there's a lot of work to do."

The key then, seems to be a combination of a shift in notions about the ideal worker mixed with wider variety in work arrangements—not a blanket flextime policy, per se, but a mix of flexibility in the type of work arrangements available and rigidity in the enforcement of those arrangements. So someone who is working a twenty-five-hour part-time gig, for example, could be paid at parity with a full-time worker (with a prorated salary) and given parallel benefits, but would be discouraged from working much more than those twenty-five hours.

Dean says the key to making flextime work for both employers and employees is a mix of standardization and customization—offering the same policy or mix of policies across the board to employees, being clear about exactly what's possible, and then customizing it to fit the needs of particular contexts for both employers and employees.

"What we're seeing right now is a gap between sort of the will and the way in companies," she says. "About 85 percent of large companies are offering some sort of flextime policy, but the uptake is low, around 12 percent. Usually that's because it's not implemented well, not standardized, and is treated as a sort of one-off favor, and so then people have concerns about bias. With those low uptake numbers, companies often come to the conclusion that flextime policies aren't working. We see it differently: How do we make the policies work?"

One solution they've found is educating managers about flextime to rid them of the entrenched idea that people who ask for flextime "really just want to work less—that idea is still so pervasive, but these people are no less committed to their jobs," Dean says. The other side of this solution is working with employees to customize a flextime schedule that really delivers what they need. "Things are so entrenched in the work environment right now that a lot of employees aren't even clear on what they need," Dean says. "We help them figure that out early on, before there's a crisis, in a way that's free of emotion so they can work out a good solution with their employer."

8

Opting Out, Leaning In, and Falling Over

Erika was in a leadership position at a job she loved. Her company-subsidized insurance helped pay for fertility treatments and enabled her to work from home with a flexible schedule when she decided to have a child on her own at thirty-nine. "I had been married for five years when I was younger and then divorced, and then I had been with someone I really loved for another five years but he didn't want children," she says. "For a while I thought I would be okay with not having kids, but as time went on I realized that wasn't the case. When I turned thirty-nine I said, 'Look, I really want to have kids and if you don't, then we need to break up.'"

He didn't, so they split up, and Erika began Googling "how to get pregnant by yourself." Several appointments, a sperm bank withdrawal, five intrauterine insemination attempts, and a round of in vitro fertilization (IVF) later, and she was pregnant. Even with insurance that Erika describes as "really good," she had to pay about $25,000 out of pocket, between fertility drugs, sperm, procedures and, eventually, storage of frozen embryos. She had to take out a loan to cover it (which, again, she was able to do because she was financially stable and had good credit).

What really gave Erika pause was not the IVF or the money, it was doing it alone. "There were two things that nearly prevented me: First, I thought, 'Am I being too selfish doing this, and then my kid doesn't have a dad?' The second was that I had to go to this IVF class where they teach you how to inject yourself, and it was six couples and me. If I had known I would have brought a friend. But I was sitting in this class squirting saline everywhere, getting it wrong, and everyone was staring at me like, What the hell is she do-ing here? *I called my friend and was like, "I don't think I can do this," and my friend said she'd do the shots. She always introduces me now as 'Erika and I made a baby together.'"*

Even with friends helping out, sometimes in big ways like giving her all her fertility injections, Erika says it's a huge struggle being a single mom. "And I only have one— I'm in this Facebook group for single moms by choice and most of them have two or more. I have no idea how you'd do that financially or otherwise," she says. "I have another friend who's a single mom by choice the less expensive [non-IVF] way. But this is not for the faint of heart; doing everything on your own is just hard. It doesn't take away from the positives and the incredible joy, but there is this element of fatigue to doing everything on your own. So, having emotional support helps, having people around, but it's not enough. You have to have some internal strength, along with the finances."

Just ten years after publishing *Of Woman Born*, which was almost breathless in its excitement for the bold new future the women's movement would deliver for mothers, Adrienne Rich was downright somber in her preface to the 1986 reprint. In addition to having realized in the ensuing decade that she had missed quite a bit of the experiences of mothers who didn't look like her, Rich was palpably disappointed that rather than continuing to grow and build, the women's movement had been all but stamped out by a swift and powerful backlash.

"By 1980 a new wave of conservatism—political, religious, deeply hostile to the gains made by women in the 1970s—was moving across the country," she writes. "Although an ever-increasing majority of families in the United States do not fit the 'nuclear' pattern, the ideology of the patriarchal family system was again ascendant. The 1980s 'war against the poor' has been above all a war against poor women and their children, woman-headed households from whom, relentlessly, federal services and supports have been withdrawn. Anti-homosexual and antiabortion campaigns, heavily funded by the Right and by the churches, have eroded the grounds of choice widened by the gay rights movement and the 1973 Supreme Court decisions on abortion."

Rich also takes aim at corporate feminism, noting that instead of toppling the patriarchal system, some women have just found a way to join it. "The working mother with briefcase was, herself, a cosmetic touch on a society deeply resistant to fundamental changes.... She had not found herself entering an evolving new society, a society in transformation. She had only been integrated into the same structures which had made liberation movements necessary. It was not the Women's Liberation movement that had failed to 'solve anything.' There had been a counter-revolution, and it had absorbed her."

Susan Faludi would describe this in greater detail in her 1991 bestseller *Backlash*, noting that despite the media and politicians proclaiming women officially "liberated," they really wanted women to finally, finally admit that their new-found equality was not all it was cracked up to be. "Behind this celebration of the American woman's victory, behind the news, cheerfully and endlessly repeated, that the struggle for women's rights is won, another message flashes," she writes. "You may be free and equal now, it says to women, but you have never been more miserable."

This, of course, was not the first time that an advancement in women's rights had spurred a social backlash encouraging women back toward marriage and children. We saw it after the Progressive Era, when the economic strain of the Great Depression made women's advancement that much more threatening, we saw it after World War II when women were encouraged to head back to their homes in order to preserve both the social fabric and their own mental well-being, and here it came again in the 1980s and 1990s, scolding women for missing out on the joys of marriage and children by selfishly focusing on their own lives. This backlash gave rise to yet another shift in cultural expectations regarding motherhood. While stories abound of 1970s moms sending their kids to the backyard all day while they dealt with household chores, talked on the phone, or had friends over, by the 1990s women's penance for being too ambitious was the requirement that they apply that ambition to their children. And because everyone from politicians to the media had been telling them for a decade by that point that marriage and children were incredible joys that they were missing out on if they chose anything else, mothers began to expect the fulfillment they had been promised from these experiences. That expectation manifested itself in a variety of ways. One is the emergence of the "helicopter parent" who is overly protective of her child: For example, in 1971, 80 percent of third graders walked to school alone; by 1990, only 7 percent did (and that is only one data point among many). Another is a sort of motherhood mystique that followed from Friedan's feminine mystique and left many mothers feeling as though motherhood should be easier, more fulfilling, and more fun in some way, and the fact that it wasn't must have to do with their own failings.

Beginning in the mid-1980s and continuing to today, Dr. William Sears has built a small empire encouraging parents to adopt his interpretation of Bowlby's attachment work, telling mothers to hold their babies constantly throughout the first year, co-sleep, and generally never be away from their children during their early years. But while American mothers have embraced these ideas, there's little evidence to support their efficacy in raising either more stable or more success-ful children. As anthropologists Robert A. LeVine and Sarah LeVine note in their book *Do Parents Matter?*, roughly 90 per-cent of the world's children live in less-developed, agrarian societies where infant and child mortality rates are still high and children work throughout childhood, yet their parents are generally far less anxious about the risks they face than parents in modern, developed countries. "The expert advice that parents attend to has grossly exaggerated the influence of parenting on child development, inflating its predictabil-ity beyond the evidence and underestimating the resilience of children and the likelihood of change in later childhood and adolescence," the LeVines write. "The time has come for American parents to reconsider the burdens they place on themselves, for dubious ends."

There are certainly gender expectations at play here, with working mothers feeling the need to prove they're good mothers by spending every free second with their kids and stay-at-home mothers often feeling the need to prove that they are not "wast-ing" their education or previous career experience by raising their children. The sad truth is that it's a lose-lose situation that tends to make both mothers and children less happy.

Progressives Can Backlash, Too

The late-1980s and early-1990s backlash to women lead-ing more public lives and the doubling down on the roles of mother and wife came from both the left and the right. From the conservative right came essays like "The Feminist Mistake," published in the *National Review,* in which writer Mona Charen complained, "In dispensing its spoils, women's liberation has given my generation high incomes, our own cigarette, the option of single parenthood, rape crisis centers, personal lines of credit, free love, and female gynecologists.

In return, it has effectively robbed us of the one thing upon which the happiness of most women rests—men." And from the left, there are charges in publications like *Time* magazine that the women's movement made the Baby Boom generation its "human sacrifice," or in *Newsweek* that feminism is "the great experiment that failed."

But while everyone was squawking about the triumphs and tribulations of gender equality, as of 1991 two-thirds of women were still living in poverty, a stat that hadn't changed since Diana Pearce first spotted it in 1978. Women in the 1990s were also still being paid less than their male counterparts, still stuck in the "pink ghetto" of women's work, completely lacking in either maternity leave or day care options, and facing constant threats to their reproductive rights.

From the 1980s to today, the pendulum has continued to swing back and forth as both women and American culture in general try to come to terms with exactly what sort of mother is acceptable. From the right-wing backlash of the Reagan 1980s to the rise of single motherhood, the "Year of the Woman" (1992), and the rise of the CEO mom, America has kept its obsession with defining "good" and "bad" mothers and found new and inventive ways to place mothers in impossible binds.

The Serena Joys

She doesn't make speeches anymore. She stays in her home, but it doesn't seem to agree with her. How furious she must be, now that she's been taken at her word.

—OFFRED, DESCRIBING SERENA JOY IN *THE HANDMAID'S TALE*
BY MARGARET ATWOOD

Part of the backlash against second-wave feminism was the rise of a whole new breed of power woman. I'm not talking about the shoulder-pad-wearing, suitcase-carrying corporate ballbuster, I'm talking about the conservative, patriarchal, Christian woman who makes a living telling other women that they shouldn't. Patriarchal women are often the most effective enforcers of the patriarchy, policing other women and providing both rhetorical and visual evidence that women accept and enjoy their role as supporting characters in the world.

In *The Handmaid's Tale*, Margaret Atwood's 1985 science fiction story of an autocratic American dystopia ruled by theocrats who, like the first Americans, took the Bible at its literal word, fertile women are outsourced to infertile women as breeders ("handmaids" in biblical and Atwoodian parlance). The main character Offred has been assigned to live with the Commander, Fred, and his wife Serena Joy. Offred recognizes Serena as an outspoken anti-feminist, evangelical speaker before the revolution. Atwood created her based on a mix of religious women speakers of the day (such as Tammy Faye Bakker) and anti-feminist pundit Phyllis Schlafly. A precursor to Kellyanne Conway, Ann Coulter, Sarah Palin, Dr. Laura Schlessinger—a whole generation of women who would follow in her footsteps—Schlafly was fond of complaining that feminism had forgotten that some women were perfectly content in traditional wife and mother roles.

Long before Atwood began writing *The Handmaid's Tale*, Schlafly had established herself as a public figure by leading a successful campaign against the Equal Rights Amendment (ERA). Unlike some of her foremothers, Schlafly didn't seize on the potential of more political power to deliver conservative victories. Instead, she saw the ERA as an affront to "traditional" women. Although drafted in 1923, the amendment, which guarantees equal rights under law for both sexes, hadn't been passed by Congress until 1972. It still needed to be ratified by the states to go into effect, and Schlafly was instrumental in killing that process. "The women's libbers don't understand that most women want to be wife, mother, and homemaker—and are happy in that role," she said in 1972.

While the ERA was just a formality for some, many feminists continue to fight for its ratification today. Ruth Bader Ginsburg has been a vocal proponent of it for decades, saying, "If I could choose an amendment to add to the Constitution, it would be the Equal Rights Amendment. I think we have achieved that through legislation, but legislation can be repealed, it can be altered. So I would like my granddaughters, when they pick up the Constitution, to see that notion—that women and men are persons of equal stature—I'd like them to see that is a basic principle of our society."

Feminists missed few opportunities to point out that Schlafly herself was leaving her home and, often, her children, in the care of paid help while she made a career for herself telling other women they shouldn't have careers, but the hypocrisy didn't seem to bother her many devoted followers. The brilliance— or at least the rhetorical efficacy—of Schlafly, and those who followed and continue to follow her, lies in her ability to use the language of female empowerment to push messages and policies that directly curtail women's rights. Much as Sarah Palin, thirty years later, would use the rhetoric of motherhood to emphasize her push to limit reproductive rights, Schlafly effectively used pro-woman messaging to crush a constitutional amendment aimed at ensuring equal rights for women.

Schlafly and her ilk gave rise to a number of patriarchal "women's organizations" that have carried on the fight against equal rights for women, such as the Independent Women's Forum (IWF), which sprang up to defend Justice Clarence Thomas during the hearings in which Anita Hill detailed numerous graphic instances of sexual harassment. The IWF vilified the women who jumped into politics as a result of the all-male grilling of Hill, which many saw as grotesque evidence of the obvious sexism entrenched in Congress. Today, it heralds women who trumpet the causes of deregulating the chemical industry, dismantling environmental regulations, and criminalizing abortion at galas paid for by companies like Koch Industries or Philip Morris. These groups aren't just shouting into the void; they've accrued significant capital and power. In Fall 2017, the Trump administration announced its intention to appoint Penny Young Nance, president and CEO of anti-feminist group Concerned Women for America, which "protects and promotes Biblical values and Constitutional principles," as its ambassador for women's issues. Nance ultimately declined to accept the appointment, saying she needed to be available to her children, but she continues to wield a significant amount of power in the anti-abortion movement.

Much as patriarchal men police other men for signs of nonconformity, patriarchal women attempt to keep other women in line. The uniquely American bent here is that a personalized and literal interpretation of both the Bible and the Constitution gives cover to these activities. The vast majority of evangelical Christians are also constitutionalists, who believe in the concept of limited government under a higher law, defined by the Constitution (signed in 1787) and the Bible. That's no surprise, given that the only people more religious—and more committed to the idea of religion informing the government—than modern-day evangelicals were colonial Puritans. Nance is an evangelical Christian, which she defines in part as a "belief in Scripture as God's inerrant, final word on all matters." On the Concerned Women for America website, each of the organization's seven core issues is pegged to a Bible verse. To support their belief that abortion is akin to genocide, evangelicals often point to scriptures that emphasize the idea of humans being made in god's image, and the CWA is no different, citing Genesis 1:27 as one of its biblical backup for its work to end legal abortion: "So God created man in His own image; in the image of God He created him; male and female He created them." Meanwhile, Jeremiah 1:5 is one of a handful of passages the CWA, and other evangelicals, point to as evidence that life begins at conception: "Before I formed you in the womb I knew you; before you were born I sanctified you; I ordained you a prophet to the nations."

Although they routinely invoke literal interpretations of the Bible, conservative evangelical women leaders often also ascribe their own interpretations of what those verses mean today. It generally adds up to a desire to go back in time two hundred years to the colonial era, never mind that they would not be CEO of anything.

Maternal Thought and the Second Shift

Despite all the backlash, the work of feminism and of motherhood studies continued. A new batch of thinkers emerged, including Patricia Hill Collins, bell hooks, Susan Faludi, and Naomi Wolf, while those who had risen to prominence in the 1970s—Audre Lorde, Angela Davis, Gloria Steinem—continued their work as well. Several women continued to build on the work Adrienne Rich had begun on motherhood. In 1989, Sara Ruddick took the first serious look at what had previously been dismissed as "mommy brain," the fog of kid schedules and parenting concerns that cloud modern mothers' brains. In her book *Maternal Thinking,* Ruddick analyzed, for the first time, the emotional and intellectual labor required of mothers, the secret and wholly unacknowledged job of keeping everyone's life running smoothly.

Ruddick defined maternal thinking as "the intellectual capacities [the mother] develops, the judgments she makes, the metaphysical attitudes she assumes, and the values she affirms in and through maternal practice." Various other writers have since expanded on Ruddick's premise, ascribing value to the "emotional labor" that women perform, not only as parents, but also in the workplace and in their relationships in general.

Ruddick took Rich's idea of dividing motherhood from mothering and ran with it, delving into the practice of mothering in great detail. In looking at what the practice of mothering really entailed for mothers on a daily basis, Ruddick came to a key realization: Outsourcing some amount of physical motherwork—via day care, for example, or delegating certain tasks to one's spouse or relative—had no impact on mothers' mental loads. Also key to Ruddick's framework of maternal thinking was the fact that it held value, not just in the way that caregiving holds value generally, but in terms of actually training those undertaking it to think in different ways.

"A mother engages in a discipline," she wrote. "That is, she asks certain questions rather than others; she establishes criteria for the truth, adequacy and relevance of proposed answers; and she cares about the findings she makes and can act on."

Ruddick also presented mothering practices as sex-neutral, a big first in the country's understanding of the word "mother." For Ruddick, anyone could undertake maternal thought, irrespective of their sex. "Anyone who commits her- or himself to responding to children's demands, and makes the work of response a considerable part of her or his life, is a mother," she wrote in the preface to the 1995 edition of the book.

Sociologist Arlie Hochschild's bestseller *The Second Shift* came out in the same year as Ruddick's book (1989). In it, she studied several heterosexual, married parents in households where both the mother and father worked. In chronicling their daily lives, Hochschild saw clearly that women were taking on a "second shift" of household and childcare work when they got home from their jobs. It was eye-opening and prompted several media stories about the need for fathers to do more. Since the first printing in 1990, things have improved, but women still bear the brunt of the second shift. In 2015, US fathers reported spending, on average, seven hours a week on childcare—almost triple the time they spent back in 1965. And fathers reported putting in about nine hours a week on household chores in 2015, up from four hours in 1965. By comparison, mothers spent an average of about fifteen hours a week on childcare and eighteen hours a week on housework in 2015, for a total of sixteen hours a week for fathers and thirty-three hours a week for mothers, on average, both of whom are also working outside the home for pay.

In the 2003 edition of *The Second Shift,* Hochschild examines the work still left to do. Noting that the modern workplace was created to fit men who had a spouse at home tending full-time to the second shift, and that it hasn't yet evolved along with the culture, she wrote,

> *Women who do a first shift at work and all of a second shift at home can't compete on male terms. They find that their late-twenties to mid-thirties, the prime childbearing years, are also a peak period of career demands. Seeing that the game is devised for family-free people, some women lose heart. Thus, to look at the system of work is to look at only half the problem. The other half occurs at home. If there is to be no more mother with the picnic basket, who is to take her place? Will the new working woman cram it all in, baby and office? Will the office take precedence over the baby? Or will babies appear in the daily lives, if not the offices, of male colleagues too? What will men and women allow themselves to feel? How much ambition at work? How much empathy for children? How much dependence on a spouse?*

What these discussions of the division of labor leave out, of course, is the number of single-parent households in which one parent is entirely in charge of the second shift.

All the Single Ladies

The same fifty years that brought a spike in single motherhood also delivered a 50 percent increase in the number of women choosing to remain childfree. Today, about 15 percent of women and 24 percent of men are hitting forty without having kids, the highest numbers on record since the US Census Bureau started collecting that information in 1979.

Although we still ask women to defend this choice, for the first time ever in US history it's not completely abnormal for women not to have children. There are a number of examples of childfree women in media and in government, modeling for young girls that you can have a very full life without children. There is still a tendency to expect that women who don't have children should be overachievers—after all, if they aren't going to give the value of their reproductive systems to society, the least they could do is accrue capital in some other way, right? But at the same time, it's becoming increasingly less common to assume that a woman will have kids at some point.

Any concern over who is having babies and how many these days, as always in America, has as much or more to do with race as with gender: Everyone is having more babies than white women. White supremacists are once again warning of a "demographic winter," with the Centers for Disease Control and Prevention predicting that by 2040, white people will no longer be the majority demographic in the United States.

Amid these conversations, the same eugenicist thread that has been pulsing under American ideas about who should and shouldn't be a mother has, unsurprisingly, exploded to the surface again. This time it's in the form of a conversation about economics—who can afford to be a mother and who cannot. The myth of the Black welfare queen mom is alive and well, and now she has been joined by the overly fertile Latina mother and the excessively strict Asian mother. The same people who encourage middle- and upper-class white women to have more kids and stay at home with them accuse women of color of having too many kids, having kids to game the welfare system, or being irresponsible by bringing kids into poverty. In the case of Asian mothers, the criticism tends to center around a vague sense that they are giving their kids an "unfair advantage" via various "Tiger Mom" tactics, which generally amount to the same intensive mothering strategies that is applauded in white women.

All of these perceptions are clearly flawed, beginning with the notion that Black mothers are underemployed, which has never been true. According to 2017 data from the Economic Policy Institute, not only do more Black mothers work (including married Black mothers) than any other category of mother, but Black working moms work more hours than any other type of working mom. African American women are also less likely than white or Hispanic moms to be non-earners (working zero hours and earning zero wages over the course of a year).

In her work as director of the Better Life Lab for the non-profit New America, Brigid Schulte has often pointed out that we currently tell women who have means and resources that they really should stay home with their kids because that's what's best for the children, while at the same time telling poor women that they really ought to be out working. The undercurrent here is that they also shouldn't have kids they can't afford. And when the guys controlling things like welfare, leave policies, and various other forms of family support are also the guys worried about a decline in white births, there's little to no incentive for them to make it easier for women with brown skin to have children.

Maternal Incarceration

Women represent the fastest-growing population of inmates in the United States, with the number of incarcerated women increasing more than 700 percent since 1980. In the 1990s alone, the number of incarcerated American women more than doubled, and the number of incarcerated women with children increased by 87 percent during that time. As of 2017, across state, local, and federal prisons there were 219,000 women incarcerated in the United States, 80 percent of whom—some 175,200 women—were mothers. Some women are pregnant when they enter prison, and must give birth as prisoners (often shackled to the bed) and then relinquish their baby to a family member or other caregiver (sometimes a foster caregiver) after twenty-four hours. A very small number of women's prisons in the country allow inmates to keep their newborns for up to eighteen months.

In contrast to male prisoners, only 22 percent of female prisoners are incarcerated for violent crimes. As California Democratic congresswoman Karen Bass put it in a Vice documentary about incarcerated mothers, "Women's pathways to incarceration are often a long line of abuse that's never dealt with. And then she winds up getting trapped in the criminal justice system."

In the criminal justice system, women are often victims of mandatory drug sentencing laws, some of which have been reinstated in states with conservative governors who run on "tough-on-crime" platforms, as was the case with the state of Indiana under then governor Mike Pence in 2016. The country's badly broken bail system, which leaves low-income people stuck in jail as they await trial, simply because they cannot afford to make bail, also disproportionately impacts women, who are more likely to be living in poverty than men, particularly if they are women of color or single mothers. A staggering 66 percent of women in jail have not been convicted of a crime, according to the nonprofit Prison Policy Initiative.

Women inmates are also far more likely than men to suffer from mental illness, often a contributing factor to their crimes in the first place. More than 70 percent of women in prison suffer from mental illness, but the prison system has few resources to devote to mental health services, and the experience of being imprisoned exacerbates mental health issues, contributing to high attempted suicide rates among incarcerated women.

In addition to the 219,000 women incarcerated in the US, nearly 1 million more women are on probation, but the Prison Policy Initiative, in its report on incarcerated women, points out that probation often undermines its own purpose— ostensibly to keep women out of prison. Like bail, probation imposes steep fees, which many women can't afford. "Failing to pay these probation fees is often a violation of probation," the Prison Policy Initiative report noted. "Child-care duties further complicate probation requirements that might require meetings with probation officers, with no extra money to spend on babysitters or reliable fast transportation across town."

Women of color are disproportionately represented in these stats: 36 out of every 1,000 Black women and 15 out of every 1,000 Hispanic women will be incarcerated at some point in their lifetimes, compared to 5 out of every 1,000 white women. In her research on the impact on children of having parents in jail, Cristina Jose-Kampfner found that approximately 75 percent of children with an incarcerated parent had trauma-related stress. Around 67 percent of incarcerated women's children are placed with a relative while their mothers are imprisoned. However, 75 percent of incarcerated mothers are the primary caregivers in their households, so if a relative is not available their children are often placed in foster care. Eleven percent of incarcerated mothers in state prison have children in a foster care home or agency, compared to only 2.9 percent of incarcerated men, whose children are usually being raised by their mother or grandmother. Women often struggle to stay in touch with their children in foster care, particularly given the frequency with which children move from one foster home to another. And then child welfare laws are often stacked against incarcerated mothers who hope to reunite with their children. The Adoption and Safe Families Act (ASFA) of 1997, for example, allows for parental rights to be terminated if a child resides in foster care for fifteen of the most recent twenty-two months. Given that the average incarcerated mother's sentence is eighty to one hundred months, ASFA could lawfully terminate parental rights during a mother's incarceration even if she is completely capable of caring for her child after release.

It is an assault on the mind and heart, reading a litany of stats like these, and they paint a grim picture of the reality of America's take on motherhood. While some women are made to feel that nothing they do is ever enough to earn the "good mom" badge, others are simply not allowed to mother their children in the first place. In their research for the Correctional Association of New York, Julie Kowitz Margolies and Tamar Kraft-Stolar found that it was "entirely plausible that a mother sentenced to three years as a first-time felony drug offender for selling $10 worth of drugs will face the real and disturbing prospect of permanently losing all rights to her children." Some states, including California, New York, and Colorado, have drafted ASFA amendments that protect incarcerated mothers and their children, but most others have not.

New Family Structures

With divorce rates rising, young people putting marriage off longer than ever, women opting to have kids solo or not at all, and the majority of queer people living publicly for the first time in US history, mainstream America in the 1980s and 1990s was moving away from the nuclear family model more than ever before. Intersectional feminists played a role in bringing alternative visions of family to the mainstream. Although there was then and remains now plenty of work left to do in terms of making feminism more inclusive and intersectional, the 1980s and 1990s brought a huge expansion of both the number and types of voices that joined the canon of feminist theory. Patricia Hill Collins and bell hooks delved into the Black motherhood experience, revealing a different take on motherhood and on the idea of a "good mother" for anyone paying attention.

The work of queer women like Audre Lorde, Kate Millett, Cherríe Moraga, and Gloria E. Anzaldúa brought the lesbian experience out into the open, if not into the mainstream. In the late 1990s Moraga published *Waiting in the Wings,* a memoir of her experience having her son at age forty and building a new family with her friend the sperm donor, her partner, and her young son.

Most of the early lesbian mothers had left marriages when they decided to come out and had to fight like hell to keep even partial custody of their children. Research during the 1980s was heavily focused on proving the normalcy of lesbian mothers and their children in an effort to bolster these women's claims to custody. Homosexual men had no such luck; fathers were less likely to get custody, and until 1973 homosexuality was still listed in the *Diagnostic and Statistical Manual of Mental Disorders* (*DSM*) as a mental illness, a sexual deviance.

Beginning in the mid-1980s, however, more and more women began trying to have children with their female partners, through adoption, insemination, or various other arrangements. There was what sociologist Kristin Esterberg calls a "lesbian baby boom" from 1980 to 2000, which brought along with it a whole host of lesbian-specific parenting books and a lesbian take on the ideal mother. As was the case with other marginalized mothers, initially these books took on lesbian motherhood from the perspective of overcoming a deficit, of proving that lesbian moms were just as good as heterosexual moms. But gradually they took on a different bent, proclaiming some unique benefits to parenting with a same-sex partner, particularly the fact that the amount of planning and commitment required for same-sex couples to become parents meant that they tended to be more prepared for parenthood, and that they had the freedom to compose their families in ways that would best support both parents and children, without worrying about conforming to the nuclear family ideal. As April Martin, considered the Dr. Spock of lesbian parenting, wrote in her 1993 book, *The Lesbian and Gay Parenting Handbook: Creating and Raising Our Families*, "because of our experience of being different from the dominant culture, we bring to our commitment to parenting an ability to embrace diversity in our families."

"It really depends on the family," Kera Bolonik says.

Sometimes the division of labor falls along the lines of people's jobs, whether somebody works more hours during the day times during the week or on the weekends—so it's driven by practicalities. Sometimes it is based on what each person is better at doing. Sometimes things fall into heteronormative divisions of labor, where one person tends to be more like the kinds of dads we grew up with and the other, more maternal. I've seen male couples who are in very heteronormative dynamics and one is more active than the other but that is because one is a stay-at-home dad and the other works full time.

For Bolonik, things have changed so much in the last twenty years that she says she doesn't really feel like she or her partner are any different than any of the other moms on her block. "With our family, there are definitely two very active hands-on parents with complementary skills, and part of that is because we both work from home and have a part time babysitter who helps, but even still our son can cling to one of us more than the other, it just depends. I never knew that having a family with a same-sex partner would become as banal as anyone else's version!" she laughs. "It just doesn't seem like anything different until we go from a big city to somewhere else and we become a curiosity and I have to explain that we're both his parents. I would love to say we do it better but we all struggle to be good parents and pull our weight. And I think these dynamics are deeply ingrained in all of us."

Bolonik spends a lot more time thinking about how to talk to her son about race than sexuality. Her son Theo, now six, is Black and Bolonik is a white Jewish woman married to another white woman. Her experience as the mother of a Black son sounds a lot like the experiences captured in Dawn Dow's research on Black middle-class mothers. "What we've been working on is just reading books and being in spaces where he's not othered," she says. "So not just issue-driven books but books with Black heroes and female heroes and a mix of representation. So just kind of instilling a sense of confidence and pride in himself and giving him, I hope, the emotional equipment to handle anything and feel really good about himself. Then we'll get to the really hard parts—I want him to have this balance between knowing that this kind of shittiness is out there, but also how to handle it. I don't want it to eat at his soul but I want him to know how to manage it so he doesn't get hurt."

She says it helps that Theo goes to a very diverse school in Brooklyn where they have resources for parents to help navigate these conversations. Bolonik and her wife have also talked to Theo about the fact that they look different than he does, but she says they'll continue to talk through that as they get into more difficult topics. "He understands what's right and wrong, and the basic tenets of justice," she says. "We started talking to him about MLK and Malcolm X, and about voting rights, but then you start taking the story deeper and there's a lot of violence and it's a scary thing for a child to wrap their head around. And then when we get to slavery— how do you explain this as a white mother to a Black kid without him wondering, 'Did you have anything to do with that? Did anyone in your family? Are you a racist? Is grandma? Am I just the exception here? It's hard and we want to make sure we help him through all of that."

Families that look like Bolonik's became increasingly common throughout the 1990s and 2000s, not just because more gay couples were adopting but also because the whole landscape of adoption was changing. As birth rates dropped among white, middle-class mothers thanks to improved access to birth control and the decriminalization of abortion, many white families began adopting children of other races, a practice that had been less common during the 1940s and 1950s, when white families had a distinct preference for adopting white children.

Meanwhile, plenty of divorced or never-married women were creating single-mother families. From 1965 to 1995 the percentage of families being led by single mothers spiked from less than 10 percent in 1965 to more than 30 percent in 1995. The number of Black single mothers in particular grew over this time period, due to a combination of no-fault divorce laws and the mass incarceration of Black men. In 1965, just under 30 percent of Black mothers were single. By 1995 that number had hit 70 percent.

Although far more common across all racial groups and socioeconomic classes, the single mother is at best pitied and at worst vilified in American culture. When actress Candice Bergen appeared as a single and pregnant Murphy Brown on the TV show of the same name in 1992, Vice President Dan Quayle famously decried it as the death knell for the American family, and slammed the show for attempting to render fathers "irrelevant."

Although the single mother is everyone's favorite example of how the American family is being destroyed, the reality is that these families represent a new and persistent form of American family, and we are utterly failing to support them. Nothing is more likely to drive a woman into poverty than being a single mother. Even for the most well-off single mother, society makes her life incredibly challenging. If single motherhood is hard for an educated, upper-middle-class white woman like Erika, with a flexible work schedule, then it gets exponentially harder as additional challenges are thrown into the mix, ranging from racial discrimination to poverty (exacerbated by the motherhood penalty) to job inflexibility (the lower wage the job, oftentimes the less flexible it is). Women age eighteen to sixty-five are currently 38 percent more likely than men in the same age range to live in poverty in the United States, and that number increases for single mothers. Currently, a startling 48 percent of Native American families headed by a single mother are living in poverty, as are 40 percent of Black single-mother families, 41 percent of Hispanic single-mother families or immigrant single-mother families, 30 percent of white single-mother families, and 24 percent of Asian American single-mother families.

None of which is to say that this country needs to reboot marriage and double down on the nuclear family, which is what several conservative pundits have suggested. Research has shown that children in two-parent homes fare better across virtually every metric—they are less likely to struggle academically, live in poverty, and have behavior problems. But the research is also clear that this in no way means that children would necessarily be better off if their biological parents married, given the negative impacts of growing up in an abusive or toxic marriage.

The solution? Researchers have recommended providing better education and career opportunities, particularly in low-income neighborhoods, to give young women good reasons to postpone marriage and childbearing and to provide better economic opportunities for their potential mates too. Reproductive health experts have pushed for the provision of low-cost IUDs to reduce the frequency of unwanted pregnancy. And both sociologists and feminists are looking for community structures that could offer an alternative to marriage while providing a certain amount of social and economic stability.

The Year of the Woman

In 1991, law professor Anita Hill accused her former boss Clarence Thomas of sexual harassment during his Supreme Court confirmation process. A highly publicized trial ensued, during which Hill was horribly mistreated. Her witnesses were given little time to speak, and some were kept from testifying. The all-white, all-male Senate panel, many of them with their own sex scandals or reputations for harassment, badgered Hill, while Thomas insinuated that he was on trial because of pervasive, racially motivated ideas about the sexuality of Black men, never mind that Hill, a Black woman, was being discriminated against.

But Hill was also a single, childfree woman, and it was here that both the senators and the public focused their outrage and suspicion. An attractive woman of a certain age who was single and had no children—what was wrong with her? Surely, she must be either crazy or a man-hater. Wild theories of Hill's erotic fixations on men of power began flying about. Senators accused Hill of being obsessed with Thomas or seeking revenge on him for rejecting her. John Doggett, a friend of Thomas and acquaintance of Hill, said that Hill had fantasized about his romantic interest in her as well, which Republican senators, particularly Orrin Hatch, latched on to as proof that Hill was lying about Thomas. "It was my opinion at that time, and is my opinion now, that Ms. Hill's fantasies about my sexual interest in her were an indication of the fact that she was having a problem with being rejected by men she was attracted to," Doggett said in interviews after the hearing. His affidavit was released to the press, and thus the public, before Hill or the entire Senate Committee had seen it. Capitalizing on Doggett's description, Senator John Danforth obtained an affidavit from psychiatrist Park Dietz, who had published a newspaper article following Hill's testimony describing the condition of erotomania: "a rare delusion of some women that particular men in positions of power...have romantic interests in them." Believing that the "erotomania hypothesis" could discredit Hill, Senator Danforth attempted to make Dietz's affidavit public prior to the confirmation vote. In Senator Danforth's own words, "I thought it my job to show that Anita Hill was not telling the truth. I wanted to present what I thought was relevant evidence to the public—evidence that was not presented to the committee...My intention was to present documents that refuted her credibility in a contest where credibility was the sole issue." Although the affidavit was not released, Dietz was called upon to provide an interview with the media. Meanwhile, Hill was not allowed to call any corroborating witnesses, even Angela Wright, who had worked with Thomas after Hill and experienced similar sexual harassment. What the Republican senators who wanted Thomas confirmed knew was that focusing on Hill's single, childfree status, and her "ambition," which was pointed to frequently during the hearing and in interviews given at the time, would be the easiest way to discredit Hill with the public. Then, once public support was waning, the senators whose votes they needed to confirm Thomas would be under less pressure to deny his confirmation. They were right, and Thomas still sits on the Supreme Court bench today, a position from which he frequently—surprise, surprise—votes against women's rights.

What those senators perhaps didn't count on was how much their treatment of Hill would enrage women and galvanize a push for more women in politics and, in particular, in the Senate, which at the time only had two women. The year following the Thomas hearing saw dozens of women mount political campaigns, and in 1992 four new women senators were elected, including Carol Moseley Braun, the first Black woman ever elected to the Senate. The shake-up prompted the media to dub it "The Year of the Woman," to which Senator Barbara Mikulski of Maryland replied, "Calling 1992 the Year of the Woman makes it sound like the Year of the Caribou or the Year of the Asparagus. We're not a fad, a fancy, or a year."

That same year, Bill Clinton began campaigning for president with his wife Hillary, the first "two-for-one" presidential ticket the country had ever seen. Bill used Hillary as a selling point on his ticket, not a colorful accessory for his speeches, a fact that grated on both patriarchal women and conservative voters, particularly when she made comments like "I'm not sitting here, some little woman standing by my man like Tammy Wynette," or the now-infamous "I suppose I could have stayed home and baked cookies and had teas, but what I decided to do was to fulfill my profession, which I entered before my husband was in public life." The fact that Clinton was actually responding to a criticism from Jerry Brown that she should have been a more traditional first lady when her husband was governor of Arkansas, or that she went on to say she had no judgment for stay-at-home moms but felt that all women should have a choice and not just be expected to follow one path or another, almost never showed up in media accounts, but that line about the cookies got replayed over and over. TV news shows had a field day during the campaign, interviewing voters who saw Clinton as "an aggressive woman, overly ambitious," as one *Today* show interviewee said, or "a smug bitch," as another commented, and drawing comparisons between these voters and the "liberal or professional women" who appreciated Clinton's assertiveness. It kicked off a manufactured "mommy war" between stay-at-home moms and working moms that would last for decades.

The "Opt-Out Generation"

Adding fuel to the mommy war fire was the so-called Opt-Out Generation, which in the late 1990s and early 2000s said, "Hey, feminism is about having choices, and I choose to stay home and raise my kids and opt out of a career for a while." Or at least that's what the *New York Times* magazine reported in 2003. Writer Lisa Belkin interviewed twenty-two highly educated women who had said "no thanks" to fast-paced careers and opted to be stay-at-home moms instead, and suddenly the idea that a whole "generation" of women was following suit swept the nation. Conservative pundits like Schlafly said

"Aha! See!" and celebrated the victory of the American family over feminism. In reality, no large-scale data set backed up Belkin's claim—there were no big dips in the number of women working or getting educated. Anecdotally, mothers were increasingly expressing a sense of damned-if-you-do, damned-if-you-don't pressure over work and motherhood as various cultural forces began stacking up on one side or the other. And it was certainly true that nothing had happened to make balancing work and motherhood any more feasible for mothers in this generation, many of whom were pursuing careers, which demanded more of them than the part-time or wage work jobs their mothers may have had. Many mothers were also pushing back against the expectation that they should be able to work as though they didn't have kids and parent as though they didn't have jobs.

A big part of this dynamic was the rise of what feminist scholar Sharon Hays calls "intensive mothering," defined by three key themes: the mother as central caregiver, mothering as more important than paid employment, and the idea that "mothering requires lavishing copious amounts of time, energy, and material resources on the child." You've probably seen examples of intensive mothering in the last ten years: It's what drives the competition between many middle- and upper-class moms over which languages their five-year-olds are learning or which classes their toddlers are enrolled in. It's spurred the rise of "mommy and me" yoga classes. It's what has transformed playgrounds throughout the country from a place where moms might congregate to socialize while their children play in the distance to a place where moms are climbing jungle gyms and sliding down slides. A mother engaged in intensive mothering is baking cookies for the bake sale from scratch, engaging in imaginative play with her children whenever possible, signing her children up for a variety of mind-expanding classes, getting on preschool waitlists when her child is one year old, and on and on. And in white middle- and upper-class communities, this has more or less become the expectation of all mothers, whether they work outside the home or not.

If that sounds very much like the notion of mothering that emerged during the Industrial Revolution, that's no accident. Matricentric feminist scholar Andrea O'Reilly traces the rise of intensive mothering to the emergence of neoliberal capitalism, which is essentially a return to early capitalism and its notions of little to no government support and the importance of individual responsibility. O'Reilly notes that with privatization and deregulation, many of the services once provided by government—schooling, health care, culture, arts, recreation, and perhaps most importantly, carework—have now been offloaded to mothers.

During the Industrial Revolution and through the years after World War I, mothering was expected to be "scientific" and expert-driven, and moral motherhood dictated that mothers take great care in shaping their children, yet it was only when women had more access than ever before to education and to better-paid and more powerful positions in the workplace that intensive mothering truly took hold. As O'Reilly puts it, "The emergence of intensive mothering parallels the increase in mothers' paid labor force participation." She views intensive mothering as something of a backlash to shifts in women's roles—with more female-initiated divorces, more female-headed households, and an increase in women's educational and professional opportunities: "It seems that just as women were making inroads and feeling confident, a new discourse on motherhood emerged that made two things inevitable: that women would forever feel inadequate as mothers, and that work and motherhood would forever be seen as in conflict and incompatible."

It's important to reiterate here that intensive mothering is something that has been embraced predominantly by white, middle-class mothers. This particular demographic of American mothers has tended more toward seeing work and motherhood as locked in permanent battle than women in other communities. In white communities, intensive mothering may also be tied to women having children later in life, after establishing careers. "Often these professional, highly educated women, who are unfamiliar and perhaps uncomfortable with the everyday, devalued, invisible work of mothering and domesticity, fill up their days with public activities that can be documented as productive and visible work," O'Reilly writes.

Michaela, a forty-one-year-old mother of two (a seven-year-old daughter and five-year-old son) echoes this. After leaving her job as a marketing manager upon the birth of her first child, Michaela found herself increasingly pressured by other moms in her middle-class Bay Area suburb to conform to the ideals of intensive mothering. "It seems like all these type-A professional women had kids and now they're taking the same approach with motherhood that they did in their careers and they are just going to parent the shit out of these kids," she says. "So they just get really competitive and it's all about whether you have your kid enrolled in all the right classes, and eating the right food and having enough play dates. It's exhausting."

It also may be contributing to the rise of a different sort of "opt-out generation," one in which many American women are simply saying no to motherhood. The allure of motherhood has waned in recent decades. Those concerned about the country's birth rate, white or otherwise, would do well to pay attention to Japan, where similarly fed-up women have just been saying no to motherhood for decades. Japan has famously restrictive immigration policies, so its low birth rate won't be compensated for, as America's has been, by immigration. Women there began opting out of motherhood primarily because men were so utterly uninvolved with childcare and household duties. Twenty years ago, Japanese men were putting in about one hour a week to their wives' thirty. In the intervening years, thanks to various new policies and initiatives, men have doubled their efforts around the house, but the gap is still large and problematic. In the United States, men do much more childcare and housework than they did fifty years ago. But so do women. Women today spend as much time with their children as stay-at-home moms did in the 1960s, and they still spend two to three times as much time doing housework as men. Meanwhile, the motherhood gap is the most persistent part of the gender pay gap, and in the culture of intensive parenting, mothers who do anything other than work and take care of their kids (exercise, for example, or shower regularly, or—gasp!—spend an hour alone doing nothing productive at all) are plied with so much guilt it takes the fun out of any activity they might have once enjoyed.

In recent studies surveying women about why they're not having children, there are as many respondents citing financial concerns as there are those saying they just don't want children or don't think motherhood is for them. For Millennials in particular, student debt is a major blocker. The average class-of-2015 student graduated with $35,000 of student debt, and 71 percent of the class had to take out loans. Ten years ago, the average debt was $20,000, and twenty years ago students who had to take out loans were in the minority. Even those without student debt are concerned about being able to support anyone but themselves, and the structural challenges of balancing work and children in the United States. That's a sad statement for a country that has long prided itself on "family values."

The Lean-In Generation

Nearly two decades into the new millennium, we have said mothers are "allowed" to work, but we have not really welcomed them into the workplace. Nor have we changed expectations of mothers at home. In fact, in addition to the whole intensive mothering thing, women are being consistently plied with messages about how much fulfillment they should be getting out of motherhood and, more recently, a very early twentieth century message from op-ed columnists and politicians alike about how important their fertility is to the nation. In a December 2017 press conference, Speaker of the House Paul Ryan encouraged American women to have more babies, saying, "I did my part [he has three children], but we need to have higher birth rates in this country," while in the same month voting for multiple bills that would cut support for women and children. Government-supported maternity leave still doesn't exist in the United States (it bears repeating that the United States is the only developed country without it, and one of only four countries in the world without it), and corporate paid leave is subpar in most cases. In addition, corporate leave is provided by only 58 percent of companies, and among those companies only 6 percent offer fully paid leave. Several US states and cities have begun passing legislation to subsidize maternity leave, but it's often inaccessible to gig economy workers, which is a problem given that more than half the workforce is expected to be contract labor in the next ten years and women dominate the gig workforce. Even when they are lucky enough to have a great maternity leave policy through work, working mothers often struggle with the perception that they will not come back, that their minds will be elsewhere in the final months of their pregnancy or the first months of their children's lives, and any number of other assumptions.

Women are encouraged into a whole host of jobs that most men would never consider, and anything considered a "woman's job"—things like home health aides or day care worker—provide lower wages than male-dominated jobs. Gig economy jobs are also heavily marketed to women, who are encouraged to take part-time or contract jobs that offer lower salaries, limited power, and no benefits or paid time off because it "makes it easier to balance family and kids." Women of childbearing age are often discouraged from leadership tracks because it is

assumed that they may at some point have children. Companies have begun paying for women to freeze their eggs to delay
motherhood, but only a very small number go the other route
and offer onsite day care or flexible family leave time, or support for women who want to have their children younger in life.

In the midst of all this, Sheryl Sandberg's best-selling
book *Lean In* encouraged women to stop telling themselves
that motherhood would be an obstacle to their success, to
stop putting themselves on the mommy track, and to start
demanding what they're worth. It was the clarion call of corporate feminism: Women can be CEOs too, and hell, so can
moms. Why shouldn't they be?

Sandberg inspired millions of women to reach higher, but
she also incurred quite a bit of backlash. Some of it came
from conservatives and sexists who thought it was "sad" that
Sandberg didn't spend more time with her children or who
mused that she probably was just a "token" woman executive
at Facebook and that's how she was pulling it off. Subsequent
tech CEO mothers received similar treatment. Most of the
men who are tech execs in Silicon Valley have kids; not unlike
in the 1950s, fatherhood is often seen as a sign of both masculinity and financial success. As a business and tech writer
for several years, I started noticing this about a decade ago.
The wealthier and more successful a tech exec or venture capitalist was, it seemed, the larger his brood. Tesla founder Elon
Musk, for example? Six children. The late Bill Hewlett, cofounder of Hewlett-Packard? Five. Famed tech investor Vinod
Khosla? Four. It's hard to find a well-known male tech executive who doesn't have at least a couple of children and, often,
a beautiful and much younger wife at home taking care of
them. Yes, even in the nation's hub of innovation, the family
ideal is still very much one hundred years old. Silicon Valley
has not gotten around to "disrupting" gender norms. None of
these men are asked how they balance fatherhood and CEO-
ing. Marissa Mayer, former CEO of Yahoo, however, is asked

in nearly every interview. Particularly of interest was Mayer's pregnancy upon taking on the mantle of CEO and what she would do once the baby was born. Some thought she should take more than the one to two weeks' leave she planned on taking. Others thought it was sexist to assume she would need it. Some thought it was great that she would build a nursery attached to her executive office; others thought it was unfair if she didn't provide similar onsite baby care to her female employees. Setting aside the merits of any one argument, there was far more discussion about what sort of mother Mayer was than what sort of CEO she would be, except insofar as her maternal status would negatively impact her job.

Feminists didn't universally love *Lean In*. I myself snarked in an essay "Lean In? Fuck off, I'm leaning so far in I'm falling over." For me, the trouble lay in the subtle insinuation of Sandberg's book that, first, all women should want to be top corporate executives, and second, that the obstacles in women's way were at least partly of their own making. Sandberg also caught flak for not going far enough in admitting that her wealth, race, and marital status made many of the strategies she suggested for balancing a demanding work life and a family possible. After her husband suddenly died in 2015, she wrote eloquently about having not previously realized the extent to which having an involved and flexible partner had made her particular juggling act possible. "I did not really get how hard it is to succeed at work when you are overwhelmed at home," she wrote on Facebook on Mother's Day 2016. "I did not understand how often I would look at my son's or daughter's crying face and not know how to stop the tears. How often situations would come up that Dave and I had never talked about and that I did not know how to handle on my own."

Sandberg also acknowledged her financial privilege in that essay and how it has made her experience of motherhood different from that of many other women. "I realize how extremely fortunate I am not to face the financial burdens so many single mothers and widows face," she wrote. "Poverty is one of the hidden and devastating aftereffects of loss for women. By the time they are sixty-five, about one in five widows in the United States lives in poverty. Cohabitating and many same-sex couples who lose partners are particularly vulnerable as they are often not afforded the same rights of survivorship that married heterosexual couples have."

But perhaps the biggest issue critics took with *Lean In* was its total devotion to corporate capitalism and what some call "choice feminism." Gone was any sense that the patriarchal system needed to be replaced, or that capitalism contained any bugs that might need fixing; in its place were tips for getting to the top of that system and staying there. The argument was, of course, that once in power women could do much more to change the system than they could if they continued to play an unimportant role in it. But as Jessa Crispin pointed out brilliantly in her rebuke of corporate feminism, *Why I'm Not a Feminist: A Feminist Manifesto*, asking people to reach for the brass ring only to give it away once they get there, to change the system just at the point where they may finally benefit from it, is a flawed strategy. "The reason it's easy to say once we have equal power we will work toward inclusiveness for all is because that will not happen in our lifetime," Crispin writes. "But if we used the power we do have for the good of all rather than just for ourselves, we will not see the rewards we want. We will not get to live the way men have lived all of this time."

Part of the issue with corporate feminism, in my mind, is the extent to which it assumes not only that work is somehow inherently noble but that it is also more noble than caregiving. It's a notion that reinforces the patriarchal value system of competition and capital over care and community; in the push to gain women access to the workplace, there wasn't much of a pause to consider whether that would indeed be a gain. Again, we come back to the unvirtuous circle: Caregiving is undervalued because it's associated with women, and because it's undervalued, it's assigned to women. Many women, understandably, see the value afforded to competition and capital and the freedom associated with both and think, "I want that," but to truly shift anything, we need to attach equal value to caregiving, community, and connection.

In her famed 1979 essay, "The Master's Tools Will Never Dismantle the Master's House," Audre Lorde touched on this, highlighting how the only valued connection allowed in a patriarchal society is maternity. "For women, the need and desire to nurture each other is not pathological but redemptive. And it is within that knowledge that our real power is rediscovered. It is this real connection, which is so feared by a patriarchal world. Only within a patriarchal structure is maternity the only power open to women."

In an insightful look at the "Oprah effect" on all of this, feminist philosopher Marjorie Jolles notes the extent to which Oprah, and various other self-help gurus, emphasize the need for women to find self-empowerment by minimizing connection, reducing the number of people who rely on them, and generally saying "no" more. It's understandable in a culture that tells women they should support everyone and always put themselves last, but Jolles worries that it sends the wrong message. Again, the problem is not connection; the problem is that patriarchy doesn't value or support connection. "A common popular narrative of female empowerment is the story of the woman who goes looking for personal satisfaction and 'completion' in others and, after much disappointment, only truly finds it in herself," Jolles writes. "Detachment from community, in this brand of American popular feminism, therefore appears to be required for self-knowledge."

The idea that detachment from one's community is the ultimate in freedom and power is nothing new in America—it's basically the country's brand. But that doesn't make it true; it just makes it rooted in patriarchal capitalism. What if being beholden to no one was actually lonely and not fulfilling?

What if community were actually the thing people are looking for when they try to find God, love, themselves? It's possible that we've been doing freedom all wrong.

Mommy Blogs and the Many Faces of the Bad Mom

When she started her blog Dooce in 2001, Heather Armstrong was a single ex-Mormon who had recently left the church and moved to Los Angeles. She was working as a web designer by day and blogging by night. A small circle of friends read her blog, which centered primarily on her discoveries of Los Angeles and the people she met, but also occasionally included rants about her job.

Armstrong got her first taste of Internet fame when she became the first person to be fired for complaining about her boss on the Internet. "I didn't even name the company on the blog, or use the names of anyone I worked with, so it was definitely a colleague who pointed them to it," she told me when I met her in Salt Lake City last year. Although it sounds so normal now, at the time, people hadn't really thought about the fact that your boss could find your personal blog and fire you for comments made there. On the plus side, Armstrong's blog got several thousand new followers out of it, and her case is now routinely taught in law schools.

"I was planning to just quit the blog after I had my first daughter," she says. "I mean, I was moving back to Salt Lake City and I was going to take some time off and be a mom and I felt like, who cares? Who could possibly want to read about that?"

But things did not go as planned. After a difficult delivery, Armstrong had severe postpartum depression that landed her in the hospital for forty-eight hours. "I couldn't sleep; I was having really intense panic attacks about a combination of keeping her alive and feeling like I just didn't know how to do this." Released back home to a role she was surprised to be bad at, she took to her blog. "At the time, really no one was writing about childbirth or motherhood in a real way," she says. "There was almost nothing out there about postpartum, or about these feelings I was having that this thing I had always assumed I'd do, always wanted to do, always thought I'd be good at was not coming as easily as I thought it would."

That's when Dooce really took off. Her blog audience grew exponentially, and she was getting emails regularly from readers who felt like she was giving them a space to finally be honest about the struggles of motherhood, warts and all. She also heard from the partners or family members of women who had experienced a similar reaction to becoming mothers. "I still get those emails and those are the ones I love to get, where reading something I've posted has helped them understand what was going on with a woman in their life," she says.

Companies began approaching her to advertise or promote their products. Bigger media outlets and TV shows came calling, and she got a book deal. Then came a tough miscarriage, followed by the birth of her second child, and then, just when mothering seemed to be getting easier, a divorce. She blogged through it all, creating a huge audience of more than a million readers and followers—and haters—on various social media platforms.

"I did not take to motherhood like I thought I would. It was like stepping into clothing that didn't fit, and I expressed that, and a lot of people just really flocked to that," she says. "The email was just incredible, so many people saying, 'This is totally normal, I didn't understand motherhood either,' and I think that's what drew people in the beginning because people were like 'She's not the perfect mom, she knows she's not doing it right, she's not trying to portray that she's doing it right.'"

It's hard to remember today, when there's a personal essay or ten about almost every aspect of motherhood, but just after the turn of the millennium, that sort of honesty was unusual. Aside from the journal snippets Adrienne Rich had included in *Of Woman Born*, there were very few women publicly talking about maternal ambivalence or feelings about not really taking to motherhood in the expected way. "People were like, 'Wow, she's even talking about it in a really sort of fucked up, funny way,'" Armstrong says. "And that's what made me successful was that I was willing to do that."

In part, women had tended to steer clear of honesty about motherhood because they were worried about being judged, or because they were perhaps holding themselves to a manufactured cultural ideal of motherhood that was impossible to obtain. Many were also scared of being a labeled a "bad mom" in a more damaging way. Throughout history the bogeyman of the incompetent, bad mother has been a shadow over US mothers. As Molly Ladd-Taylor and Lauri Umansky point out in their collection *"Bad" Mothers: The Politics of Blame in the Twentieth Century*, the bad mom label can also come with real legal, political, and social consequences. While Umansky and Ladd-Taylor don't deny that some mothers truly are bad—those who abuse or murder their children, for example—they see the label being applied too easily, and often in cases where women have a lot to lose, including custody of their kids.

Just think of the burst of recent news stories about mothers who are bad because they aren't physically present with their children at all times. The "free-range" mom who let her children walk around their Maryland neighborhood unattended, for example, or the mom who left her child in the car sleeping for five minutes to grab milk from the store and came out to find Child Protective Services had been called. We have a history of being hypervigilant about bad moms in this country, but not often in a way that actually helps children or their mothers.

These days the bad mom label has been reclaimed by some bloggers and mother activists (and by a movie of the same name), many inspired by the early pioneers of this form like

Armstrong. But that has not always been a positive thing for mothers, either. Sometimes it minimizes issues, particularly of verbal or emotional abuse, that really deserve a closer look. Other times it prevents a critical analysis of the impact the bad mom trope has had on women. "It has totally been commodified and commercialized with this 'bad mom,' or 'confessions of a slacker mom' thing," Armstrong says.

I've seen firsthand-hand on various list-servs and social media mom groups how honesty and sharing can suddenly become permission for borderline abusive parenting, or for a bad mom joke to mask a more serious problem. In part, that's because we still don't really take moms seriously. In our national obsession with turning mothers into ephemeral, idealized beings, either angels or monsters, we often fail to take practical steps to support healthy parenting.

If a mom is having a real issue controlling her anger, for example, the tendency is to minimize it—you just need more sleep, or, well, children are trying. If she expresses ambivalence, in our general discomfort with it, we tell her that what she's feeling isn't real and that she's probably just tired or stressed. This is an extension of the issue bell hooks pointed to in a chapter on feminist parenting in *Feminism Is for Everybody* (published in 2000): One of the aspects of motherhood that has been taboo for feminists for a long time is the existence of actual bad mothers. They exist. Some of them physically abuse their children. As hooks pointed out, some of them are the most virulent protectors of patriarchy. "Within white supremacist capitalist patriarchal cultures of domination, children do not have rights," she wrote. "The feminist movement was the first movement for social justice in this society to call attention to the fact that ours is a culture that does not love children, that continues to see children as the property of parents to do with as they will. Maternal sadism often leads women to emotionally abuse children, and feminist theory has not yet offered both feminist critique and feminist intervention when the issue is adult female violence against children."

In some ways, the rise of more honest discussions around parenting has begun that conversation, but to the extent that it also helps to normalize maternal sadism, it can be problematic.

The other side of this is the persistent assumption that moms are, by nature, silly and thus their problems are too. The growth that could have been inspired by mothers opening up online has been diminished by the joke of the "scary mommy" and the dismissive way we talk about mommy blogs. This extends into other realms of society, too. The "mom use case" is a common phrase in product and technology offices—it refers to a usability test for a product or marketing message that assumes you're dealing with a "mom," code for a woman who doesn't know anything.

Armstrong bristles at how patronizing people have always been about the concept of the mommy blog. Since Philip Wylie first used it as such in *Generation of Vipers*, placing the term "mom" or "mommy" in front of anything is meant to instantly demean it. The term "mommy blog" is not and never has been a compliment. "You know, it's really annoying because—and I know this is a bold statement, but I think it's true—we were the first people to actually monetize content on the Internet," Armstrong says. "And the first to monetize social media followings, and now those are the only ways anyone makes money on the Internet, but people still like to pat us on the head for our mommy blogs."

The End of Men and the Rise of the Robot

In what everyone from Pulitzer Prize–winning economist Thomas Friedman to most presenters at the latest Salesforce conference have taken to calling the "Fourth Industrial

Revolution," the robots are coming for our jobs. The Bureau of Labor Statistics (BLS) predicts that within the next ten years, as automation and artificial intelligence start to replace human labor in some capacities, the labor landscape will look very different in the United States. Amid a lot of hand-wringing over general economic concerns, what people are most worried about is what this coming crisis will do to men.

It seems to be the final blow to a certain type of male narrative in the United States, one in which you learned a particular skill, usually a physical skill of some sort, not taught at a university, and then you got a lifelong job that required that skill and paid decently. This was the American dream that many citizens felt had been promised to them. But for men born from 1950 to 1980, that dream was unceremoniously yanked away (those born after 1980 never really expected it). The country has lost hundreds of thousands of manufacturing jobs, and the world is transitioning away from fossil fuels, in part because most government leaders are concerned about the impacts of climate change on their lands and on the health of their citizens and in part because of the vagaries of energy markets and the fact that at some point we will run out of fossil fuels.

The first part of this dream to go was the nuclear family, with the wife at home taking care of the house and kids while her husband worked. And while conservatives love to blame that shift on second-wave feminism, capitalism was at least as much of a driver. Women entered the workforce in part because they needed money and in part because the economy needed their labor. Dual-income households as a proportion of all households have risen from 25 percent in 1965 to more than 60 percent in 2012 and have continued to rise since then. By 2014, only 14 percent of US households fit the historical nuclear family mold of a married heterosexual couple with children in which only the father worked. The story here is as much one of rising equality for women as it is one of diminishing economic returns for workers in a country in which the cost of living has outpaced growth in wages for several decades.

When I was born in 1978, my parents got a $10,000 loan from my grandfather to make a down payment on a house. After my mom had surprise twins (really, she had no idea), she stayed home with us until we were in middle school. They were never rich, but they could make do with just my dad's income. When my mom did go back to work, she worked at a travel agency, mostly to be able to afford family vacations.

That sort of setup is unheard of in working- or middle-class neighborhoods anymore. The cost of homes has skyrocketed in the past several decades: In 1940, the median home price in the United States was $2,938. In 1980, it was $47,200, and by 2000, it had risen to $119,600. Even adjusted for inflation, the median home price in 1940 would have been only $30,600 in 2000 dollars, according to data from the US Census Bureau. According to the most recent Pew Research Center data on cost of living and wages, real wages for Americans have been stagnant for decades. The average wage peaked more than forty years ago, according to Pew. The $4.03-an-hour rate recorded in January 1973 has the same purchasing power as $22.41 would today. A report from the Economic Policy Institute found that while wages had increased 21 percent from 1990 to 2017, the cost of living had increased 67 percent in the same amount of time. Meanwhile, Americans are working more hours, logging a lot of "digital overtime" hours, and their productivity has increased. In other words, they've earned a raise, but they haven't gotten one. Few have been able to afford the American family of yore for a long time.

In addition, beginning in the 1960s women were increasingly encouraged to get more education. Many were even going back to school later in life to get the education or training needed to obtain a well-paying job. In 2015, for the first time in history, American women were more likely than American men to have a college degree. As jobs in manufacturing and energy began to disappear, jobs in the service sector—many dominated by women—were increasing, as were jobs in highly skilled sectors and in clean energy. White men without a college education were left out.

All these changes have impacted motherhood in two ways. First, there's a clear parallel between the persistently low wages of caregiving jobs, despite their increasing value to society, and the low value given to caregiving in American culture in general. This explains some of the reluctance of unemployed men to consider taking any of these jobs. Several reports have been written since 2015 about the reticence of men to take jobs that seem too womanly. In some cases, the problem is financial—these jobs pay less than their previous jobs. But there are issues of culture and gender here too, with some men seeing direct, caring contact with other humans as something only women can do. As noted in previous chapters, addressing this requires both a reassessment of the value of caregiving and an acknowledgment that for some men this change may just be one too many and we may need to just let that go. By that I do not mean we throw these men away. I mean this: The economy does not owe people jobs that reinforce their gender identity, but a matrifocal society takes care of its people, no matter how pigheaded they are. I believe there's a way to bring these men gently into a culture of caregiving (more on that in the next chapter).

Second, the rise of women in the workplace has created an additional, nonfinancial motherhood penalty. Mothers have been driven into the workplace as much by economic necessity as their own desires, which means more mothers are working today than ever. In 40 percent of family households, the primary earner is the woman. However, mothers still do two to three times the childcare and household chores as fathers. Time-use experts have also pointed out that in many households, fathers are doing chores alongside mothers, the inference being that this extra input from the man of the house is not necessarily freeing up time for mothers. On top of the obvious time suck here, this creates another, less quantified "motherhood penalty." I'll give you an example from my own life: In 2016, three months after giving birth to my son, I had to take a consulting gig that required me to work around fifty to sixty hours a week and be away from home one to two days a week. I did not want to do this, but we were broke, my husband didn't have a job, and I had to take whatever I could find that would pay good money quickly. Every week, I'd pack some clothes plus my breast pump and bags and a little construction-orange cooler to store pumped breast milk. Then, to minimize the time spent away, I'd wake up at 4 a.m. and drive to the office. I'd pump once along the way (yes, while driving). This would almost always result in breast milk getting dribbled on my shirt. Also, the 4 a.m. wakeup plus the night feedings meant I was operating on about two hours sleep. So, I would drink coffee (yes, while breastfeeding, I know), which, combined with exhaustion, would make me sweat. All of which is to say that by the time I'd get to the office and into my first meeting, I looked like the frazzled working mom I was. My male colleagues, however, most of whom also had young kids and infants at home, were showered, calm, and fully immersed in work. It was easy to see how any one of them would have had better ideas than me on such a morning, or done better work. Arlie Hochschild mentions this in her preface to the 2003 reprint of *The Second Shift*, noting her jealousy of both male colleagues who had a spouse at home taking care of everything, and female friends who were able to solely focus on their children.

We still ask mothers to parent as though they don't work and work as though they don't parent, and meanwhile the ideal worker myth driving all of this—that idea of the worker who has no life outside a job—is bad for everyone's life satisfaction, irrespective of their parental status, and it's bad for productivity too. Recent research indicates that workers in Norway and

Belgium, where workweeks are capped and employees are given a fair amount of flexibility and time off, are more productive than US workers. Meanwhile, the United States is clinging to a workplace ideal that makes everyone miserable, as evidenced by the rapidly increasing number of highly skilled, educated workers opting to leave the workforce and go freelance. According to the annual "Freelancing in America" report put out by Upwork and the Freelancers Union, more than 50 percent of the US workforce will be freelance within the decade. Some of those workers are being forced into contract labor against their will, but the survey found that more than 60 percent are highly skilled workers who are choosing to freelance. Diane Mulcahy, a business professor at Babson College and author of the book *The Gig Economy*, asked me, "These numbers beg the question: what is wrong with the American workplace that as soon as people reach a certain level, as soon as they can make freelancing work financially, they leave?" The answer seems clear: The American workplace ideal was created one hundred years ago under very different social and economic circumstances. It's well past time we updated the workplace to accommodate how people live today, especially when all the available data points to such a transformation bringing increased profits and productivity to companies, too.

Cultural Fix: Abandon Corporate Feminism

The idea that any choice you make as a woman is a feminist choice simply because you're a woman is counterproductive to the dismantling of patriarchy and creating something better in its place. This becomes even truer when you replace "choice" with "purchase." Hitching feminism to capitalism or consumerism's wagon is unlikely to increase the value of caregiving or connection in our communities, or to create a more egalitarian society.

Feminists hoping to truly shift social norms need to be thinking at least as much about what they would like to do with power as they are about getting women into existing roles of power. Once in power, will women choose to help other women, particularly those that don't look like them? Will they, unlike their male predecessors, go out of their way to not only find people from marginalized communities and bring them into positions of power, but also train people in those communities? Will they advocate for policies that might negatively impact their own bank accounts but make things more fair for the general public? Women need to start thinking about the world they want to create—the education system they would build, the health care policies they would adopt, the political and legal changes they'd like to see, the workplaces they would create—not just the perks they would like to receive from, as Crispin put it, living "as men have lived."

The idea of simply slotting women in for men in a patriarchal hierarchy that continues to value competition and individual success above all else is not progress; it's just a distraction. What would a caring, woman-centered reality look like? This is the imaginative work women need to be undertaking. Instead of the endless drive toward higher salaries and more lofty titles, what if we built a world in which those things had less value?

Policy Fix: Cap Workdays for Men and Women

More than anything else I've written in this book, this—a policy that already exists in at least a dozen other countries—is the one that feels most radical to me. One of the many ways this country's Puritan roots have influenced the workplace is in our slavish devotion to work for work's sake, to the cleansing and morally beneficial power of hard work. Our notion that work, which for most people boils down to putting money in someone else's pocket, is somehow inherently noble and moral may be the biggest obstacle to modernizing the American workplace. The neat trick here is that it makes every demand for more comfortable work situations seem lazy, selfish, and entitled. I remember once talking to my dad when I was looking for a job and saying "I'd really like to find a job where I can help people in some way," and him saying, "Hey, they call it work for a reason. You can help people in your spare time."

The Puritan work ethic keeps us working longer and under worse conditions than the rest of the developed world, and contrary to popular belief, it doesn't actually deliver improvements to productivity or profits. It's also terrible for talent recruitment and retention, and thus often winds up costing companies. As Mulcahy puts it, "Every single study shows that as soon as people have enough niche knowledge, and experience, and valuable enough skills, they can't escape the American workplace fast enough." Replacing those people costs American companies money—ultimately more money than it would cost them to create workplaces people actually want to stay in.

So, while it's hard for me to believe that American politicians or CEOs would agree to a capped workday—eight hours a day, for example, or a forty-hour workweek spread across four days—for men and women, there are a whole host of bottom-line reasons to implement such a policy. In addition to creating workplaces where people actually want to be, those benefits include productivity increases, lower health care costs, and more innovative ideas that tend to spring from the minds of people not ground down by their jobs.

CHAPTER

9

The Fertility-Industrial Complex

Lorien McKenna, a TV and film writer and producer, was at a fertility clinic, her feet in the stirrups, in the process of being inseminated, when her fertility specialist leaned over and casually said, "This is never going to work. You're too old. You need to do IVF."

"That's what she told me when she was literally inside me, inseminating me, which is already a pretty intensely embarrassing experience," McKenna says.

The specialist turned out to be wrong. It was a successful intrauterine insemination (IUI), a procedure during which sperm is inserted into the female's reproductive tract, much closer to the egg than where it would naturally be deposited. McKenna gave birth to a healthy baby girl nine months later.

"[Specialists] kept telling me I was old and that my eggs were bad, and that IVF was my only option," she says.

But McKenna didn't buy it. Sure, she was forty, but she had been pregnant in the recent past, so her eggs didn't seem to be the issue. One specialist cautioned her that an abortion she'd had in her twenties might make it difficult for her to get pregnant now (despite the fact that this notion has been proven false by multiple studies, it's a popular myth that's still spread by both religious groups and *some medical professionals). At her urging, the clinic fi-nally tested her husband and discovered that his low sperm count was the problem. Yet, they still encouraged her to do in vitro fertilization (IVF), rather than the lower-cost, less-invasive IUI. It's a common move, not just because IVF delivers higher profits, but also because most fertility specialists believe that the more eggs they have to work with, the better, and since clinics use their success rates to market to potential new customers, they often tend to skip immediately to the procedure that they feel will reliably give them the higher success rate—IVF.*

Very few clinics mention the option of "natural" IVF, a type of IVF that requires fewer drugs and is both less expensive and gentler on women's bodies. McKenna said no one told her about it. "But honestly, I probably wouldn't have done it even if they had," she says. "By that point I was completely baby crazy, and I felt like I needed to do what-ever the fastest thing was."

"Really the only reason I didn't do IVF at the time was I just couldn't scrape together the additional $12,000," Mc-Kenna says. "So, I said okay well let's do this last-ditch IUI at least, and that will buy me some more time to save up for IVF. But their attitude was that I was wasting my time."

Fertility has played an integral role in feminism since the movement first started including discussions of family planning and birth control back in the 1920s. In modern times, one solution many women have found in the quest to balance family planning and career is to wait as long as possible to have children, a strategy that has been enabled in large part by advancements in fertility-assistive technology. But in this realm too, women's "choices" are often dictated to them by a cultural and corporate structure that is designed to suit men more than women, and to suit capitalism most of all.

In the meantime, corporate America has forgotten a more obvious option: allowing women to take time off to have children when they want without risking their careers. A workplace that could allow for both of these options, while also treating childfree women fairly, would be truly inclusive, but few exist.

Although often hailed as a win-win solution for the modern woman, fertility treatments have an impact on women's physical and mental health and often their professional lives as well. Many have to take time off during the most intense months of treatment. The dirty little secret here is that more than half the time the fertility issue can be traced to the male partner, despite the prevailing assumption that if a woman, and therefore her eggs, are "old" (over thirty-five, according to fertility experts), she must need IVF. Because less invasive procedures are also less costly (and can be less effective), many fertility clinics try to encourage women to go straight to IVF. In a survey I conducted of more than one hundred women who had undergone fertility treatments, some 80 percent said their doctor had told them at their very first appointment that they should do IVF.

While IVF can help to increase a fertility clinic's advertised success rate, for individual cases the average success rate is around 20 percent. The bigger issue, according to various reproductive health experts I've spoken with, is that the treatment doesn't get at any underlying health issues that may be leading to infertility.

According to Dr. Geeta Nargund, an international fertility expert based in London, too many women who don't need drug-assisted IVF are being sold on the idea. "In a lot of cases, the woman has no fertility issue; it's their partner that has the issue," she says. In fact, this is true in roughly half of fertility cases in the United States. "There's a significant population of perfectly fertile women who are having fertility treatment and they don't need it," Nargund adds. She counsels women who ovulate on their own and have no issue with their fallopian tubes to try "natural IVF," which requires far fewer drugs than the standard IVF process.

"We tend to forget because the field is male-dominated and they often take the approach of, 'Oh well, women are doing all these injections, but they don't mind that,'" Nargund says. "Well, how do you know that?...Most women are working during this time and I've seen a number of them have to resign because of the intensity of this process—I think we owe it to women to make fertility treatments as safe and easy as possible."

Michaela, now a mother of two, spent almost four years trying to conceive before eventually succeeding with IUI, but it wasn't until she went to see Dr. Aimee Eyvazzadeh, a well-known Bay Area fertility specialist (and creator of EggFreezingParty.com), that she realized that the problem had never been her. Michaela's husband had a very common condition that was heating his sperm and killing it off. A simple outpatient procedure to fix a faulty vein, and boom, they had their second baby easily and with no help at all. "I was furious and really sad for months," Michaela says. "I spent years of my life not knowing what was wrong, thinking it was something wrong with me, believing that I was somehow flawed. Not to mention the thousands of dollars we spent on fertility treatments I didn't need, and all those drugs I pumped into my body that I didn't need."

Eyvazzadeh says that sort of scenario is extremely common. "IVF is probably the most effective tool in the fertility toolbox, but as with any tool it's only useful if it's the right tool for the job," she says. "This is not something you want to rush into, and I do think that's the case with some IVF clinics. It's imperative to first address any underlying factors that may be causing fertility issues. You don't want to come out of a cycle without success and say, 'Oh, we should have removed those polyps from your uterus, or your husband should have seen a urologist.'"

"I have a love-hate relationship with IVF," Dr. Paul Turek, a world-renowned male fertility expert, says. "It's been very enabling for couples that have a genetic infertility issue, or have been made infertile by something like chemotherapy. But it's overused because it's fast."

Turek gets pretty blunt in his assessment. "IVF is fast and it's powerful," he says. "But is it cost-effective? No. Is it perfectly safe? No. Does it improve health? No. It is the McDonald's of fertility. And I would say it's probably the worst thing to happen to men's health in America."

Turek would like to see men not only referred to their own specialists earlier on in fertility treatments, but also visiting urologists regularly, in the same way that women have annual gynecological checkups, because the reproductive system can often be a great indicator of physical health in general. A weird and peculiarly American mix of gender issues for both men and women prevents this from happening. The tendency to place infertility solely and always at the feet of women, to tie them so explicitly and completely to the physically productive ability of their bodies, has led to a fertility approach that only looks at one-half of the whole picture, while the connection between fertility and masculinity has kept men from preventive care that in some cases could save their lives.

The women's health system hasn't protected women from the negative health impacts of IVF, either. Gynecologists' go-to first move for fertility issues is often to prescribe Clomid, a synthetic hormone that tricks the body into producing artificially low amounts of estrogen, stimulating the hypothalamus and, in turn, the pituitary gland to secrete hormones that kick the ovaries into overdrive. "Many gynecologists do women a disservice by jumping to prescribe medicine before doing a complete fertility screening," Eyvazzadeh says. She recommends that those struggling with infertility first have a fertility screening—getting a clear read on the health of their eggs, fallopian tubes, and partner's sperm. "Instead of this approach, too often I have patients that come to me having been told by their OBGYN to take Clomid when in reality that was not and is not the right solution to their fertility problems," she says. "Frankly, prescribing Clomid can be downright dangerous for some women as it can accentuate or cause depression, anxiety and migraines…I call it 'crazy Clomid' for a reason."

Sanofi, the pharmaceutical company that makes Clomid, did not respond to requests for comments, but the company does list psychosis as a possible side effect of the drug. It's also contraindicated for women with a personal or family history of ovarian, uterine, or fallopian cysts, but it is not standard practice for obstetrician-gynecologists to ask about those histories or conduct ultrasounds to check for cysts before prescribing the drug. "Unfortunately, I see far too many patients who have been taking Clomid as prescribed by a gynecologist without having done a fertility screening," Eyvazzadeh says. "Often I find something that could have been addressed years earlier and the patient has now lost precious years of fertility taking a medication they ultimately didn't need. For example, in an initial appointment with a patient, I performed an ultrasound and immediately discovered a uterus full of fibroids. Boom—that right there was the problem. Not a case for Clomid, yet she'd been taking it for years unnecessarily."

Putting All Our Eggs in One Freezer

The dream currently being sold to women is that they can "just" freeze their eggs when they're in their twenties or early thirties, particularly if they work in tech, where companies are increasingly willing to pay for the service. Then, once their careers are stable or they've met a stable partner, whichever comes first, they can do IVF. In 2009, only about five hundred women in the United States froze their eggs—in 2013, almost five thousand did, according to data from the

Society for Assisted Reproductive Technology. Fertility marketer EggBanxx estimates that seventy-six thousand women will be freezing their eggs by 2018.

But while the media narrative has largely been one of career women putting their professional lives first—often in ways deemed selfish by cultural critics—in reality women go this route for a wide variety of reasons. According to Nargund, many of the women she sees at her clinic are freezing their eggs because they just haven't been able to find a partner yet. Others have had to postpone children because they are looking after elderly parents or other relatives. Anthropologists at Yale University recently interviewed 125 women at an egg-freezing clinic and concluded that the vast majority were educated women who were having a hard time meeting equally educated men (increasingly common as women surpass men in the accumulation of degrees). As author Antonio Garcia Martinez put it in a Facebook post, "Women refuse to marry down, and most men refuse to commit. This is the real reason for our collapsing birth rates." Nargund put it slightly less bluntly: "Women tell us frequently that they are freezing their eggs because they have just not been able to find a compatible partner."

Irrespective of the drivers, in most cases egg freezing is being oversold as a solution for anyone hoping to extend their fertility. While egg freezing can absolutely be a useful tool (and hey, that external uterus Shulamith Firestone once dreamed of may well be a reality in our lifetimes), it's not quite the sure thing some want us to think. Many clinics have no idea whether their patients' eggs will still be viable once defrosted.

Although the American Society for Reproductive Medicine removed the "experimental" label from egg freezing in 2012 because advancements had dramatically improved success rates, it still cautioned against overselling the procedure to women and giving them "false hope" of more control over their future fertility. Sadly, several clinics have not heeded that warning.

Ernest Zeringue, medical director and founder of the California IVF Fertility Center in Davis, has some advice for women envisioning egg freezing as a fail-safe. "Egg freezing services are relatively new," he says. "It is no longer considered experimental, however, that doesn't mean that clinics are proficient yet. There are many centers, I'd go as far as to say most centers that are freezing eggs, that have not yet thawed them and attempted pregnancy." In other words, they don't yet know whether the eggs will be viable once thawed— something the woman won't find out until years later.

Zeringue explains that in his center, it took quite a bit of time and effort to come up with an egg-freezing process they know works: "We set up trials of different techniques and tested eggs after thawing to see if the fertilization rates and pregnancy rates were the same as with fresh eggs. Using commercially available materials and protocols, most of the eggs failed to make good-quality embryos." It was only after several adjustments to their process that his center was able to ensure a higher survival rate following egg freezing. Still, only about 75 percent of frozen eggs survive the freezing and thawing process.

In addition to not being guaranteed effective, egg freezing isn't cheap. It costs about $10,000 to harvest eggs, a procedure that is typically done after a woman has taken many of the same follicle-stimulating drugs taken during IVF, which can cost up to $1,000, depending on your insurance. Then the storage fee is around $500 a year. If and when you decide to use the eggs, you'll still need to go through the implantation procedure and, if you're single, pay for sperm.

Fertility Technology and Reproductive Rights

The rise of fertility technology has created new and complicated questions around reproductive rights. Each round of

IVF produces a certain number of fertilized embryos, which are then stored. High-profile court cases over which parent has a legal claim to these embryos have begun to show up with increasing regularity in the press, and anti-abortion groups are moving in on these legions of frozen embryos as a new battleground in the war over reproductive rights.

Women who undergo IVF will need to decide at some point whether to use, donate, or destroy these embryos—a decision that carries increasingly uncertain legal implications. And one that for religious women can create a whole other host of complications around IVF.

Take Amber, for example, whose name I've changed to protect her identity. She married her college sweetheart and worked for a while after graduation, and then the two of them planned to have a family. She and her husband were in their late twenties and thought they'd have two, maybe three kids, ideally close together so that Amber wouldn't be out of her career for too long. After trying to get pregnant for a year, they went to a fertility clinic and discovered that she has a condition called hydrosalpinx; both her fallopian tubes were blocked.

"Our reproductive endocrinologist said the only way I'd ever be able to get pregnant was through IVF—without fallopian tubes there's really no other way," Amber says. "We were devastated, but we talked it over and decided we really wanted biological children so we said we'd try this and see what happened."

In the course of her first round of IVF, Amber had to make an unexpected decision. "The process of creating the embryos is really tricky and risky: You don't know how many eggs will be retrieved and viable, how many will fertilize, and then how many will make it to 3 or 5 days," she says. Would-be parents have to decide early on how many embryos they want to try with, and doctors mostly encourage patients to shoot for the moon to increase their chances. "We did not want to end up with more embryos than we wanted to carry," Amber says.

She didn't want to have to make a decision later on about either donating fertilized embryos to someone else or destroying them, which she didn't think she could do. "So we opted to just have five carried from fertilization to five days."

That decision was so unusual the doctors made Amber and her husband sign forms confirming that they were requesting that only five embryos be moved forward through the process.

"Well, all five made it," Amber says. "So we are on the path to having five." After having twin girls in 2012, Amber had her third child in June 2015 and her fourth in late 2017.

"I had never planned on having this many kids, but we had to hedge our bets and also think about how many kids max we could handle," she says. "And at that point we were in our twenties and hadn't had kids yet."

Amber says it can be a challenge to balance gratitude for her growing family with concerns about the impact on their lives. "The financial part makes an impact in terms of whether we're able to buy a house, a car of a certain type, how much I work because having three kids in day care is a big financial burden, and then it puts a lot of strain on my husband as the person who's working outside the house and has the financial burden and has to keep that job and stay happy," she says.

She feels less comfortable talking about the burden on her, but being pregnant two to three times more than you'd like is not nothing. She sounds exhausted and a bit wistful talking about it. She loves her children, loves being a mother, and says she feels like she can't complain: "I asked for this, and I've been lucky to have IVF work so well; I have friends who have tried multiple rounds and never had it work." Yet part of her feels like her control was taken by this technology that was supposed to give women more control over their fertility.

"I never wanted five children; it's not what I would have chosen," she says. "I try to see it as a gift. But some days, I'm just really tired."

The Consumer Choice Model of Reproduction

Feminist theorists have grappled recently with whether fertility technology represents more control for women over their reproductive systems or whether the commodification of fertility is ultimately bad for women.

Kristin Esterberg points out in a chapter on lesbian motherhood in the 2008 book *Feminist Mothering* that more recently the advice literature for lesbian mothers has largely leaned toward what she calls a "consumer model of reproductive choice," in which the idea that lesbian mothers can have whatever sort of child they want is a key message. Prospective parents budget for the high cost of reproductive assistance, and then browse through catalogs of donors to select for the traits they'd like. "Not surprisingly, fertility services are well beyond the reach of most poor and working-class women," she writes. The consumer model is available to straight women who require reproductive technologies as well, and feminists such as Robyn Rowland and Barbara Katz Rothman have argued that the commodification of reproduction in a patriarchal capitalist society will ultimately harm women.

Rowland's description of the rise of reproductive technologies and the ownership of them by science, medicine, and corporations echoes back to the early medicalization of motherhood. She points out in her 1993 book on the subject, *Living Laboratories: Women and Reproductive Technologies,* that while advancements in reproductive technology have been marketed as a way to give women more control and choices, their choices are ultimately being controlled by a combination of science and capitalism (those who can afford fertility treatments may have more choices, but those who cannot are in the same boat they would have been in fifty years ago).

In the use of purchased eggs and surrogate mothers, Rowland sees a continuation of the objectification of women. "Advertising uses women's bodies and sexual availability this way, and an entire industry of pornography reaps its profit from this objectification. With the new reproductive technologies women are further objectified and fragmented, dismembered into ovaries and eggs for exchange and wombs for rent."

Ultimately, for Rowland, it boils down to control, particularly our almost pathological desire to control nature. The idea that money and technology can get us out of any of the unpleasantness of being human—from the possibility of infertility to the inevitability of death—has been intoxicating men in power since humans first began telling stories and making tools. It's an obsession that dovetails nicely with the very American idea of absolutely everything in a person's life being attributable to personal responsibility and the choices they've made. In the realm of fertility, that's an idea that almost inevitably makes women feel like shit—for having waited too long, for having a physical abnormality, for not being able to afford fertility treatments, for not being able to do "the most natural thing in the world."

Because fertility technology has helped so many infertile couples conceive, and because it has been particularly instrumental in helping single women and lesbian women conceive, it's hard to see it as wholly bad. However, the current economic realities of the system often remove control from women while simultaneously selling them the fantasy of having greater control over their reproductive systems. To give some of that control back to women, the fertility industry could and should be more forthcoming with information about everything from how to address male infertility to the option of "natural IVF" to the potential side effects of fertility drugs like Clomid.

Cultural Fix: True Reproductive Control

We need to enable women to truly have or not have children whenever they wish in whatever situation suits them. It would be a great thing if asking any woman about her plans to have or not have children could go the way of the dodo (any woman who wants you to know will tell you, believe me!). We also need to get much better about sharing all kinds of information about fertility and motherhood in general, particularly in realistically discussing everything from age and infertility to the success rates of fertility treatments to the day-to-day grind of mothering.

The question of access to fertility treatments, including IVF, also needs to be addressed. Making this option available only to those who can afford it is population engineering, whether intended or not, and it has led to all manner of unintended consequences. Because most insurance plans don't cover IVF, for example, it's standard procedure in the United States for doctors to ask their patients whether they want to implant two fertilized eggs to increase their chances. That practice has led to a spike in multiple births that are costly to the health care system and put undue stress on both mothers, for whom a multiple pregnancy is high risk, and on children, given that most multiples are delivered prematurely.

We need to be more flexible about how people create families. Companies should be at least as supportive of maternity leave when a woman is in her best child-producing years as they are willing to pay for egg freezing and fertility treatments. Women should have children late only if they want to, not because that's the only way to keep their jobs.

As more and more women are finding themselves without a partner in middle age, but still wanting to have children, we need to do a much better job of supporting single mothers and creating the sorts of situations that don't just leave these women to fend for themselves. Cohousing for single mothers, or for a mixed community of lots of different types of families, for example, could be amazing (and is something a few scattered groups are experimenting with).

Getting comfortable with the idea of young mothers again would be helpful in shifting our system. At some point, it became culturally unacceptable for women to have children young—a shift that enabled women to plan out their lives a bit more, to do something other than get married and have children if they so desired, and to create complete identities themselves before being responsible for the shaping of others. But there are ways in which we may have overshot the mark. In some ethnic minority communities, for example, having a child in your late teens or early twenties is not frowned upon, but those women have to deal with the stigma placed on young motherhood by the broader culture. If a woman truly wants to have children young, there's nothing inherently wrong with that, nor is there anything objectively better about having children later in life.

Policy Fix: Raise Awareness of Family Responsibilities Discrimination and Strengthen Laws Preventing It

One way to increase the amount of control women and men have over their reproductive choices is to lift some of the systemic limits to those choices, many of which swirl around the workplace and how it does or doesn't support caregiving. There are many ways in which we've changed our thinking about reproduction to better suit the "ideal worker" scenario in the American workplace, rather than rethinking the American workplace to better fit women's lives.

The brainchild of attorney Joan Williams, family responsibilities discrimination (FRD), also called caregiver discrimination, is employment discrimination against workers based on their family caregiving responsibilities. The Center for WorkLife Law at the University of California at Hastings College of the Law, which Williams heads up, explains it like this: Pregnant women, mothers and fathers of young children, and employees with aging parents or sick spouses or partners may encounter family responsibilities discrimination. They may be rejected for hire, passed over for promotion, demoted, harassed, or terminated—despite good performance—because their employers make personnel decisions based on stereotypical notions of how the employee will or should act despite their family responsibilities. Lawsuits alleging caregiver discrimination have increased 269 percent over the last decade, according to the center.

The win rates for employees in these cases tend to be high: Plaintiffs win 67 percent of the FRD cases that go to trial and 75 percent of those that wind up in federal court. According to Cynthia Thomas Calvert with the Center for WorkLife Law, the high win rate for plaintiffs indicates that employers are not yet understanding their liability for FRD and are not responding appropriately to employees' claims. One surprising aspect of the center's latest report on FRD cases is that more than half of FRD plaintiffs are currently men. Calvert, the report's author, notes that fully 25 percent of calls to the Center for WorkLife Law's FRD hotline are now from men. In the last decade, cases involving paternity leave have increased 336 percent. Male plaintiffs now account for 55 percent of cases involving spousal care, 39 percent of eldercare, and 28 percent of childcare, as well as 38 percent of cases stemming from the Family and Medical Leave Act. Male plaintiffs, however, are less likely than female plaintiffs to actually win: 44 percent of all cases (both those that go to trial and those that don't) as opposed to 52 percent.

Within the world of FRD cases, pregnancy discrimination cases have ballooned as well, increasing 315 percent in the past decade, with lactation cases increasing 800 percent. At issue in many of these cases is a lack of federal law governing FRD across the board, and inconsistencies among state laws and, in some cases, county- or city-level laws as well, which leaves decisions largely up to each individual judge's discretion. Some states have pregnancy accommodation requirements for employers, some don't, twenty-four states require lactation accommodation, but the rest don't. Some district court judges have allowed lactating women to sue under the Affordable Care Act, and some have not. Calvert writes in her 2016 report that "the number of FRD cases is expected to continue to rise at a rate higher than other types of employment cases. Several trends contribute to this conclusion: the prevalence of American households with all adults in the paid workforce; the projected increase in the number of people over the age of 65 who need care; the growing number of other family members who have disabilities; the number of men who are becoming caregivers; and the expectations of employees that working and providing family care should not be mutually exclusive."

Williams, who has played a leading role in documenting workplace bias against mothers, leading to the Equal Employment Opportunity Commission's 2007 Guidance on Caregiver Discrimination, has often said that the modern American workplace was "designed around a man's body." In her book *Unbending Gender: Why Family and Work Conflict and What to Do About It,* she argues, "Instead of assuming that the only two alternatives are an immediate replacement of all equipment [geared toward men doing a particular job] versus perpetuating into the indefinite future a system that excludes women, courts and plaintiffs should explore the many intermediate solutions. The guiding principle is to proceed in a measured and orderly fashion toward a society where workplaces are designed around the body of the average person, not the average man."

FRD policies must inform nationwide law if we are going to enable both women and men to truly choose the sort of family life they want. If men can't take leave without being discriminated against, and are then discriminated against in court as well, that undermines all attempts to create equality in caregiving. If women feel as though they really can't take maternity leave when they want to, if various work penalties are associated with childbirth, that gives companies far too much influence and power in the reproductive decisions women make.

CHAPTER

10

The Patriarchs

"No one asks in a serious way how a man should consider where he chooses to live, what he chooses to do, and what kind of father he wants to be," says John Eden, a lawyer and start-up consultant in Silicon Valley. He's a single guy with no children, which isn't necessarily how he wanted it. He says he wishes someone had talked to him about the logistics of parenthood at a young age, and as a philosophy grad student he spent a lot of time thinking and talking through how both men and women behave when it comes to family responsibilities. Raised by his mother and grandmother, with minimal contact from his father, whom Eden describes as "not interested in the impacts of his behavior on my mother or on me," he's also thought a lot about what fatherhood means in general.

"Look at the NFL, they're trained to be effective gladiators. So it shouldn't be surprising when you see a lot of horrific domestic abuse in their families.

Of course, when Ray Rice is caught on tape knocking out his female partner, the social fabric erupts with moral condemnation and what I personally think is a kind of feigned disbelief. But at the same time, we never talk in a serious way about whether gladiatorial combat might not be the right path for young men who, if you asked them, actually do have an aspiration to become dedicated, engaged fathers.

Another example is people in finance. They work really long hours, in this hyper-competitive culture, there's a lot of substance and alcohol abuse. What's more, anyone who has seen this world up close as I have can tell you there's a lot of womanizing going on. So, again, at a high level this world is not really that compatible with the kind of fatherhood we all want. It would be great if we talked to guys when they were like eighteen about whether or not they thought they might want to be fathers, and what makes a good father, and whether that might preclude certain professions or behaviors. I really think something radical needs to happen because men do not think about their own social worth in terms of how well we function as fathers and husbands."

Eden says he'd like to see more of a focus on moral development for both sexes, too, as well as a better understanding of the value of caregiving. "These days I think both men and women are not valuing the sorts of things that are good for society," he says. "And there's a lack of understanding around the intellectual side of caregiving. The actual skills and abilities you need to take care of people require a lot of analytical thinking, and I don't think people realize that. There's the idea that raw empathy is enough, but it isn't. You have to think carefully about where someone is at before you can step in and try to effectively help that individual."

And while we may not talk to guys enough—or at all—about what the future might look like should they become fathers, Eden says the way we talk to mothers is equally problematic. "We need to be more honest with women before they become mothers," he says. "We need to actually treat potential mothers as the adults they are and talk about motherhood in a more honest way. We need to

*make sure women don't feel like becoming a mother is a
ticket to immortality or a solution to everything. Motherhood is irredeemably complex and it's trying and beautiful and frustrating—it's everything all at once. Stop the
propaganda."*

*"Women need to care more about the moral integrity
of who they have kids with, too," he adds. "But men need
to think about their well-being and functioning as human
beings in terms of how they function as fathers and husbands. Right now, the guys who are becoming stay-at-home
dads have an unusual amount of courage. Most men will
not do something where being ostracized is the natural and
inevitable consequence."*

———————————

It's amazing to me how surprised people often are when I
say that patriarchy is oppressive for men, too. Feminists have
been saying as much for years, but the dominant narrative of
feminists as man-hating harpies seems to always win out in
the popular consciousness.

Patriarchy doesn't have as much to do with actual men being in power as it does with traditionally masculine traits—
competition, individualism, logic—being the dominant values
of the society, and being used to create a culture of domination that oppresses both biological women and anyone who
exhibits traits often associated with women—expressiveness,
compassion, connection. As patriarchal values have mixed
with capitalism, the economic system best matched to patriarchy, we've seen a rise in private property, a focus on individual success, and an emphasis on the protection of the rights
of some at the expense of others.

It's patriarchy that makes it easy for some men to think
other men have less worth, too: men who look different, or
are perceived as a threat in some way, or who do not fit into
clearly defined structures of what it means to be a "man." Men

who take on the traits of "women" (or at least the traits that patriarchy assigns to women) are particularly threatening because they represent an aggressive rejection of patriarchy.

It's patriarchy that allows us to think of men as disposable human shields, too. The one way in which patriarchy allows for the sacrifice of the individual for the good of the whole is in the practice of nation building, otherwise known as murder and theft. Here, patriarchy tells us the individual sacrifice is noble and deserving of praise, that these men risking their lives so that a handful of other men can reap a reward is admirable. To make it sound morally superior, we wrap it in the freedom-fighting cape of "defending democracy" and "keeping people safe." In reality, our democracy is more often attacked from within, and our wars often only bring more risk of violence to citizens. This is not to discredit the sacrifices and efforts of individual soldiers, but to say that I believe their sacrifice is unfairly asked of them by a system that does not adequately value their humanity.

Patriarchy expects nothing of fathers except to create as many children as possible to showcase their masculinity. It does not encourage paternal bonds, nor does it reward men for fathering. This does not give men freedom so much as it robs them of deep and meaningful relationships with their children and the experience of unconditional love.

Our patriarchal society doesn't just value aggression, competition, and individual success but also devalues and penalizes traits like caring, empathy, and nurturing. Again, this is not a man versus woman thing. Men have plenty of natural nurturing capabilities and empathy and desire for connection. They are told in a patriarchal society, however, to quash those traits because those traits are not valuable. "The first act of violence that patriarchy demands of males is not violence toward women," bell hooks writes. "Instead patriarchy demands of all males that they engage in acts of psychic self-mutilation, that they kill off the emotional parts of themselves. If an individual is not successful in emotionally crippling himself, he can count on patriarchal men to enact rituals of power that will assault his self-esteem."

As a mother of boys, this makes me want to hold my sons and cry. And that makes me a sentimental mother, the least valuable being of all in a patriarchal society.

It is also patriarchy that makes some women want to oppress men, and other women, any way they can because that is how they achieve individual success, how they compete in a market that does not value caring. Matrifocal societies are not societies in which men are subservient to women or lack agency; they are societies in which humans of both sexes and all races have equal status and collaborate to protect the health and well-being of the community.

As women gained access to patriarchal structures by earning the right to vote, entering the workforce, gaining their own credit and bank accounts, and finally joining the ranks of government, some men began to lose their positions in the system—not because women kicked them out per se, but because in a patriarchal system that values competition and individual success over all else, more competitors equals more losers. Now, as we undergo yet another Industrial Revolution, one dominated by automation and artificial intelligence, many men are falling victim to the patriarchy in other ways. Those who are no longer useful are being discarded. This includes the mentally ill, the disabled, the destitute, and those who are either too old to learn new skills or too tired or stubborn or proud to. The system asked them to be stubborn and proud and is now condemning them to poverty for failing to be flexible and adaptable.

Black men have been the victims of patriarchy forever, targeted as both victims and threats. Gay men and trans men, both threats to patriarchal dominance, are terrifying to patriarchal men who would rather see these threats disappear than examine their notions of "man."

In his book *Politics of Masculinities: Men in Movements*, Michael Messner refers to the "costs of masculinity," noting that any status and privilege that come with masculinity aren't given freely: "Often, men pay with poor health, shorter lives, emotionally shallow relationships, and less time spent with loved ones."

Still, despite the toll that patriarchy takes on men, it also instills in them an urge to protect it. This makes the coexistence of patriarchy and the changes wrought by the women's movement difficult for more patriarchal men, who feel they are getting mixed signals. I'm not saying, "Poor men, they've had all that power for so long," so much as "Hey, dominator culture mixed with capitalism is bad for everything and everyone, and expectations of men have changed without much coaching or teaching about how best to meet those expectations." The broader society continues to tell boys and men, "Be a man!" defined as being unaffected by emotion; the willingness to sacrifice one's health to create capital—either as a soldier or a worker; the ability to procreate, but not necessarily build a relationship with one's children; and the idea that they should protect and dominate women, attract them but not love them.

Masculinity, Capitalism, and Nation Building

In the same way that republican motherhood has been used to both exalt the role of mothers and restrict the opportunities of women, the notion of strong, patriotic masculinity has been used to both glorify and cripple men, figuratively and literally.

When we were seventeen, my twin brother and I both went on various college campus tours with our parents. They had the same path in mind for both of us, despite the fact that neither one of them had gone this route: go to high school, get good grades, go to college somewhere not too expensive and maybe (hopefully) with a scholarship. I was thrilled at the possibility, but my brother was frightened—he had always struggled to make friends, he was always the kid who just wanted to be liked, and moving to a new place by himself with thousands of strangers was daunting. Other guys could get him to do almost anything in high school with the promise that he would be "in" with them. As an emotional guy in a society that does not allow men to have emotions, he was constantly doing harmful things to prove he was cool and manly. He hadn't wanted to do hard-core drugs but felt the pull of them as a way to prove his manliness and was self-aware enough to be worried about what that might lead to if he were out on his own on a college campus with easy access to drugs and alcohol. So, he opted instead for the ultimate badge of masculinity: the US Marine Corps. Here was a group he could belong to without having to do drugs (he hadn't yet considered the physical risk he would ultimately be taking on). He convinced my mom to sign the papers to allow early enlistment at seventeen, and off he went to boot camp while I packed up a U-Haul and headed to Berkeley.

When he visited me at school after boot camp, I was deeply concerned about him. Although fairly tall, he was still a pretty thin, scrawny guy, and he seemed scared, not of being deployed to war, but of the other guys in his unit. "There are a lot of criminals in there, and some pretty crazy dudes," he said. He couldn't tell if his drill sergeant was a good guy or not, couldn't tell who in his platoon really had his back, which is something he hadn't expected. "I thought that was the deal, that everyone is there for each other," he said. He wasn't sure he'd made the right decision, and it was hard to send him back to base.

A few months later, I collapsed on campus, overwhelmed by emotion for no apparent reason, and for the first time in my life. It surprised and scared me, and I worried that I was having some sort of psychotic break. I would learn later that I'd had my first-ever encounter with "twin sense." Something terrible had happened to my brother.

We still don't know the exact chain of events and probably never will, but at 5 a.m. on a Monday morning, my brother was found badly beaten on his military base. He had been stabbed fourteen times, had his head bashed in by some sort of blunt object, and had been pushed out a second-story window. He was found near the building with the mental health ward, and where soldiers are kept before being discharged for various infractions, so theories range from the notion that he might have been poking around out of curiosity and triggered someone's psychosis to the fact that someone may have thought he was the reason they were being sent home. Whatever the case, the Marines sent two soldiers in dress blues to my parents' home to tell them their son had attempted suicide.

Over the next several weeks, I would receive phone calls from anonymous men telling me the suicide story was untrue. My parents, meanwhile, learned from one of my brother's doctors that it was physically impossible for his injuries to have been self-inflicted. The lacerations on his wrists, they said, had been the last injury he received, an obvious and lazy attempt to make it look like a suicide.

Armed with this knowledge and a commitment from the doctors that they would testify in court should it come to it, my parents found a lawyer and went after the US military. Their lawyer rightly counseled them to focus on securing benefits for my brother rather than justice. "This is the military. If they don't want you to know something, you won't find out," he said.

After a year in the hospital and nearly another year of rehab, my brother eventually moved into his own apartment and began rebuilding his life. Ideals of masculinity still plagued him. Now, as a quadriplegic, he mourned not just the ability to walk, or the fact that his life path was so violently changed, but that he could no longer lift heavy things for women or reach things on high shelves. As someone who has always wanted to be a husband and a father, he worries that those roles are no longer options for him.

My brother's case is, obviously, extreme. But expectations of masculinity cripple men in plenty of less obvious ways, too. It leads them into dangerous jobs, convinces them that their worth lies only in a combination of physical ability and bread-winning, and denies them the basic human right of express-ing emotion, which in turn dampens creativity, spirituality, and psychological health.

"Patriarchy has taught him that his masculinity has to be proved by the willingness to conquer fear through aggression; that it would be unmanly to ask questions before taking ac-tion," hooks writes.

Its intertwining with capitalism makes patriarchal mas-culinity particularly hard to shift. Not only do patriarchal values help to keep the engines of capitalism purring, but also rigid masculinity helps to sell men stuff they don't need, except to reinforce their masculinity. In much the same way that women have long been sold products they don't need to reinforce their femininity, the 2010s has seen a boom in once gender-neutral products with newly masculine packaging and marketing. As capitalism has taken away some of the means of reinforcing masculinity—jobs, financial success—it has created a new way to sell it back to men. Lost your job? Wife left you? Feeling like less of a man? No problem, buy these Q-tips for men and men's shampoo, and this men's deodor-ant guaranteed to attract submissive women, and you will be back on top of the man pyramid before you know it!

In women's attempts to dismantle patriarchy, or envision a different sort of system, men have often been left out of the conversation. While the branch of feminism devoted to moth-erhood studies is filled with research on the mother-daughter relationship, for example, there is a dearth of research on mothers and sons (or fathers and sons, for that matter). And while there are plenty of books on the impacts of patriarchal masculinity, or toxic masculinity, and how society continues to reinforce it—recent examples include C. J. Pascoe's brilliant book on high school gender policing, *Dude, You're a Fag*; Michael Kimmel's *Angry White Men*, on the rise of men's rights activists (MRAs); and Erynn Masi de Casanova's *Buttoned Up: Clothing, Conformity, and White-Collar Masculinity*—there are precious few focused on creating a masculinity divorced from patriarchy.

The Rise of Men's Rights Activists and What We Can Learn from It

Men's rights activists are often aggressive, hateful, and disrespectful. They are also prone to violence.

In June 2014, I was visiting my brother in Santa Barbara when I turned a corner and saw more police cars and mayhem than I'd ever seen in that sleepy, wealthy beach town. A twenty-two-year-old named Elliot Rodger, tired of being rejected by hot sorority girls whose bodies he felt entitled to, had planned and carried out a murderous revenge on them, shooting some, stabbing others, and using his car to kill in total seven people and injure fourteen. We know he was a men's rights activist because he left behind a 137-page manifesto filled with the lingo commonly found in men's rights forums.

Rodger's killing spree brought media attention to the growing men's rights movement, the father of which is Warren Farrell, a man who once palled around with Gloria Steinem and sat on the board of advisers for the National Organization for Women (NOW). He was in charge of organizing men's consciousness-raising workshops all over the country, and wrote his first book in 1974, *The Liberated Man*, in which he discussed the negative impacts that sexism had on men, too, most notably the stress of being the primary breadwinner, and various other economic and social obligations that kept men from discovering themselves and their true potential. Feminists couldn't get enough of Farrell.

It was a disagreement over divorce and custody battles that ultimately sent him packing. In the late 1970s when NOW came out in favor of awarding custody to the primary caregiver (typically the woman), Farrell began to feel as though, rather than overturning the patriarchy, feminists were simply trying to grab as much power as they could within it. Many radical feminists would have agreed with him up to this point, and it remains a valid critique of feminism that some of the movement's leaders have opted to push for power within the patriarchy rather than the dismantling of it. Farrell's views also resonated with men who were feeling increasingly defensive in the face of feminism.

Then in 1978 he and his first wife Ursula, the primary breadwinner in their marriage, divorced and Farrell pulled a 180. Farrell described their breakup in a 2015 article in *Mother Jones*, saying he still remembers the conversation that precipitated the decision. He asked her whom she would marry if he were to die—somebody like him or the type of man she worked with? "She said, 'I feel I'd have a lot more in common with another IBM executive,'" he recalled. "And I took a big, deep breath." A few years later, she had done exactly that, and Farrell came out as feminism's staunchest enemy. In 1988, he published *Why Men Are the Way They Are*, which criticized women for lording power, particularly sexual power, over men, and for taking advantage of men financially.

Then came *The Myth of Male Power*, the MRA Bible, in 1993. In it, Farrell misses plenty. He blithely describes women in industrialized societies as having attained "control-over-their-life power" that men have never had, for example; he's quick to blame feminism or "female empowerment" for impacts on men that have more to do with systemic failure; he claims to have entirely disproven the "myth" of the gender pay gap; and in his discussion of men as the primary victims of violence, he forgets to mention that they're also the primary perpetrators, particularly of violence against women. In his most bizarre moment, and there are quite a few to choose from, he calls men America's "new nigger," complaining, "When slaves gave up their seats for whites, we called it subservience; when men give up their seats for women, we call it politeness."

It's offensive. But dismissing it out of hand ignores a key truth of both Farrell's work and that of his followers, even the most virulent misogynists: Patriarchy is bad for men, too, and they need help transitioning out of it. The standard feminist response to that tends to be that men are not our problem, that it's not the job of women to educate men or help them build a more positive masculinity. While that's understandable, as a heterosexual woman and a mother of sons I can't ignore the men in my life or my desire to help them. And as a proponent of transition to a more just system than patriarchy, I am aligned with Farrell in one way: I too want to find a positive place for masculinity.

Working Fathers

Not a week goes by without a new study or media article about working mothers. That attention and research is necessary and great, but the gendered framing of the need for support of working families is not so great. As men have become more involved in fatherhood, few researchers have bothered to ask them how they're finding the task of balancing fatherhood and work. Professional expectations for men have not changed as familial expectations have. Men, like women, continue to butt up against the ideal worker myth in the workplace. And while they do benefit from the so-called fatherhood bonus—men tend to be more likely to be hired, promoted, or paid more as fathers, while women are hired less often, promoted less, and paid less when they become mothers—they still struggle to balance work demands and family time.

Moreover, it remains far less okay, culturally, for a father to take extended paternity leave, leave work early to pick up his children, or take a sick day to stay home with a sick child. For evidence of this, we need look no further than family responsibilities discrimination lawsuits: Men file more of these suits and are less likely to win them than women. Annie Dean, of Werk, says she has banned her team from using the term "working mother" because "we never use the term working father, we just use men," she says.

Dean says many of the men she speaks with, particularly Millennial men, want to be more involved fathers. "It's a catch-22: They get rewarded, socially and personally, for showing up to the soccer games and being the involved dad, but at work if they want to leave early to pick up their kid, that's still often frowned upon."

Highlighting working fathers, and supporting them and working mothers equally, is critical to ending discrimination in the workplace. As Kristin Rowe-Finkbeiner, CEO and cofounder of MomsRising, puts it, "We know that in countries with family economic security policies in place for both moms and dads, it's a win for everyone. If we only focus on moms, or we push through a leave policy that covers moms only, it reinforces discrimination against moms."

The other side of this coin is the need to end the notion that men "help out" with children and households, while women raise children and run households. When Anne-Marie Slaughter's husband Andrew Moravcsik was asked in an interview whether it might be true that men just aren't wired to handle things like remembering which yogurt the kids like, he bristled. "If I said that to you about women in the workplace—that they can do okay but are biologically incapable of reaching the levels men can attain, you'd see that as incredibly sexist, right?"

Moravcsik went on to explain that in his marriage, he is the one who is more likely to remember a piano recital or a homework assignment that's due, that being the primary parent is more about context and conditioning than biology. I've heard this from many men over the years, including both stay-at-home dads and working dads: We need to move past the idea that men can't be good nurturers, or the notion that men who are spending time with their children are "babysitting" as opposed to just parenting. The solution may be a sort of virtuous circle of fathering: Men who do more caregiving appreciate the need to support caregiving in the workplace, and are thus more likely to advocate alongside women for policies like flextime and family leave.

Stay-at-Home Dads and Single Fathers

No statistic is more often pointed to as proof that our notions about family and gender are changing than the increasing number of stay-at-home dads. In 2016 there were 209,000 stay-at-home dads in the United States. That's 3 percent of the country's fathers, but this number does not account for a large number of dads who work part-time and are part-time caregivers. An equally significant change in recent years is the growing number of single fathers. In 2016, the Census Bureau reported there were 2 million single fathers running households in the United States, representing 17 percent of the country's single-parent families.

But despite the growth in the number of men taking on the role of primary caregiver, as well as increased child-rearing involvement from dads in general, culturally we still have many hang-ups when it comes to supporting caregiving in men. There are support groups for stay-at-home dads, less because they are struggling to learn the ropes of full-time parenthood than because they deal with an intense amount of discrimination. At a recent breakfast for executive women I attended, one woman said that her husband, a stay-at-home dad, "practically needs a therapy session every night to process all of the horrendous things people will say to him and the way he's treated. If anyone treated a woman like that, we would be up in arms, but he's just expected to deal with it because he's a guy," she said. "I feel badly for him, and it also undermines the whole point of him being at home, because I now spend a lot of time and energy worrying about how this setup is negatively impacting him. That shouldn't be the case."

Annie Dean has high hopes that standardized, well-implemented flextime policies will help. "Flextime gives men the same opportunity to opt into parenthood that it gives women to opt into leadership." But we may need a more concerted approach to shift cultural norms. There have been gradual improvements in media depictions of dads. The "clueless dad" trope seems to have been effectively skewered and put to bed, and Super Bowl ad breaks these days are filled with commercials that highlight fathers, respectfully. Still, dads out in the world often find that it is not set up for them. There are rarely baby-changing tables in men's restrooms, for example; there are almost no diaper bags made with men in mind; and, growing up, men are not taught or encouraged to learn anything at all about taking care of children.

Cultural Fix: Positive Masculinity—Creating a Pathway from Competition to Care

Amid all the criticism of toxic masculinity, right as it may be, we have forgotten to tell men, or teach men, what is good about masculinity. In fact, we have left masculinity largely unexplored except for mining its faults. We have said no to anger and aggression but have not channeled that energy into new directions, and so it has turned inward and then outward in a vicious and endless cycle that's damaging to both men and women.

This is not an easy fix, and is an area that needs more research. However, there are some ways to begin today.

When my first son was a year and a half, he was very into hitting everyone. We were told this was common, but that didn't make it any less off-putting. Because we lived in the Bay Area at the time, we had an integrative wellness pediatrician who had a naturopath and a child development specialist on hand, in the interest of treating the whole child (I know). When I asked the child development specialist if there was anything I could do about the hitting thing, she agreed that it was normal, developmentally, and suggested two things: First, she said we should essentially shun him when he hit, to model what would happen if he were an adult who went around hitting people (people wouldn't want to hang out with him); then, she said we should find positive outlets for his male energy. "Have him wrestle with his dad, maybe have a pillow fight—these are natural instincts that need an outlet," she said. "Repressing them can lead to other issues later on."

I've thought of that appointment often as I follow the various gender debates going on in the news and media. Where are the positive outlets for male energy? Honestly, I have no idea. I know my husband has found that martial arts, specifically aikido, is helpful for channeling aggression in a way that makes him feel both strong and calm. But part of the answer may also be giving men an on-ramp to caregiving, and positive reinforcement for it. Valuing caregiving across the board would support both sexes in undertaking these tasks. The bonus there is that if men have performed caretaking tasks themselves, they're more likely to support it in others.

Kate Sheppard, an executive editor for HuffPost, says the most important form of support for her as a working mom was having a boss who was a working dad. "Having a boss who's also an involved parent is really huge," she says. "It doesn't matter what sex they are, really. I had a boss who was a dad of three kids and he just totally got it that sometimes I'd need to disappear in the middle of the day for some unexpected thing but that I would reappear later and finish whatever needed to be done."

So, having at least some parents in leadership roles might help. But people can work toward this in their own homes, too. I have to say that personally, the most powerful shift in my own parenting reality came about because my husband and I were each able to experience firsthand what it's like to be the primary caregiver and what it's like to be the primary breadwinner. We didn't plan it that way, and, frankly, it was hard. During the time when I was the primary earner and he was the primary parent, we both felt the pressure of bucking gender norms; I felt like a bad mom for not being physically present for my children, and he felt like a failed man for not bringing home a paycheck. Those feelings were tough to process. But because we came through it, we now have more empathy for both roles. I'm not saying it's impossible to have empathy for anything you haven't directly experienced—I'm sure some people can—but going through these experiences really helped us.

I should underscore here that this was equally important for me, as I don't think I had truly appreciated the stress of being not just the primary but the sole breadwinner for a family. When I had my first son, I took a few months off work and then worked part-time for two years, while my husband worked full-time. I remember being often annoyed that he wasn't home more and wholly unsympathetic to the stresses of being the breadwinner. Because we each now know from experience that being wholly one or the other doesn't feel great, we each do more to share both roles and to appreciate what the other is doing.

Policy Fix: Parent Pensions

At the same time that we have skyrocketing day care costs, record numbers of women with higher education degrees in the workplace, and more mothers than ever working, we have record numbers of men, many of them fathers, out of work. Turning men into the new 1950s housewives would likely prove disastrous, but what if there were a way to pay both men and women for caregiving? One that didn't undermine masculinity but rather rewarded men for providing a necessary service and being a positive male role model? And what if at the same time we dramatically improved the lot of single mothers, too?

Back in the early 1900s, we rolled out mothers' pensions in an effort to provide a way for low-income mothers to stay home with their children. The program was adequately funded but implemented in a biased way. If we were to revive the idea of a mother's pension as a parent's pension, it could serve much of the same function as a universal basic income policy, providing a social safety net as the economy transitions away from some industries and toward new ones, while also providing an incentive to maintain birth rates.

If paired with a cultural campaign (okay, yes, also known as propaganda) aimed at highlighting the importance of fathers, and with more part-time, contract, and flextime work options so that both fathers and mothers could more equitably share in caregiving and work duties, it might not only smooth out parenting and gender roles but also provide support through the coming economic transition.

11

Redefining "It All"

Four hundred or so years ago, the ideologies of patriarchal capitalism and the nuclear family worked well for some people. The nuclear family enabled families to be adaptable and mobile, which was helpful as new countries were being built or colonized and old ones were being revolutionized. Sociologists credit it with enabling some groups of white, non-aristocratic Europeans to break free from the chains of aristocracy and create their own fortunes. While the landed gentry, with their large houses, extended families, and displays of wealth could not, and would not, just pick up and move to a new country, for a Puritan nuclear family, the New World held a lot of upside (barring the life-threatening passage and the threat of disease or violence upon arrival, of course).

In the Industrial Revolution, the neatly divided roles of the nuclear family again enabled white Americans to weather a significant economic change and come out the other end mostly the better for it. But as populations grew and the world became larger and smaller at the same time, global economic trends and war began to poke holes in patriarchal family structures.

Those for whom these structures had never worked began to find allies in those who had come to believe the safety these systems promised was an illusion, a gilded cage. Suffragettes and abolitionists teamed up to push for equal rights for all; Progressives and Marxists took to the streets to demand fair treatment of workers and some amount of social welfare. Even through the various backlashes that would inevitably come, these forces for change continued to push forward, sometimes in quiet, subversive ways (teens having lots of illicit sex in the conservative 1950s or, conversely, lesbians having perfectly boring families in the 1990s), and sometimes in loud and destructive revolutions.

I believe we've reached the useful end of patriarchy. It is no longer providing any sort of benefit for the vast majority of people, irrespective of their race, sex, creed, or class. The patriarchy need not be replaced by a matriarchy per se, so much as a more matrifocal structure that rebalances society around the community rather than the individual. This would complete the original mission of feminism, which was not to place women atop the patriarchal structure, but to create a new system in which all humans are equally valued.

This society would encourage a rethinking of motherhood that would incorporate the strategies and traditions of the many cultures that make up the United States. It would put the community first and encourage both men and women to think about what sorts of roles they want to play in that community and how biological children may or may not fit into those roles. It would value caregiving in both women and men, and that value would be clear in systems that adequately support not just parents and children, but also those who perform caregiving services for people that are not their relatives. In placing value on human connection, this new version of society would enable many different forms of alliances and relationships beyond marriage. It would create a system in which humans are in communion, not competition.

Too often, Americans have conflated patriarchy and religion, as though dispensing with patriarchy would in some way undermine religion, but Jesus himself was a big proponent of gender equality, and there are just as many Bible verses espousing equality as trumpeting male dominance. As sociologist Dawn Dow points out, many of our existing social structures have either been created or interpreted or implemented by humans. "That means we can change them," she says.

The patriarchy, it has been said, will die hard. That rings true, but it's also a rather patriarchal view of things, one that assumes that only those to which the system has given power actually have power. What if we began thinking matrifocally, taking whatever power each of us may have and using it to make any transformations we can? It's easy to say these sorts of changes are only for the rich or the educated, those with leisure time. Again, that's a fairly patriarchal view of things. It's exceedingly patronizing to believe that poverty removes all desire for change or hope for the future from a human being. Even in the direst of circumstances, people dream of a better life and do what they can to move toward it.

For some, change might mean turning parenthood into activism, fighting the patriarchy in their own homes and children wherever possible. Others might be able to take on the mantle of community mothering, sheltering their neighbors as best they can from poverty, sexism, and racism. Others might be able to push for change in their companies or in their local and state governments. Some may be able to run for public office. Some uniquely revolutionary souls will start building truly new models, showing those of us with less imagination what can be done—they will create the communal housing units that are optimized for community mothering, they will form the new family structures that provide all adults with love and support and the option to extend that love and support to children if and when they choose to, they will recast religion to better align with their values, and they will write and paint and sing this world into being.

It is hard to see how clearly this system needs to change, how much is required to change it, and how much opposition there is likely to be. What gives me faith is history. For every man or woman who has single-handedly stopped progress, there have been millions who have inspired and worked for change—that's true no matter which aspects of history you view as progress or backsliding.

I also find a good number of reasons to be optimistic in the present and the future. For all the pain it's brought to the surface, the #MeToo movement has marked a turning point, an emphatic "no" to patriarchal abuses of power, and a willingness to ask tough questions and have uncomfortable conversations. We've taken sexual harassment and assault for granted for a long time, chalking it up to just one more way those in power can take what they want. That assumption has been particularly widespread with respect to the entertainment industry. It's so ingrained in our national psyche that women must sleep with men (often unwillingly) to get jobs in Hollywood that there's a term for it (the casting couch) and it's a theme that shows up regularly in shows and films. It's nothing short of radical that women are saying no to the standard notion that that's "just how it is," not only in Hollywood, but also in government, academia, publishing…and hopefully soon the patriarchal strongholds of Wall Street and the military.

In the future, amid all the panic about robots coming for our jobs, I see a silver lining in the skills that economists say will be most needed and valued: emotional intelligence, collaborative thinking, communication—those "soft skills" that have been so undervalued for so long will be in demand. It turns out they're the hardest thing to teach a machine, which can have all the strength and power in the world but likely not the ability to understand nuance or to harness compassion and intelligence to work collaboratively. This also makes me worry about men. The millennia when what mattered most was brawn and aggression are coming to an end. As anthropologist and behavioral biologist Melvin Konner put it in his book *Women After All*, "In spite of their greater strength, men had to make laws to suppress women, because on a truly level playing field, women were destined to compete successfully and very often win." Konner also sees the direction of evolution and civilization as being distinctly geared toward the success of women, which he doesn't describe as a bad thing. We are in a moment in which many men are grappling with this idea already, some relieved that many of the unfair expectations put on men may dissipate and others irate that what they see as their birthright is being taken from them. Radical change is always hard for the generation that first experiences it, and there will be men who fight it to their graves, but there are many more men who are up to the task, and more of them are being born and raised every day. A good many feminists have said that men are not our problem. They are not there for us to fix; women need to figure out what works best in general and leave men to sort themselves out. While I can appreciate the logic of that, I don't believe it fits in a care-centered world. We need to ensure that men are not left behind by either the education system or the environment, that they are welcomed into a new and more caring era, and that they are supported through the transition, not left to struggle alone.

If the matriarchal utopia I've outlined here seems like a pipe dream, remember this: For all of their faults, and there are many, the people who founded this country believed that they could leave everything they'd known and go build an ideal country, one centered around liberty. We, their descendants, could still make that country. America has spent more than two hundred years grooming exceptional individuals: just imagine what will happen when they come together for the common good.

Acknowledgments

This book could not have existed without the support of several people, starting with my husband, who insisted on disappearing with our children for long stretches of time, despite all of my protests that it was unnecessary. It was completely necessary. My agent Laurie Abkemeier has been a tireless champion of my work, even when I've been a cranky, broke, sleep-deprived pain. Stephanie Knapp, my editor at Seal Press, offered real insight and valuable guidance on the manuscript, as did the rest of the editorial team at Seal, saving me from myself on multiple occasions. Multiple friends read and offered valuable feedback on initial drafts, too, especially Kera Bolonik, Michaelanne Petrella, and Maya Francis. My mom spent many hours sharing her thoughts on mothering with me over the phone, sometimes in the way that all moms do and other times as a sounding board for some of the ideas I grappled with in writing this book. She will not be pleased that the phrase "abolishing marriage" is in here, but she'll get over it. Masako Ishii-Kuntz was an inspiration. All of the wonderful people who agreed to speak with me or share their stories for this book, or bear with me as I talked about it, are too many to list, but I particularly want to thank Lora Kolodny, Danielle Lovell-Jones, Leticia Aguilar, Anh Gray, Julia Richey, Ashley Cooper, John Eden, Tim Ross, Alyssa Johl, Heather B. Armstrong, Lina Fisher, Lorien McKenna, Wesley Allsbrook, and Darren Westervelt.

Notes

CHAPTER 1

3   **cultures that value women and men equally:** Chodorow, Nancy J. *Femininities, Masculinities, Sexualities: Freud and Beyond*. Lexington: University Press of Kentucky, 1998.

4   **"For the daughter of a Western middle-class family":** Chodorow, Nancy. *The Reproduction of Mothering: Psychoanalysis and the Sociology of Gender*. Berkeley: University of California Press, 1978.

4   **Several decades ago:** Rich, Adrienne. *Of Woman Born*. New York: W. W. Norton, 1976.

4   **O'Reilly pioneered the field of motherhood studies and matricentric feminism:** O'Reilly, Andrea. *Matricentric Feminism: Theory, Activism, and Practice*. Bradford, Ontario: Demeter Press, 2016.

6   **"Both men and women are naturals at child care":** Schulte, Brigid. *Overwhelmed*. Toronto: HarperCollins Canada, 2015.

12   **"The problem with stereotypes is not that they are untrue":** Adichie, Chimamanda Ngozi. *We Should All Be Feminists*. London: Fourth Estate, 2014.

12   **"the Woman Question" in America:** Tarbell, Ida M. *The Business of Being a Woman*. N.p.: Nabu Press, 1912.

12   **Abigail Adams was lecturing her husband John:** Gunderson, Joan. "Independence, Citizenship, and the American Revolution." *Signs: Journal of Women in Culture and Society* 13,

no. 1 (September 1, 1987). http://www.journals.uchicago
.edu/doi/pdfplus/10.1086/494386.

12 **ever-shifting roles and power between mother, father,
and child:** Badinter, Elisabeth. *Mother Love: Myth and
Reality*. New York: Collier Books, 1982.

13 **calling Americans by turns lonely, isolated, and self-
sufficient:** Tocqueville, Alexis de, and Henry Reeve.
Democracy in America. London: Saunders and Otley, 1838.

13 **were critical to survival:** Collins, Patricia Hill. *Black
Feminist Thought: Knowledge, Consciousness, and the Politics
of Empowerment*. New York: Routledge, 2000.

13 **"alloparents":** Hrdy, Sarah Blaffer. *Mother Nature*. New York:
Pantheon, 2000.

15 **began preaching the gospel of birth control:** Sanger,
Margaret, and Esther Katz. *The Selected Papers of Margaret
Sanger*. Champaign: University of Illinois Press, 2007.

15 **providing a new model for First Lady:** Roosevelt, Eleanor.
The Autobiography of Eleanor Roosevelt. New York: Harper
and Brothers Publishers, 1961.

16 **white America rushed to the safety of the past:** DeGenova,
Mary Kay. *Families in Cultural Context: Strengths and Challenges
in Diversity*. Mountain View, CA: Mayfield Publishing, 1997.

CHAPTER 2

21 **early American colonialists saw themselves as the next
iteration of the Israelites:** *A New Adam: God in America—
How Religious Liberty Shaped America*. PBS, 2010.

22 **believed in the all-powerfulness of God:** Linker, Damon.
"Calvin and American Exceptionalism." *The New Republic*.
July 09, 2009. https://newrepublic.com/article/50754
/calvin-and-american-exceptionalism. And Hart, Darryl.
"Calvinism in the United States." *Oxford Research
Encyclopedia of American History*. June 08, 2017. http://

americanhistory.oxfordre.com/view/10.1093/acrefore
/9780199329175.001.0001/acrefore-9780199329175-e-318.

22 **As early governments and courts were established:**
Nelson, William E. *The Common Law in Colonial America.*
New York: Oxford University Press, 2016.

23 **The average colonial American white woman:**
Vandenberg-Daves, Jodi. *Modern Motherhood: An American
History.* New Brunswick, NJ: Rutgers University Press, 2014.

23 **The notion of "breaking a child's will":** Vandenberg-
Daves, Jodi. *Modern Motherhood: An American History.* New
Brunswick, NJ: Rutgers University Press, 2014.

24 **the idea of children as innocents:** Matthews, Gareth, and
Amy Mullin. "The Philosophy of Childhood." *Stanford
Encyclopedia of Philosophy.* September 13, 2002; revised 2014.
https://plato.stanford.edu/entries/childhood/.

24 **As their American sisters were setting up homesteads:**
Badinter, Elisabeth. *Mother Love: Myth and Reality.* New
York: Collier Books, 1982.

25 **Frenchwomen were the first to send their children away
to wet nurses:** Badinter, Elisabeth. *Mother Love: Myth and
Reality.* New York: Collier Books, 1982.

26 **John Bowlby, the sociologist whose work:** Bowlby, John.
Attachment and Loss. London: Pimlico, 1997.

27 **Two genes in particular, Peg1 and Peg3:** Keverne, E. B.
"Significance of Epigenetics for Understanding Brain
Development, Brain Evolution and Behaviour." *Neuroscience*
264 (2014): 207–217. doi:10.1016/j.neuroscience.2012.11.030.

27 **the behavioral biology work of Melvin Konner:** Konner,
Melvin. *The Tangled Wing: Biological Constraints on the
Human Spirit.* New York: Holt, 1983.

27 **while Suomi's work has been instrumental:** Snowdon,
Charles T., and Stephen J. Suomi. "Paternal Behavior in
Primates." *Child Nurturance* (1982): 63–108. doi:10.1007
/978-1-4613-3605-1_3.

28   **the competing demands, between their own survival and
      that of their offspring:** Hrdy, Sarah Blaffer. *Mother Nature*.
      New York: Pantheon, 2000.

30   **In England, public health officials:** Davin, Anna.
      "Imperialism and Motherhood." In *Tensions of Empire:
      Colonial Cultures in a Bourgeois World*, ed. Frederick Cooper
      and Ann Laura Stoler. Berkeley: University of California
      Press, 1997, 87–139. doi:10.1525/california/9780520205406
      .003.0003.

30   **the "motherhood mandate"—the idea that all women
      must be mothers:** Marsh, Margaret, and Wanda Ronner.
      *The Empty Cradle: Infertility in America from Colonial Times
      to the Present*. Baltimore: Johns Hopkins University Press,
      1996.

30   **Tocqueville and "The Three Races":** Tocqueville, Alexis de,
      and Henry Reeve. *Democracy in America*. London: Saunders
      and Otley, 1838.

31   **In her research on matriarchal societies:** Goettner-
      Abendroth, Heide. *Matriarchal Societies: Studies on Indigenous
      Cultures Across the Globe*. New York: Peter Lang, 2013.

32   **"The cultural expectation that you should be economically
      self-reliant":** Dow, Dawn Marie. "Integrated Motherhood:
      Beyond Hegemonic Ideologies of Motherhood." *Journal of
      Marriage and Family* 78, no. 1 (2015): 180–196. doi:10.1111
      /jomf.12264.

33   **explains indigenous feminist theorist Kim Anderson in
      her essay:** O'Reilly, Andrea, ed. *Maternal Theory: Essential
      Readings*. Toronto: Demeter Press, 2007.

34   **social support was crucial to human success:** Hrdy, Sarah
      Blaffer. *Mothers and Others: The Evolutionary Origins of
      Mutual Understanding*. Cambridge, MA: Belknap Press of
      Harvard University Press, 2011.

34   **"In my view, cooperative breeding":** Hrdy, Sarah Blaffer.
      "Meet the Alloparents." *Natural History*, 2012.

40 **a proponent for years of equal paternity and maternity leave:** Williams, Joan, and Rachel Dempsey. *What Works for Women at Work: Four Patterns Working Women Need to Know.* New York: New York University Press, 2018.

41 **one of the few parenting podcasts that does try to take an intersectional lens:** Frank, Hillary. *It's a Real Mother. The Longest Shortest Time.* Recorded November 1, 2017. Hillary Frank, 2017, MP3.

CHAPTER 3

46 **defines maternal ambivalence:** Almond, Barbara. *The Monster Within: The Hidden Side of Motherhood.* Berkeley: University of California Press, 2011.

47 **a view of maternal ambivalence:** Parker, Rozsika. *Mother Love/Mother Hate: The Power of Maternal Ambivalence.* New York: Basic Books, 1996.

48 **Republican motherhood as an idea:** Lewis, Carolyn Herbst. "Republican Motherhood." *Encyclopedia of Motherhood.* Thousand Oaks, CA: Sage Publications, 2010. doi:10.4135/9781412979276.n577.

48 **"Between the 1780s and 1820s":** McMahon, Lucia. *Mere Equals: The Paradox of Educated Women in the Early American Republic.* Ithaca, NY: Cornell University Press, 2012.

49 **"A girl who curtailed brain work during puberty":** Smith-Rosenberg, Carroll. *Disorderly Conduct: Visions of Gender in Victorian America.* New York: Oxford University Press, 1986.

50 **"Though her station is subordinate":** Emerson, Joseph. "Simeon Doggett, A Discourse on Education, Delivered at the Dedication and Opening of Bristol Academy, the 18th Day of July, A.D. 1796. (New Bedford, 1797)." In *Essays on Education in the Early Republic*, ed. Frederick Rudolph. Boston: Harvard University Press, 1822. doi:10.4159/harvard.9780674864597.c6.

51 **The emphasis on moral motherhood and maternalism:** "Maternalism as a Paradigm." *Journal of Women's History* 5, no. 2 (1993): 95. doi:10.1353/jowh.2010.0143.

52 **the first women's rights convention:** Sklar, Kathryn Kish. "Report of the Woman's Rights Convention: Seneca Falls, N.Y., July 1920, 1848." *Women's Rights Emerges Within the Antislavery Movement, 1830–1870*. New York: Bedford/St. Martin's, 2000, 172–179. doi:10.1007/978-1-137-04527-0_43.

54 **Ultimately, the women's rights and abolitionist movements split:** Dudden, Faye E. "Women's Rights, Abolitionism, and Reform in Antebellum and Gilded Age America." *Oxford Research Encyclopedia of American History*. New York: Oxford University Press, 2016. doi:10.1093/acrefore/9780199329175.013.20.

55 **supported suffrage for Black men first and then all women:** Douglass, Frederick. *My Bondage and My Freedom*. San Francisco: Bottom of the Hill Publishing, 2010.

55 **association with the temperance movement ultimately worked against the women's rights movement:** Gage, Matilda Joslyn. *Woman, Church and State: A Historical Account of the Status of Woman through the Christian Ages;… with Reminiscences of the Matriarchate*. London: Forgotten Books, 2015.

55 **points to Sarah Palin as a recent example:** Buchanan, Lindal. *Rhetorics of Motherhood*. Carbondale: Southern Illinois University Press, 2013.

56 **"I think '08 fundamentally changed the terrain":** Jennifer Lawless, quoted in Terkel, Amanda. "Why Can Paul Ryan Have It All?" Huffington Post. August 14, 2012. Accessed March 14, 2018. https://www.huffingtonpost.com/2012/08/14/paul-ryan-have-it-all_n_1776145.html.

58 **espouses more of a both-and understanding of maternalism:** Buchanan, Lindal. *Rhetorics of Motherhood*. Carbondale: Southern Illinois University Press, 2013.

59   **in defense of activist, community mothering:** Collins, Patricia
        Hill. *Black Feminist Thought: Knowledge, Consciousness, and the
        Politics of Empowerment.* New York: Routledge, 2000.

60   **That stat is nowhere to be found:** For a database of US
        representatives and senators with young children, see
        author's website: www.amywestervelt.com.

60   **draws attention to this gap:** Schulte, Brigid. *Overwhelmed.*
        Toronto: HarperCollins Canada, 2015.

CHAPTER 4

64   **The Industrial Revolution brought more people:** Cohen,
        Philip N. "The Gender Division of Labor." *Gender and Society*
        18, no. 2 (2004): 239–252. doi:10.1177/0891243203262037.

65   **"Women's reproductive labor":** Glenn, Evelyn Nakano.
        Forced to Care: Coercion and Caregiving in America.
        Cambridge, MA: Harvard University Press, 2010.

66   **Collins points out that for most women of color:** Collins,
        Patricia Hill. *Black Feminist Thought: Knowledge, Consciousness,
        and the Politics of Empowerment.* New York: Routledge, 2000.

66   **could be paid less:** "Rise of Industrial America, 1876–1900:
        Work in the Late 19th Century." Library of Congress, www.loc
        .gov/teachers/classroommaterials/presentationsandactivities
        /presentations/timeline/riseind/work/.

66   **Even late-nineteenth-century Marxists:** Hartmann, Heidi I.
        "The Unhappy Marriage of Marxism and Feminism: Towards
        a More Progressive Union." *Capital and Class* 3, no. 2 (1979):
        1–33. doi:10.1177/030981687900800102.

67   **The activity of woman today in industrial pursuits:** Kautsky,
        Karl, and Daniel De Leon. *The Class Struggle.* New York:
        National Executive Committee of the Socialist Labor Party, 1892.

67   **In 1908 a high-profile Supreme Court case:** "Muller v.
        Oregon." Legal Information Institute. January 1, 1987. https://
        www.law.cornell.edu/supremecourt/text/208/412.

68   **"By making women a special class of employee":**
        Vandenberg-Daves, Jodi. *Modern Motherhood: An American
        History.* New Brunswick, NJ: Rutgers University Press, 2014.

69   **emergence of the notion of private property:** Engels,
        Friedrich. *The Origins of the Family, Private Property, and the
        State (1884).* New York. Penguin Classics, 2010.

69   **there is an inherent economic value and power:** Jolles,
        Marjorie. "Going Rogue: Postfeminism and the Privilege of
        Breaking Rules." *Feminist Formations* 24, no. 3 (2012): 43–61.
        doi:10.1353/ff.2012.0031.

70   **held the White House Conference on the Care of
        Dependent Children:** Dalton, Kathleen. *Theodore Roosevelt:
        A Strenuous Life.* New York: Vintage Books, 2004.

71   **a stay-at-home mom who divorces in mid-life:** "Stay-at
        -Home Mothers Through the Years: Monthly Labor Review."
        US Bureau of Labor Statistics. September 1, 2014. https://
        www.bls.gov/opub/mlr/2014/beyond-bls/stay-at-home-mothers
        -through-the-years.htm.

72   **the history of childcare in the United States:** Michel,
        Sonya. "The History of Child Care in the U.S." Social Welfare
        History Project. September 26, 2017. https://socialwelfare
        .library.vcu.edu/programs/child-care-the-american-history/.

74   **mothering was work of value:** Eastman, Crystal. "'Now We
        Can Begin' (1920)." Lumen. January 1, 2000. https://courses
        .lumenlearning.com/ushistory2americanyawp/chapter
        /primary-source-crystal-eastman-now-we-can-begin-1920/.

75   **the average assistance grant:** Mink, Gwendolyn. *The Wages
        of Motherhood: Inequality in the Welfare State, 1917–1942.*
        Ithaca, NY: Cornell University Press, 2006.

76   **tens of thousands of Native American children:** Gregg,
        Matthew T. "The Lasting Effects of American Indian
        Boarding Schools." *SSRN Electronic Journal*, 2016.
        doi:10.2139/ssrn.2776417.

78   **It was this constellation of factors:** Bingman, Melissa.
        "Memorializing Motherhood, Anna Jarvis, and the Struggle

for the Control of Mother's Day by Katharine Lane Antolini." *West Virginia History: A Journal of Regional Studies* 11, no. 1 (2017): 73–74. doi:10.1353/wvh.2017.0003.

79 **"Equality per se may have a different meaning":** Shanley, Kate. "Returning." In *A Gathering of Spirit: Writing and Art by North American Indian Women*, ed. Beth Brant. Ithaca, NY: Firebrand, 1988.

79 **Anglo America has largely forgotten:** Mann, Barbara Alice. *Iroquoian Women: The Gantowisas*. New York: P. Lang, 2011.

80 **But while female leadership and community motherwork:** Collins, Patricia Hill. "Shifting the Center: Race, Class, and Feminist Theorizing on Motherhood." In *Representations of Motherhood*, ed. Donna Bassin, Margaret Honey, and Meryle Mahrer Kaplan. New Haven, CT: Yale University Press, 1996.

81 **women and their complexities:** Hsieh, Lili. "A Queer Sex, Or, Can Feminism and Psychoanalysis Have Sex Without the Phallus?" *Feminist Review* 102, no. 1 (2012): 97–115. doi:10.1057/fr.2011.52.

82 **In an informal survey I conducted:** For more information on the results of the author's survey of working parents, visit her website: www.amywestervelt.com/research.

82 **women are still definitely doing more:** Suh, Michael. "Division of Labor in Households with Two Full-Time Working Parents." Pew Research Center's Social and Demographic Trends Project. November 2, 2015. http://www.pewsocialtrends.org/2015/11/04/raising-kids-and-running-a-household-how-working-parents-share-the-load/st_2015-11-04_working-parents-02/.

82 **under-the-radar tasks:** Suh, Michael. "Raising Kids and Running a Household: How Working Parents Share the Load." Pew Research Center's Social and Demographic Trends Project. November 4, 2015. http://www.pewsocialtrends.org/2015/11/04/raising-kids-and-running-a-household-how-working-parents-share-the-load/.

83   **What is produced and reproduced [by housework]:** West, Candace, and Don H. Zimmerman. "Doing Gender." *Gender and Society* 1, no. 2. (June 1987): 125–151.

83   **In a 2011 study of boys growing up in single-mother households:** Berridge, Clara W., and Jennifer L. Romich. "Raising Him…to Pull His Own Weight—Boys' Household Work in Single-Mother Households." *Journal of Family Issues* 32, no. 2 (2010): 157–180. doi:10.1177/0192513x 10380832.

83   **That finding dovetails:** Penha-Lopes, Vânia. "To Cook, Sew, to Be a Man: The Socialization for Competence and Black Men's Involvement in Housework." *Sex Roles* 54, nos. 3–4 (2006): 261–274. doi:10.1007/s11199-006-9343-1.

84   **professional husbands and wives sharing housework:** Gager, Constance T., Teresa M. Cooney, and Kathleen Thiede Call. "The Effects of Family Characteristics and Time Use on Teenagers' Household Labor." *Journal of Marriage and the Family* 61, no. 4 (1999): 982. doi:10.2307/354018.

84   **calls "disaffiliation":** Hochschild, Arlie Russell, and Anne Machung. *The Second Shift*. New York: Penguin, 2003.

85   **arrange what she calls "strategic absences":** Bueskens, Petra. "Mothers in Transition: Changing Gender Dynamics in the Home Through Strategic Absence." *Journal of the Australian Sociological Association*, May 1, 2015.

86   **women continuing to take on more of the household and childcare:** Hays, Sharon. *The Cultural Contradictions of Motherhood*. New Haven: Yale University Press, 1998.

CHAPTER 5

90   **estimates that abortion rates may have increased:** Mohr, James C. *Abortion in America: The Origins and Evolution of National Policy, 1800–1900*. Oxford: Oxford University Press, 1979.

91   **a concept promoted by the behaviorists:** Watson, John B.
        Psychological Care of Infant and Child. New York: Arno Press,
        1972.

91   **These women endured countless surgeries:** Axelsen,
        Diana E. "Women as Victims of Medical Experimentation: J.
        Marion Sims' Surgery on Slave Women, 1845–1850." *Women's
        Bodies*, 1985. doi:10.1515/9783110976328.93.

93   **development milestones:** Gesell, Arnold. "A Method for
        Studying Child Development." In *Readings in General
        Psychology*, ed. Wayne Dennis. New York: Prentice-Hall, 1949,
        486–492. doi:10.1037/11352-066.

94   **hugely disruptive to "female traditions of maternal
        advice sharing":** Vandenberg-Daves, Jodi. *Modern
        Motherhood: An American History*. New Brunswick, NJ:
        Rutgers University Press, 2014.

94   **a resurgence of Puritan morality:** Cain, Tambra K.
        "Comstock Laws." *Encyclopedia of Women's Health*, ed. Sana
        Loue and Martha Sajatovic. New York: Springer, 2004,
        301–303.doi:10.1007/978-0-306-48113-0_101.

95   **referred to women who avoided having children:**
        Roosevelt, Theodore. "T. Roosevelt Letter to C. Davenport
        About 'Degenerates Reproducing': DNA Learning Center."
        DNALC Blogs. January 3, 1913. https://www.dnalc.org/view
        /11219-T-Roosevelt-letter-to-C-Davenport-about-degenerates
        -reproducing-.html.

96   **some people ought to breed more than others:** Sanger,
        Margaret, and Alan F. Guttmacher. *Margaret Sanger: An
        Autobiography*. New York: Pergamon, 1938, 106–120.
        doi:10.1016/b978-0-08-018730-3.50014-0.

96   **human populations would outstrip the available food
        supply:** Ehrlich, Paul R. *The Population Bomb*. New York:
        Ballantine Books, 1971.

97   **In one high-profile example:** Gamble, Clarence J. "Clarence
        James Gamble Papers, 1920–1970s." Center for the History of

Medicine, Harvard University. http://oasis.lib.harvard.edu
/oasis/deliver/~med00082.

98   **A large number of these so-called bachelor maids:**
Library of Congress. "Topics in Chronicling America—
Bachelor Maids." Bachelor Maids—Newspaper and Current
Periodical Reading Room (Serial and Government
Publications Division, Library of Congress). 1907. https://
www.loc.gov/rr/news/topics/bachelor.html.

99   **Some of the most visible public women were single:** Harper,
Ida Husted. *The Life and Work of Susan B. Anthony: Including
Public Addresses, Her Own Letters and…Many from Her
Contemporaries During Fifty Years.* London: Forgotten Books, 2017.

99   **defining the era we're living in today:** Traister, Rebecca.
*All the Single Ladies: Unmarried Women and the Rise of an
Independent Nation.* New York: Simon and Schuster, 2018.

99   **one in five adults age twenty-five and older:** Wang, Wendy,
and Kim Parker. "Record Share of Americans Have Never
Married." Pew Research Center's Social and Demographic
Trends Project. September 24, 2014. Accessed March 14, 2018.
http://www.pewsocialtrends.org/2014/09/24/record-share-of
-americans-have-never-married/.

100   **"Freedwomen derived emotional fulfillment":** Jones,
Jacqueline. *Labor of Love, Labor of Sorrow: Black Women,
Work and the Family, from Slavery to the Present.* New York:
Basic Books, 2010.

105   **In 2015, I produced a series:** Westervelt, Amy, and
Guardian Readers. "Readers Responses: Can You Be an
Environmentalist and Still Have Kids?" *The Guardian.*
November 13, 2014. https://www.theguardian.com/vital-signs
/2014/nov/13/sea-level-stories-population-climate-change.

106   **Many radical feminists today:** Crispin, Jessa. *Why I Am Not a
Feminist: A Feminist Manifesto.* New York: Melville House, 2017.

107   **most children born to "single mothers":** Edin, Kathryn,
and Maria Kefalas. *Promises I Can Keep: Why Poor Women*

Put Motherhood Before Marriage. Berkeley: University of California Press, 2011.

108　**legalizing gay marriage effectively put an end:** Johnson, Fenton. "The Future of Queer." *Harper's*. January 1, 2018. https://harpers.org/archive/2018/01/the-future-of-queer/.

109　**"Most arguments in a marriage":** Popova, Maria. "If This Isn't Nice, What Is? Kurt Vonnegut's Advice to the Young on Kindness, Computers, Community, and the Power of Great Teachers." Brain Pickings. November 11, 2016. Accessed March 14, 2018. https://www.brainpickings.org/2014/04/17 /if-this-isnt-nice-what-is-kurt-vonnegut-commencement/.

110　**nearly 60 percent of pregnancies are unplanned:** "Unintended Pregnancy in the United States." Guttmacher Institute. September 20, 2017. https://www.guttmacher.org /fact-sheet/unintended-pregnancy-united-states.

110　**if we really want to get at the unwanted pregnancy problem:** "The Choice Project." The Choice Project. http:// www.choiceproject.wustl.edu/.

111　**unplanned births affect children's development:** Monea, Emily, and Adam Thomas. "The High Cost of Unintended Pregnancy." Brookings Institution. July 28, 2016. https://www. brookings.edu/research/the-high-cost-of-unintended-pregnancy/.

CHAPTER 6

113　**again when the Depression hit:** Milkman, Ruth. "Rosie the Riveter Revisited." In *On Gender, Labor, and Inequality*. Urbana: University of Illinois Press, 2017. doi:10.5406 /illinois/9780252040320.003.0004.

114　**Authorizing $52 million for childcare:** Cohen, Rhaina. "Who Took Care of Rosie the Riveter's Kids?" *The Atlantic*. November 18, 2015. https://www.theatlantic.com/business /archive/2015/11/daycare-world-war-rosie-riveter/415650/.

114   **At its peak in July 1944:** Stoltzfus, Emilie. "Child Care:
        The Federal Role During World War II." Washington, DC:
        Congressional Research Office. http://congressionalresearch
        .com/RS20615/document.php.

114   **A smaller network of centers:** Greenblatt, Bernard.
        *Responsibility for Child Care: The Changing Role of Family
        and State in Child Development.* San Francisco: Jossey-Bass,
        1977.

116   **Employment data from the post-war era:** US Bureau of
        Labor Statistics. "Women in the Labor Force." *BLS Reports*,
        May 1, 2014.

116   **At the same time, more socialist attitudes:** Bloom,
        Nicholas Dagen, Fritz Umbach, and Lawrence J. Vale. *Public
        Housing Myths: Perception, Reality, and Social Policy.* Ithaca,
        NY: Cornell University Press, 2015.

117   **Eugenicist ideas would persist:** Thass, Anandita. "Forced
        Sterilization and Poverty." *SSRN Electronic Journal*, 2012.
        doi:10.2139/ssrn.2244448.

117   **In 1948, future Planned Parenthood director:** Vogt,
        William, and Bernard M. Baruch. *Road to Survival.*
        Whitefish: Kessinger, 2010.

118   **a nationwide yearning for stability:** May, Elaine Tyler.
        Homeward Bound: American Families in the Cold War Era.
        New York: Basic Books, 2017.

120   **"Just about everyone who lived through this era":** Fessler,
        Ann. *The Girls Who Went Away: The Hidden History of Women
        Who Surrendered Children for Adoption in the Decades Before
        Roe v. Wade.* New York: Penguin, 2007.

121   **Of the approximately 1.5 million women mentioned
        above:** Solinger, Rickie. *Pregnancy and Power: A Short History
        of Reproductive Politics in America.* New York: New York
        University Press, 2007.

123   **women who wished to pursue a career during this time:**
        Cowan, Ruth Schwartz. *More Work for Mother: The Ironies of*

Household Technology from the Open Hearth to the Microwave.
New York: Basic Books, 2008.

125 **prototypical bro Paul Popenoe wrote:** James, George
Wharton, Ralph D. Cornell, and Paul Bowman Popenoe.
"Date Culture in Southern California, by George Wharton
James...Paul B. Popenoe...[and] Ralph D. Cornell." 1912.
doi:10.5962/bhl.title.36959.

125 **Channeling John B. Watson:** Wylie, Philip. *Generation of
Vipers, Newly Annotated by the Author.* New York: Holt,
Rinehart and Winston, 1964.

127 **Wylie also opened the floodgates for various other critics:**
Strecker, Edward Adam. *Their Mothers' Sons: The Psychiatrist
Examines an American Problem.* Philadelphia: Lippincott,
1951.

127 **Books like:** Lundberg, Ferdinand, and Marinya F. Farnham.
Modern Woman: The Lost Sex. New York: Harper and
Brothers, 1977.

127 **blamed the nation's mothers:** Levy, David M. *Maternal
Overprotection.* New York: W. W. Norton, 1966.

127 **At the other end of the spectrum:** Waltz, Mitzi. "From
'Pathological Motherhood' to Refrigerator Mothers." *Autism*
(2013): 73–86. doi:10.1057/9781137328533_5.

127 **J. Edgar Hoover, in a 1944 *Woman's Home Companion*
article:** Walker, Nancy A., ed. *Women's Magazines 1940–1960:
Gender Roles and the Popular Press.* New York: Palgrave
Macmillan, 2014.

130 **It's no wonder that amid all the experts:** Spock, Benjamin,
and Dorothea Warren Fox. *The Common Sense Book of Baby
and Child Care.* New York: Ishi Press International, 2013.

130 **As Ann Hulbert points out about the twentieth century:**
Hulbert, Ann. *Raising America: Experts, Parents, and a
Century of Advice About Children.* New York: Vintage Books,
2004.

131 **Black families that could afford to escaped the Jim Crow
South:** Orleck, Annelise. *Storming Caesars Palace: How Black*

Mothers Fought Their Own War on Poverty. Boston: Beacon Press, 2005.

132 **"White women raised in the 1950s":** Coontz, Stephanie. *The Way We Never Were: American Families and the Nostalgia Trap*. New York: Basic Books, 2016.

134 **"In looking at the stark facts of women at the top and at the bottom":** Slaughter, Anne-Marie. *Unfinished Business: Women Men Work Family*. New York: Random House, 2016.

135 **"What look like female values are regulations":** Haug, Frigga, and Rodney Livingstone. *Beyond Female Masochism: Memory-Work and Politics*. London: Verso, 1992.

136 **Here's the infuriating thing:** General Services Administration. "Child Care Services." Washington, DC, August 13, 2017. https://www.gsa.gov/resources-for/citizens -consumers/child-care/child-care-services.

136 **We also have a small number of programs in place:** Cohen, Nancy L. "Why America Never Had Universal Child Care." *The New Republic*. April 24, 2013. Accessed March 14, 2018. https://newrepublic.com/article/113009/child-care -america-was-very-close-universal-day-care.

138 **Patagonia, the company that pioneered on-site day care:** Bellis, Rich. "Patagonia's CEO Explains How to Make On-Site Child Care Pay for Itself." *Fast Company*. March 07, 2017. Accessed March 14, 2018. https://www.fastcompany.com /3062792/patagonias-ceo-explains-how-to-make-onsite-child -care-pay-for-itself.

CHAPTER 7

141 **In her 1963 book:** Friedan, Betty. *The Feminine Mystique*. New York: W. W. Norton, 2013.

142 **Friedan's book was in many ways a response:** Lundberg, Ferdinand, and Marinya F. Farnham. *Modern Woman: The Lost Sex*. New York: Harper and Brothers, 1977.

143   **As psychologist Elaine Heffner wrote:** Heffner, Elaine.
        *Mothering: The Emotional Experience of Motherhood After
        Freud and Feminism*. Garden City, NY: Anchor Press, 1980.

143   **perspective-changing 1976 book on motherhood:** Rich,
        Adrienne. *Of Woman Born*. New York: W. W. Norton, 1976.

144   **In her searing book:** Firestone, Shulamith. *The Dialectic
        of Sex: The Case for Feminist Revolution*. New York: William
        Morrow, 1970.

144   **In her famous 1970 "Living the Revolution" speech:**
        Steinem, Gloria. "Gloria Steinem, 'Living the Revolution' (31
        May 1970)." Voices of Democracy. http://voicesofdemocracy
        .umd.edu/steinem-living-the-revolution-speech-text/.

145   **"Although early feminists demanded respect and
        acknowledgment for housework":** hooks, bell.
        "Revolutionary Parenting." Caring Labor: An Archive.
        November 03, 2010. https://caringlabor.wordpress.com/2010
        /07/27/bell-hooks-revolutionary-parenting/.

146   **Alice Walker, who coined the term "womanism":** Walker,
        Alice. *In Search of Our Mothers' Gardens: Womanist Prose*.
        New York: Houghton Mifflin Harcourt, 2004.

148   **Nancy Chodorow's treatise on the reproduction of
        gender:** Chodorow, Nancy. *The Reproduction of Mothering:
        Psychoanalysis and the Sociology of Gender*. Berkeley:
        University of California Press, 1978.

149   **Miriam Johnson built on and expanded Chodorow's
        theory:** Johnson, Miriam M. *Strong Mothers, Weak Wives: The
        Search for Gender Equality*. Berkeley: University of California
        Press, 1990.

151   **What many white feminists didn't realize:** Andrews,
        Katherine. "The Dark History of Forced Sterilization of
        Latina Women." Panoramas. October 31, 2017. http://www
        .panoramas.pitt.edu/health-and-society/dark-history-forced
        -sterilization-latina-women.

151   **Indian Health Services doctor routinely performed
        sterilizations:** US National Library of Medicine. "Government

Admits Forced Sterilization of Indian Women—Timeline—
Native Voices." Native Voices, US National Library of Medicine.
https://www.nlm.nih.gov/nativevoices/timeline/543.html.

151   **At one such hospital in Oklahoma:** Stern, Alexandra
        Minna. "STERILIZED in the Name of Public Health."
        American Journal of Public Health 95, no. 7 (2005): 1128–1138.
        doi:10.2105/ajph.2004.041608.

152   **It's hard to imagine that a government report:** Patterson,
        James T. "Moynihan Report, The." In *The Wiley Blackwell
        Encyclopedia of Race, Ethnicity, and Nationalism*, ed. Anthony
        D. Smith, Polly Rizova, and John Stone. San Francisco: John
        Wiley and Sons, 2015, 1–3. doi:10.1002/9781118663202
        .wberen019.

154   **first documented use of the term "victim blaming":** Ryan,
        William. *Blaming the Victim*. New York: Vintage Books, 1976.

154   **In a speech announcing the report:** Johnson, Lyndon B.
        "Lyndon B. Johnson: Commencement Address at Howard
        University." The American Presidency Project. http://www
        .presidency.ucsb.edu/ws/?pid=27021.

155   **the link between the Moynihan report and mass
        incarceration:** Coates, Ta-Nehisi. "The Black Family in the
        Age of Mass Incarceration." *The Atlantic*. March 08, 2017.
        https://www.theatlantic.com/magazine/archive/2015/10/the
        -black-family-in-the-age-of-mass-incarceration/403246/.

156   **What was perhaps most damaging to Black communities:**
        Collins, Patricia Hill. *Black Feminist Thought: Knowledge,
        Consciousness, and the Politics of Empowerment*. New York:
        Routledge, 2000.

158   **Inspired by Michael Harrington's 1962 exposé of poverty:**
        Harrington, Michael. *The Other America*. New York: Macmillan,
        1970.

158   **Lyndon B. Johnson launched his War on Poverty:** Orleck,
        Annelise, and Lisa Gayle Hazirjian. *The War on Poverty: A
        New Grassroots History, 1964–1980*. Athens: University of
        Georgia Press, 2011.

160   **defines the welfare queen trope:** Lubiano, Wahneema H.
      The House That Race Built: Black Americans, U.S. Terrain.
      New York: Vintage, 1998.

160   **Native American families were also left reeling:**
      Woodard, Stephanie. "Native Americans Expose the
      Adoption Era and Repair Its Devastation." Indian Country
      Today Media Network. December 06, 2011. https://
      indiancountrymedianetwork.com/news/native-americans
      -expose-the-adoption-era-and-repair-its-devastation/.

161   **Often, these children were not originally in abusive or
      neglectful homes:** Busbee, Patricia, and Trace A. DeMeyer.
      Two Worlds: Lost Children of the Indian Adoption Projects.
      Greenfield, MA: Blue Hand Books, 2012.

162   **the humanist theories:** Maslow, Abraham H. *A Theory of
      Human Motivation.* United States: BN Publishing, 1943.

163   **The mother-blame trend:** Friday, Nancy. *My Mother/My Self:
      The Daughter's Search for Identity.* New York: Delacorte Press,
      1977.

163   **As Judith Warner put it in her best seller:** Warner, Judith.
      Perfect Madness: Motherhood in the Age of Anxiety. New York:
      Riverhead Books, 2006.

164   **Given conservative efforts to preserve the American family:**
      Wilcox, W. Bradford. "The Evolution of Divorce." *National
      Affairs.* September 1, 2009. https://www.nationalaffairs.com
      /publications/detail/the-evolution-of-divorce.

164   **the trend in pop psychology toward finding oneself:**
      Reuben, David. *Everything You Always Wanted to Know About
      Sex (But Were Afraid to Ask).* London: Pan Books, 1971.

164   **fueled by best-selling books:** Harris, Thomas, MD. *I'm OK-
      You're OK.* New York: Harper and Row, 1969.

165   **By the mid-1980s, 20 percent of children were born to
      unwed mothers:** Akerlof, George A., and Janet L. Yellen. "An
      Analysis of Out-of-Wedlock Births in the United States."
      Brookings Institution. January 25, 2018. https://www.brook

ings.edu/research/an-analysis-of-out-of-wedlock-births-in
-the-united-states/.

167 **Since the early 2000s:** Dow, Dawn. "Negotiating 'The
Welfare Queen' and 'The Strong Black Woman.'" *SAGE
Journals* 58, no. 1 (2015).

168 **the intensive mothering ideology:** Hays, Sharon. *The
Cultural Contradictions of Motherhood.* New Haven, CT: Yale
University Press, 1996.

170 **This holds particularly true for working mothers:** Correll,
Shelley J., Stephen Benard, and In Paik. "Getting a Job: Is
There a Motherhood Penalty?" *American Journal of Sociology*
112, no. 5 (2007): 1297–1339. doi:10.1086/511799.

171 **extensive research of the "motherhood penalty":** Budig,
Michelle J., and Paula England. "The Wage Penalty for
Motherhood." *American Sociological Review* 66, no. 2 (2001):
204. doi:10.2307/2657415.

171 **For certain cohorts of women:** Budig, Michelle J., and
Melissa J. Hodges. "Statistical Models and Empirical
Evidence for Differences in the Motherhood Penalty Across
the Earnings Distribution." *American Sociological Review* 79,
no. 2 (2014): 358–364. doi:10.1177/0003122414523616.

171 **not evenly distributed across class lines:** Budig, Michelle
J., and Melissa J. Hodges. "Differences in Disadvantage."
American Sociological Review 75, no. 5 (2010): 705–728.
doi:10.1177/0003122410381593.

173 **in situations where it is poorly implemented, it harms
women:** Munsch, Christin. "Men Viewed More Favorably
Than Women When Seeking Work-Life Balance." *Journal of
the American Sociological Association*, August 14, 2014.

174 **Meanwhile, a recent German study:** Lott, Yvonne, and
Heejung Chung. "Gender Discrepancies in the Outcomes
of Schedule Control on Overtime Hours and Income in
Germany." *European Sociological Review* 32, no. 6 (2016):
752–765. doi:10.1093/esr/jcw032.

174   **another way for women to fall behind:** Burkus, David. "Everyone Likes Flex Time, but We Punish Women Who Use It." *Harvard Business Review*. February 20, 2017. Accessed March 15, 2018. https://hbr.org/2017/02/everyone-likes-flex-time-but-we-punish-women-who-use-it.

175   **A reduction in the number of days:** Dembe Allard. "Why a Four-Day Workweek Is Not Good for Your Health." The Conversation. March 01, 2018. https://theconversation.com/why-a-four-day-workweek-is-not-good-for-your-health-64516.

CHAPTER 8

180   **"By 1980 a new wave of conservatism":** Rich, Adrienne. "Preface." *Of Woman Born: Motherhood as Experience and Institution*. New York: Norton, 1986.

180   **Susan Faludi would describe this in greater detail:** Faludi, Susan. *Backlash: The Undeclared War against American Women*. New York: Three Rivers Press, 2006.

181   **In 1971, 80 percent of third graders:** Rosin, Hanna. "The Overprotected Kid." *The Atlantic*. August 20, 2015. https://www.theatlantic.com/magazine/archive/2014/04/hey-parents-leave-those-kids-alone/358631/.

181   **Beginning in the mid-1980s and continuing to today:** Sears, William. *The Baby Book: Everything You Need to Know About Your Baby from Birth to Age Two*. New York: Little, Brown, 2013.

182   **As anthropologists Robert A. LeVine and Sarah LeVine note:** LeVine, Robert A., and Sarah LeVine. *Do Parents Matter? Why Japanese Babies Sleep Soundly, Mexican Siblings Don't Fight, and American Families Should Just Relax*. New York: PublicAffairs, 2016.

182   Charen, Mona. "The Feminist Mistake," *National Review*, March 23, 1984.

Staff. "The Failure of Feminism." *Newsweek*. November 18, 1990. http://www.newsweek.com/failure-feminism -205870.

183   **charges in publications like *Time*:** Bellafonte, Ginia. "Feminism: It's All About Me!" *Time*. June 29, 1998.

183   **as of 1991 two-thirds of women were still living in poverty:** Kleiman, Carol. "'Feminization Of Poverty' Still True in the '80s, Sociologist." *Chicago Tribune*, August 5, 1985, articles.chicagotribune.com/1985-08-05/business /8502210142_1_poverty-diana-pearce-job.

184   **1985 science fiction story of an autocratic American dystopia ruled by theocrats:** Atwood, Margaret. *The Handmaid's Tale*. Boston: Houghton Mifflin, 1986.

184   **A precursor to Kellyanne Conway:** Schlafly, Phyllis. *A Choice Not an Echo*. Alton, IL: Pere Marquette Press, 1964.

184   **Ruth Bader Ginsburg has been a vocal proponent:** Schwab, Nikki. "Ginsburg: Make ERA Part of the Constitution." *U.S. News & World Report*. April 18, 2014. https://www.usnews.com/news/blogs/washington-whispers /2014/04/18/justice-ginsburg-make-equal-rights-amendment -part-of-the-constitution.

187   **what had previously been dismissed as "mommy brain":** Ruddick, Sara. "Learning to Live with the Angel in the House." *Women's Studies* 4, nos. 2–3 (1977): 181–200. doi:10.1080/00497878.1977.9978416. And Ruddick. *Maternal Thinking: Toward a Politics of Peace; with a New Preface*. Boston: Beacon Press, 2002.

188   **in the same year as Ruddick's book:** Hochschild, Arlie Russell, and Anne Machung. *The Second Shift*. New York: Penguin, 2003.

190   **Although we still ask women to defend this choice:** Khazan, Olga. "How People Decide Whether to Have Children." *The Atlantic*. May 22, 2017. Accessed March 14, 2018. https://www.theatlantic.com/health/archive/2017/05 /how-people-decide-whether-to-have-children/527520/.

190   **Any concern over who is having babies and how many:**
        Joyce, Kathryn. "The Tip of an Ideological Iceberg." *Harvard
        Divinity Bulletin* 36, no. 2 (April 1, 2008).

190   **white people will no longer be the majority demographic:**
        Colby, Sandra L., and Jennifer M. Ortman. "Projections
        of the Size and Composition of the U.S. Population: 2014
        to 2060." Population Estimates and Projections, Current
        Population Reports, US Census Bureau, March 1, 2015.

191   **According to 2017 data from the Economic Policy
        Institute:** Wilson, Valerie. "African American Women Stand
        out as Working Moms Play a Larger Economic Role in
        Families." Economic Policy Institute. May 11, 2017. https://
        www.epi.org/blog/african-american-women-stand-out-as
        -working-moms-play-a-larger-economic-role-in-families/.

191   **number of incarcerated women with children increased
        by 87 percent:** Smyth, Julie. "Dual Punishment: Incarcerated
        Mothers and Their Children." *Columbia Social Work Review*,
        2012.

192   **Some women are pregnant when they enter prison:**
        Cristina Jose-Kampfner. "Post-Traumatic Stress Reactions in
        Children of Imprisoned Mothers." In *Children of Incarcerated
        Parents*, ed. Katherine Gabel and Denise Johnston. Lexington
        Books, 1995.

192   **"Women's pathways to incarceration":** Collins, Eliza. "Rep.
        Karen Bass: Criminal Justice Reform Is Possible." Politico.
        December 10, 2015. https://www.politico.com/story/2015/12
        /criminal-justice-reform-women-rule-event-216630.

193   **nearly 1 million more women are under probation:**
        Wagner, Peter, Bernadette Rabuy, and Wendy Sawyer. "Mass
        Incarceration: The Whole Pie 2018." Prison Policy Initiative.
        March 14, 2014. Accessed March 15, 2018. https://www.prison
        policy.org/reports/pie2018.html.

193   **In her research on the impact on children of having
        parents in jail:** Cristina Jose-Kampfner. "Post-Traumatic
        Stress Reactions in Children of Imprisoned Mothers." In

Children of Incarcerated Parents, ed. Katherine Gabel and Denise Johnston. Lexington Books, 1995.

193   **Women often struggle to stay in touch with their children:** Margolies, Julie Kowitz, and Tamar Kraft-Stolar. "When Free Means Losing Your Mother: The Collision of Child Welfare and the Incarceration of Women in New York State." *National Criminal Justice Journal*, February 2006.

195   **The work of queer women:** Millett, Kate, Catharine A. MacKinnon, and Rebecca Mead. *Sexual Politics*. New York: Columbia University Press, 2016.

195   **The work of queer women:** Moraga, Cherríe, and Celia Herrera Rodriguez. *A Xicana Codex of Changing Consciousness: Writings, 2000–2010*. Durham, NC: Duke University Press, 2011. And Anzaldúa, Gloria, and AnaLouise Keating. *Light in the Dark = Luz En Lo Oscuro: Rewriting Identity, Spirituality, Reality*. Durham, NC: Duke University Press, 2015.

195   **a memoir of her experience having her son at age forty:** Moraga, Cherríe. *Waiting in the Wings: Portrait of a Queer Motherhood*. Ithaca, NY: Firebrand Books, 1997.

195   **what sociologist Kristin Esterberg calls a "lesbian baby boom":** Esterberg, Kristin. "Planned Parenthood: The Construction of Motherhood in Lesbian Mother Advice Books." In *Feminist Mothering*, ed. Andrea O'Reilly. Albany: State University of New York Press, 2008.

196   **the Dr. Spock of lesbian parenting:** Martin, April. *Lesbian and Gay Parenting Handbook: Creating and Raising Our Families*. New York: HarperPerennial, 1993.

199   **In 1991, law professor Anita Hill accused:** Shapiro, Bruce. "The Complete Transcripts of the Clarence Thomas–Anita Hill Hearings." *The Nation*, December 12, 1994.

201   **Bill used Hillary as a selling point:** *Hillary Clinton on "Baking Cookies."* Performed by Hillary Clinton. *60 Minutes*. June 19, 2008. https://youtu.be/8EGranwN_uk.

202   **Adding fuel to the mommy war fire was the so-called Opt-Out Generation:** Belkin, Lisa. "The Opt-Out Revolution."

New York Times. October 25, 2003. Accessed March 14, 2018. http://www.nytimes.com/2003/10/26/magazine/the-opt-out -revolution.html.

203 **Many mothers were also pushing back:** Williams, Joan C. "The Opt-Out Revolution Revisited: Women Aren't Foresaking Careers for Domestic Life: The Ground Rules Just Make It Impossible to Have Both." *The American Prospect*, March 1, 2007.

205 **Those concerned about the country's birth rate:** Soble, Jonathan. "Japan, Short on Babies, Reaches a Worrisome Milestone." *New York Times*. June 02, 2017. https://www .nytimes.com/2017/06/02/business/japan-population-births .html.

206 **For Millennials in particular, student debt is a major blocker:** Vedantam, Shankar. *How Student Debt Affects Personal Choices of Young People*. NPR. Recorded June 8, 2016.MP3.

207 **Government-supported maternity leave still doesn't exist in America:** Livingston, Gretchen. "Among 41 nations, U.S. is the outlier when it comes to paid parental leave." Pew Research Center. September 06, 2016. http://www.pew research.org/fact-tank/2016/09/26/u-s-lacks-mandated-paid -parental-leave/.

208 **In the midst of all this:** Sandberg, Sheryl, and Nell Scovell. *Lean In: Women, Work and the Will to Lead*. London: W. H. Allen, 2013.

210 **rebuke of corporate feminism:** Crispin, Jessa. *Why I Am Not a Feminist: A Feminist Manifesto*. New York: Melville House, 2017.

211 **In her famed 1979 essay:** Lorde, Audre. *Sister Outsider: Essays and Speeches*. Berkeley: Crossing Press, 2015.

211 **In an insightful look at the "Oprah effect":** Harris, Jennifer, ed. *The Oprah Phenomenon*. Lexington: University Press of Kentucky, 2009.

212 **When she started her blog Dooce:** Armstrong, Heather B. *It Sucked and Then I Cried: How I Had a Baby, a Breakdown, and a Much Needed Margarita*. New York: Gallery Books, 2010.

214 **the bad mom label:** Ladd-Taylor, Molly, and Lauri Umansky, eds. *"Bad" Mothers: The Politics of Blame in Twentieth-Century America*. New York: New York University Press, 1998.

214 **Just think of the burst of recent news stories:** Wallace, Kelly. "'Free-Range' Parents Face Neglect Investigation." CNN. January 21, 2015. https://www.cnn.com/2015/01/20 /living/feat-md-free-range-parents-under-attack/index.html.

217 **It seems to be the final blow to a certain type of male narrative:** Rosin, Hanna. *The End of Men and the Rise of Women*. London: Penguin, 2013.

218 **the cost of living has outpaced growth in wages:** DeSilver, Drew. "For Most Workers, Real Wages Have Barely Budged for Decades." Pew Research Center. October 09, 2014. http:// www.pewresearch.org/fact-tank/2014/10/09/for-most-workers -real-wages-have-barely-budged-for-decades/.

218 **while wages had increased 21 percent:** Michel, Lawrence, Elise Gould, and Josh Bivens. "Wage Stagnation in Nine Charts." Economic Policy Institute. January 6, 2015. https:// www.epi.org/publication/charting-wage-stagnation/.

218 **Americans are working more hours:** Organization for Economic Cooperation and Development. "Productivity— GDP per Hour Worked—OECD Data." January 4, 2017. https://data.oecd.org/lprdty/gdp-per-hour-worked.htm.

221 **more than 50 percent of the US workforce will be freelance:** Edelman Intelligence. "Freelancing in America: 2017 Survey." Upwork. August 1, 2017. https://www.upwork .com/i/freelancing-in-america/2017/.

CHAPTER 9

226 **In a survey I conducted of more than 100 women:** For detailed results of the fertility survey mentioned in this chapter, visit the author's website: www.amywestervelt.com /research.

229 **"Clomid can be downright dangerous":** Siedentopf, F., B. Horstkamp, G. Stief, and H. Kentenich. "Clomiphene Citrate as a Possible Cause of a Psychotic Reaction During Infertility Treatment." *Human Reproduction* 12, no. 4 (1997): 706–707. doi:10.1093/humrep/12.4.706.

229 **"it can accentuate or cause depression":** Grimm, Oliver, and Petra Hubrich. "Delusional Belief Induced by Clomiphene Treatment." *Progress in Neuro-Psychopharmacology and Biological Psychiatry* 32, no. 5 (2008): 1338–1339. doi:10.1016 /j.pnpbp.2007.08.037.

229 **"crazy Clomid":** Venkatesh, Ramesh, et al. "Clomiphene Citrate–Induced Visual Hallucinations: A Case Report." *Journal of Medical Case Reports* 11, no. 1 (2017). doi:10.1186/s13256-017-1228-0.

230 **having a hard time meeting equally educated men:** Petropanagos, Angel, et al. "Social Egg Freezing: Risk, Benefits, and Other Considerations." *Canadian Medical Association Journal* 187, no. 9 (2015): 666–669. doi:10.1503 /cmaj.141605.

230 **it's not quite the sure thing some want us to think:** Alter, Charlotte, Diane Tsai, and Francesca Trianni. "The Truth About Egg Freezing: Exclusive National Success Rates." *Time.* July 16, 2015. http://time.com/3959487/egg-freezing -need-to-know/.

234 **Kristin Esterberg points out in a chapter on lesbian motherhood:** Esterberg, Kristin. "Planned Parenthood: The Construction of Motherhood in Lesbian Mother Advice Books." In *Feminist Mothering,* ed. Andrea O'Reilly. Albany: State University of New York Press, 2008.

234 **"consumer model":** Rowland, Robyn. *Living Laboratories: Women and Reproductive Technologies.* London: Cedar, 1993.

234 **the commodification of reproduction:** Rothman, Barbara Katz. "Reproductive Technology and the Commodification of Life." *Women and Health* 13, nos. 1–2 (1988): 95–100. doi:10.1300/j013v13n01_08.

237   **The brainchild of attorney Joan Williams:** Kelly, E. L. "Discrimination Against Caregivers? Gendered Family Responsibilities, Employer Practices, and Work Rewards." In *Handbook of Employment Discrimination Research*, ed. L. B. Nielsen and R. L. Nelson. New York: Springer, 2005.

237   **The win rates for employees:** Williams, Joan C., and Stephanie Bornstein. "The Evolution of "FReD": Family Responsibilities Discrimination and Developments in the Law of Stereotyping and Implicit Bias." *Hastings Law Journal* (2008).

239   **the modern American workplace was "designed around a man's body":** Williams, Joan. *Unbending Gender: Why Family and Work Conflict and What to Do about It*. New York: Oxford University Press, 2005.

CHAPTER 10

243   **The first act of violence:** hooks, bell. *The Will to Change: Men, Masculinity, and Love*. New York: Simon and Schuster, 2005.

245   **The "costs of masculinity":** Messner, Michael A. *Politics of Masculinities: Men in Movements*. Lanham, MD: Alta Mira Press (Rowman and Littlefield), 2000.

249   **books on the impacts of patriarchal masculinity:** Casanova, Erynn Masi De. *Buttoned Up: Clothing, Conformity, and White-Collar Masculinity*. Ithaca, NY: ILR Press, an Imprint of Cornell University Press, 2015.

249   **brilliant book on high school gender policing:** Pascoe, C. J. *Dude, You're a Fag: Masculinity and Sexuality in High School*. Berkeley: University of California Press, 2012.

249   **on the rise of men's rights activists:** Kimmel, Michael S. *Angry White Men: American Masculinity at the End of an Era*. New York: Nation Books, 2017.

249   **A twenty-two-year-old named Elliot Rodger:** Adam Nagourney, Michael Cieply, Alan Feuer and Ian Lovett.

"Elliot O. Rodger's Killings in California Followed Years of Withdrawal." *New York Times*. June 01, 2014. https://www .nytimes.com/2014/06/02/us/elliot-rodger-killings-in-califor nia-followed-years-of-withdrawal.html.

249   **We know he was a men's rights activist:** Rodger, Elliott O. "Elliot Rodger Manifesto: My Twisted World." Document Cloud. 2014. https://www.documentcloud.org/documents /1173808-elliot-rodger-manifesto.html.

249   **He was in charge of organizing men's consciousness- raising workshops:** Farrell, Warren. *The Liberated Man*. New York: Random House, 1974.

250   **Farrell described their breakup in a 2015 article:** Blake, Mariah. "Mad Men: Inside the Men's Rights Movement—and the Army of Misogynists and Trolls It Spawned." *Mother Jones*. June 24, 2017. https://www.motherjones.com/politics /2015/01/warren-farrell-mens-rights-movement-feminism -misogyny-trolls/.

250   **criticized women for lording power:** Farrell, Warren. *Why Men Are the Way They Are: The Male-Female Dynamic*. New York: Berkley Books, 1986.

250   **the MRA Bible:** Farrell, Warren. *The Myth of Male Power*. New York: Berkley Books, 1993.

252   **For evidence of this, we need look no further than family responsibilities discrimination lawsuits:** Williams, Joan C., and Cynthia Thomas Calvert. "Caregiver Discrimination Lawsuits Up 269 percent in the Last Decade." *Time*. May 17, 2016. http://time.com/4337233/family-responsibilities-discrimination/.

252   **When Anne-Marie Slaughter's husband:** Note to Self. "Taking the Lead: Bonus." In *Andrew Moravcsik*. Manoush Zomorodi, 2016, MP3.

253   **increasing number of stay-at-home dads:** US Census Bureau. "Facts for Features: Father's Day." June 8, 2017. Newsroom. https://www.census.gov/newsroom/facts-for -features/2017/cb17-ff12-fathers-day.html.

CHAPTER 11

258   **Four hundred or so years ago:** Hussung, Tricia. "The Evolution of American Family Structure." Concordia University, St. Paul Online. June 23, 2015. https://online.csp .edu/blog/family-science/the-evolution-of-american-family -structure.

258   **the neatly divided roles of the nuclear family:** Sarkisian, Natalia. *Nuclear Family Values, Extended Family Lives: The Power of Race, Class, and Gender.* St. Louis: Taylor and Francis, 2016.

258   **Those for whom these structures had never worked:** Hansen, Karen V. *Not-So-Nuclear Families: Class, Gender, and Networks of Care.* New Brunswick, NJ: Rutgers University Press, 2005.

262   **"In spite of their greater strength":** Konner, Melvin. *Women After All: Sex, Evolution, and the End of Male Supremacy.* New York: W. W. Norton, 2016.

Index